Walter James Wyatt

Hungarian Celebrities

Walter James Wyatt

Hungarian Celebrities

ISBN/EAN: 9783742868350

Manufactured in Europe, USA, Canada, Australia, Japa

Cover: Foto ©Thomas Meinert / pixelio.de

Manufactured and distributed by brebook publishing software
(www.brebook.com)

Walter James Wyatt

Hungarian Celebrities

HUNGARIAN CELEBRITIES.

BY

CAPTAIN W. J. WYATT,

AUTHOR OF

'REVOLUTIONARY SHADOWS,'

'REFLECTIONS ON THE FORMATION OF ARMIES, A POLITICAL AND MILITARY HISTORY

OF THE HANOVERIAN AND ITALIAN WAR,'

ETC. ETC.

LONDON:

LONGMANS, GREEN, AND CO.

1871.

THIS WORK

Is most respectfully Dedicated

TO

THE LOVELY DAUGHTERS OF HUNGARY

WHO, AIDED BY THEIR BEAUTEOUS QUEEN,

SO GREATLY ASSISTED IN BRINGING ABOUT THE PRESENT

HAPPY STATE OF AFFAIRS IN THEIR COUNTRY.

PREFACE.

—◦◦—

THE interest felt in the affairs of the Austro-Hungarian empire at the present time has led the Author to believe that a sketch of the early history of that country, together with some brief biographies of those who have rendered themselves celebrated in its annals, would not be unwelcome to the British public.

a

CONTENTS.

PART I.

HUNGARIAN CELEBRITIES.

PART II.

FEMALE MAGYAR CELEBRITIES.

PART I.

HUNGARIAN CELEBRITIES.

THE history of nations is the biography of their martyrs. As the effects of the mighty convulsions to which the earth has been subjected are exhibited in its seamed and rugged surface, so may we perhaps consider that the annals of the world are written with the blood of those who have died in support of opinions with which their birthright inspired them.

Every nation in the adoration of its martyrs respects at the same time the history of the country; and thus, in attempting to narrate the history of past centuries, special prominence must be given to the names of those whose great deeds have inspired their countrymen to raise statues and monuments to their memory.

But what must be the feelings of a nation which can proudly proclaim to the world that it counts among these martyrs, beings whom the munificent Providence intended to be the symbols of peace, and yet, in the hour of destruction, inspired by burning love for their country, placed the soldier's helmet on their heads, exchanging their home-spun garments for the warrior's cloak, and casting aside the distaff to grasp the sword!

CHAPTER I.

MYSTIC HISTORY.

ONE of the most peculiar traits in the character of the
Eastern races is their extraordinary love and veneration
of mystic, or, as we might say, imaginary history. This
feeling is possessed to a great degree by the Magyars, whose legends give us the following description of
their origin: Nimrod, a descendant of Japhet, son of
Noah, after the destruction of the Tower of Babel,
wandered into the land of Havila with his family and
dependants. Here his wife gave birth to two sons, one
called Hunyor, the other Magyar. These two brothers,
during a hunting expedition in the Caucasus, were one
day following a roe, when, on reaching the swampy moors
of the Sea of Azof,[1] the animal suddenly disappeared from
their sight. In their search for the retreat of the roe
they were struck with the magnificent pasturages with
which this country abounded, and which would afford
them ample grazing grounds for their numerous flocks
and herds. On their return home they related to their
father what they had seen, and induced him to allow them
to emigrate with their flocks to the newly discovered
country.

Here they remained attending to their cattle for a

---

[1] In the history of the Visigoths, who lived in the beginning of the
fourth century on the borders of the Sea of Azof, it is mentioned that a roe,
swimming across the Don, led the Hunic hunters to discover the Sea of
Azof and to attack the Visigoths.

space of five years. Wearied, it seems, with their mono-
tonous life in this land of plenty, they undertook a journey
for the purpose of exploring new lands. Their path led
them along the Steppes. Suddenly, to their great astonishment, the wind wafted to their ears the sound of
festivity. Guided by it, they came unexpectedly upon a
number of beautiful women and girls, the daughters of
the sons of the Bush, who were celebrating the festival of
the hunting horn. These lovely children of nature,
struck with the manly beauty of the sons of Nimrod,
yielded to their embraces, and followed their new lords
and masters to the neighbourhood of the Sea of Azof.
Amongst these girls were two virgins of extraordinary
beauty: they were daughters of Dula, King of the Alans.
Hunyor married one, and Magyar the other. The offspring of these two marriages were the founders of two
great tribes, the Huns and the Magyars. The prolific
tendencies of these two families and the rapid increase of
their flocks were so great that the territory they inhabited
was soon found too small for them. They therefore
determined to emigrate. Following the course of the
rivers, they overran Scythia and occupied the greater part
of Russia. The descendants of Hunyor took possession
of the north-eastern districts of the Volga; those of
Magyar seem to have taken up their abode along the left
bank of the Don, and were now called Donmagyars, but
their country took the name of Dontumogeria. It seems
that the Donmagyars suffered but little from the inroads
of the nomad tribes. This arose from the natural barriers
which surrounded them, whereas their kindred race, the
Huns, from their exposed position, were constantly engaged in defending their territory from the advance of
the hostile wandering tribes. The consequence was that
the character of the descendants of Nimrod became totally
different.

In the beginning of the fourth century, stimulated by the stories of the riches of the Western world, the Huns commenced their celebrated invasion. After a series of great victories, they ultimately took up their abode on the Theiss and the Donau, where they remained until their great leader Attila, surnamed 'the Scourge of God,' commenced his bloodthirsty conquest of the greater part of Europe. After the death of Attila, his two sons, Alabar and Csaba, began a fratricidal war for the possession of their father's crown—a war which ended in the destruction of this powerful nation; for the conquered tribes, availing themselves of this favourable opportunity to reconquer their independence, did their utmost to destroy their oppressors. The followers of Alabar were entirely annihilated; and Csaba himself, hotly pursued by his opponents, with the greatest difficulty escaped to Greece with about 15,000 of his people. As his mother was a Greek princess, Csaba was favourably received by the Emperor Marcianus, who allowed him and his followers to remain in his dominions, and afforded them his assistance and protection. But the revengeful and ambitious spirit of Attila's son could not endure a life of inactivity, and he was pining for the power which would enable him to revenge himself on his enemies and reconquer that immense empire which his own folly had been the principal instrument of destroying.

A few thousand of Csaba's followers, who had deserted the cause of their leader, sought refuge in the mountainous part of Eastern Transylvania, where, at a later period, their descendants intermarried with the Magyars, who had migrated into that part of the country, and founded a tribe which is up to the present day called the Seklers.

After a sojourn of a few years in Greece, Csaba and his adherents joined his peaceful kindred on the Don, where, until his death, he occupied himself in attempting to induce the latter to aid him in invading Western Europe. In this he seems to have been unsuccessful, for the richness of their country had made the Magyars a peace-loving people. In fact, they had everything they could desire, and were most primitive in their ideas and habits. There is no doubt, however, that the unruly Csaba and his followers sowed those seeds of which Hungary, after the lapse of centuries, has had to reap the harvest.

The government of the Magyars seems to have been a republican confederacy, for the nation was divided into seven tribes or families. Their names were as follows: Nyek, Kurt, Tarjan, Ienö, Kara, Kaza, and Megyar, and they called themselves the seven Magyar families. Each tribe had its own leader, or woiwode, who had sovereign power over it; and each of these leaders was equal in rank to the others. In case of war, or of any great emergency, the seven tribes assisted each other.

Their religion consisted of sacrifices, which generally took place on eminences, or high grounds, either in the day or at the dead of night. They immolated to their gods all sorts of animals, but their principal sacrifice was the Aldomas. This consisted in the offering of a white stallion, which was dedicated to a deity whom they called Isten. Isten was supposed to be the Almighty. Second to him ranked the sun, whom they believed to be the instrument through which Isten bestowed his gifts on his beloved. The Magyars also worshipped the atmosphere, the earth, the fire, and the water. They acknowledged the existence of a bad spirit, who was ruled by Isten, and whom they named Arnany, or Oerdög. They also believed in the immortality of the soul, and in another world, in which they would enjoy a better life.

They buried their dead either on the banks of the

rivers or on the top of some promontory. The funeral rites were celebrated by a feast and much singing.

One of the most marked characteristics of this people was their fidelity to their promises, which were generally ratified by a solemn oath and the opening of a vein.

They had also priests, who were supposed to possess the power of foretelling what was to take place, which they did by the intestines of victims sacrificed. These priests seem to have occupied the highest posts in the tribes, for they were the counsellors of the princes, the learned men, the doctors and poets of the people, and in this latter capacity played a most prominent part among them, for the Magyars were already very fond of music and singing. This no doubt contributed greatly to awaken in their minds a love for military conquests; and we shall afterwards see that this priestly power was one of the chief instruments in instigating the Magyars to leave their adopted country. About four hundred years after the death of Attila we find the peace-loving Magyars becoming one of the most warlike and bloodthirsty of nations. They were celebrated for all those arts and exercises which in those days made a soldier, and in their insatiable love for revenge had become the terror of the inhabitants of the surrounding countries. Fear seems to have been unknown to them, and on the slightest provocation, or some imaginary wrong, they were not only ready to annihilate their supposed enemy, but were prepared to make any sacrifice on their own part in order to wreak their vengeance.

In the beginning of the ninth century one of the seven Magyar rulers, named Ugek, married Emese, daughter of another woiwode. The fruit of this marriage was a son, who received the name of Almos. It is related that a large eagle had appeared to Emese, and bowed his head towards her lap, which had the effect of making her pregnant. Shortly after a glittering stream seemed to flow from her loins towards strange lands. Hence the child was called Almos, or the Dream. The priests declared that he would be the founder of great kings in distant lands. As Almos grew up to manhood, it is stated that his personal appearance and manners induced those who surrounded him to believe in his godly descent. He was tall and slender; his aspect expressed great determination, accompanied by an expression of good nature. His hands were very muscular, with long, outstretched fingers. He possessed all the good and great qualities which render a ruler illustrious. His confederate chiefs seem to have tacitly acknowledged him as their superior, for they never undertook anything without previously asking his advice.

In the year 884 a warlike tribe called the Patzenaci had been driven from their abodes across the Volga by the Uzen, and entered the territory of the Hungarians. The latter, compelled to retreat before these powerful enemies, crossed the Don by means of small leather boats, and made their way into the empire of the Chazaren. The part of the country where they took up their abode bore the name of Lebedia, and is situated to the north of the Black Sea. The ruler of this empire seems to have afforded them every assistance, and to have formed an intimate alliance with them against the warlike Uzen and Patzenaci. In order to render this alliance more durable, he gave a daughter of one of the most noble families as wife to Elöd, one of the Magyar rulers.

After three years' residence in their newly adopted country the Hungarians were again attacked by their old enemies the Patzenaci, who completely defeated and routed them, and they had no alternative left but to seek refuge in flight. This arose from the disunion which seems to have prevailed at that time among the seven

Magyar chiefs. The smaller party of the fugitives re-crossed the Don, and formed a settlement in the Caucasus, near the frontiers of Persia, where for a long time they kept up their connexion with their kindred tribe. The remaining part of the defeated Hungarians retreated in the direction of the Dnieper, across which they swam, and then pushed forward into that part of the country which is watered by the Bug, the Dniester, the Pruth, and the Sereth: from thence they seem to have extended their habitations to the low grounds of the Lower Danube.

The Khan of the Chazaren, not being able to depend on the remaining tribes of the Hungarians, perceived that he would have to contend alone against the Pat-zenaci unless he could establish a firm alliance between the seven Magyar rulers. He therefore expressed his willingness to acknowledge as his leader any one of their chiefs whom they might elect as their own. Thereupon the Hungarians assembled a great national council, in which Arpád, son of Almos, was unanimously elected as their sovereign and leader, and accordingly placed on a shield, after the warlike custom of the people, the assembled council shouting, ' From henceforth we acknowledge you as our leader, and we will follow you wherever your fate leads you.' The woiwodes and the elders of families ratified this compact by a solemn oath—namely, by opening one of their veins and letting several drops of blood fall in a holy goblet—and solemnly cursed all those who should break this national contract. This compact was divided into six parts:

1. As long as the descendants of Arpád existed their leader should be chosen from his family.

2. All the spoils conquered in common should be equally divided amongst them all.

3. Arpád, on his side, promised for himself and suc-

cessors always to ask the advice of those who had signed the contract, and their descendants, and to maintain them always as rulers of their tribes.

4. In case of any of their descendants or themselves breaking the oath of obedience, or provoking discord with their ruler, their blood should flow like that which had fallen in the holy goblet.

5. In case of any of the descendants, either of their king or of the princes, attempting to break the contract, they should be for ever exiled from their people.

6. Whoever refused to be present at the national assemblies should be chopped in two.

The names of the woiwodes who signed the above agreement are as follows: Almos, the father of Arpád; Elöd, the father of Szabolcs; Ond, the father of Ete; Tas, the father of Lel; Huba, who was the founder of Szemere; Kond, the father of Csörsz; and Töhötön, the father of Gyula and Zombor.

CHAPTER II.

THE HUNS.

THE HUNS (Hunni or Ούννοι), a comprehensive name designating most likely all the Scythian tribes, appeared in Europe in the year 375 of the Christian era, and played for some time a remarkable and conspicuous part in the history of Europe. Their original seat was on the north side, and in the immediate vicinity, of the Chinese wall; but through their barbaric bravery and wonderful powers of endurance they extended their frontiers. It is stated that their food consisted of slices of meat which had been placed between the saddle and the back of their horses, and fresh blood; their habits and manners were akin to those of brutes; and, as they seldom or ever quitted the saddle, they were the most perfect horsemen in the world.

Their chiefs, who were called Fandschus, gradually became the conquerors and sovereigns over vast regions. In the East the ocean only stopped their progress, and the tribes living between the Amour and the peninsula of Corea were forced to join their banners. In their advance towards the West, at the sources of the Irtish,[1]

---

[1] The Irtish is one of the largest rivers of Siberia; its sources are in the Altai mountains, in the north of China, in the province of Songarei. It flows in a north-westerly direction, through the Saisany sea, passing through the Siberian governments Omsk and Tobolsk, and at the latter town takes a north-easterly course, and falls into the great river Ob, near the town of Samarowo. Before entering the Saisany sea it is called the

and in the valley of the Imaus,[1] they found large territories, but also numerous enemies. As an instance of
their success, it is stated that one of the lieutenants of
the Fandschus conquered no less than twenty-six tribes
in a single campaign.   In the north the ice-fields of the
Arctic Ocean were soon reached, and all Siberia fell
under their yoke.   The Huns now directed their attention to the south, with the richness of which they seem
to have been perfectly acquainted.   The constant and
terrible inroads which they were in the habit of making
into China at last induced the Chinese Emperor Tsin-
Schi-Hoang-Ti to erect along the frontiers of his dominions a wall of upwards of 1,500 miles in extent, in order
to protect his people from the invasion of their insatiable
adversaries; but this was of no avail, for the cavalry of
the Fandschus, we are told, was irresistible.   These troops
generally consisted of from 200,000 to 300,000 sabres, and
surpassed the Chinese cavalry in dexterity and rapidity
of movement and the use of the bow and arrows, and there
is no doubt that the tactics of the Hunish leaders were
then far superior to those of the Chinese.

Upper Irtish, and on leaving it the Lower Irtish. It receives, in its long
course of above 2,000 miles, many rivers and rivulets, amongst which are
the Narim, the Om, the Tasa, the Ishim, and the Tobol. It is remarkable
for the abundance of its fish, especially the sturgeon, with its famous caviar.
Between the Irtish, the Tobol, and the Alei rivers is situated the great
steppe called the Irtish Baraba steppe.

[1] In ancient geography, the chief mountain of the great Asiatic high-
lands. According to Ptolemy, it not only occupied a great space on the
northern frontier of India from east to west, but also extended from the
north, where there are no mountains to be found at present, and thus
divided Scythia into two large parts or halves, *Scythia intra* and *extra*
Imaum. The western parts of the Imaus were called Emodi montes. The
name of Imaus (in Greek, 'Ιμάος) was known to Strabo as well as to
Ptolemy, and is evidently no other than the one at present used in the
language of the natives of India and thereabout, as Imeia, Ima, Imaas,
Himalaya, which signifies the habitations of snow.

The Chinese Emperor Kuoti, a soldier of fortune, who had risen to the imperial dignity through the bravery which he had displayed in the wars against the enemies of his country, determined to make one grand effort to defeat them. He therefore collected a numerous army, consisting of his bravest warriors; but the Huns, by a series of rapid and skilful movements, contrived entirely to surround him. After an heroic defence, the unfortunate Kuoti was compelled to capitulate and accept the most degrading terms at the hands of his victors. From their peaceful habits, his successors seem to have offered no resistance to the Huns, who, taking advantage of this, became outrageous in their demands, one of the most galling to the Chinese national pride being that a number of the most beautiful maidens should be delivered over to the Huns. In addition to this, it was stipulated that a number of the princesses of the Chinese imperial family should intermarry with some of the Fandschus, or chiefs of the Huns. One of these unfortunate princesses is said to have described in verse her miserable condition: she stated that her only nourishment was sour milk and raw meat, and wished that she might be turned into a bird in order to be able to fly from her captivity, and return to her beloved country.

The vast power of the Huns was at last broken up by Vuti, the fifth Emperor of the powerful house of Han. This he brought about through his military talents and skilful policy, by which he had gained over the Tartars for his allies. His generals had orders to act on the offensive, and they pushed several hundred miles into the country of the Huns. A column upon a high mountain still bears an inscription proclaiming to posterity that the Chinese had advanced 700 miles far into the country of the Huns. In these wildernesses of fabulous extent they suffered unheard-of hardships, and of 140,000 men who had set out against the Huns, only 30,000 returned. These losses, however, were soon repaired. The Chinese commanders, taking advantage of the superiority of their arms, of their war-chariots, and of the services of their Tartar allies, who held at that time some of the chief military posts, surprised the Huns in their camp; and although the Fandschu cut himself a passage through his enemies, he left 15,000 slain on the battle-field. The result of this victory was, not only that the Huns of the southern provinces submitted to the laws and customs of the Chinese, but Vuti and his successors, through their intrigues, induced the various tribes which had been con-quered by the Huns to throw off their galling yoke. The chief tribes of the eastern and western parts seem in course of time to have obtained their freedom, and became the most deadly and irreconcilable enemies of the Huns. The result of these disasters was that the Fandschu was at last obliged to resign his position of independent sovereign. He was received by the Emperor at Sigau, the capital of the Chinese empire, with all the honours due to an independent ruler. A palace was made ready for him, and precedence was given him before all the imperial princes; but his patience, it is said, was sorely tried by the ceremonies of an endless banquet. The sequel of all these ceremonies, however, was that the Fandschu was obliged to do homage on his knees to the Emperor, and swear allegiance in his name and that of his successors. But whenever a favourable opportunity to commit rapine presented itself the Fandschus did not for a moment scruple to break their oath.

Step by step this formidable nation became weaker, until their intestine feuds brought about their final dis-memberment. They became divided into two hostile bodies. One of the Hunic princes was forced to retreat towards the south with eight tribes, consisting of from about 40,000 to 50,000 families. The Chinese Emperor allowed him, near the frontiers of China, a district sufficiently large for himself and followers, and granted him the title of Fandschu. The Northern Huns held their ground for the space of about half a century, but being unable to withstand the constant attacks of their overwhelming enemies, they had to retreat from the seat of their dominions, which had been in their power for upwards of thirteen hundred years. Their most bloody assailants were the Sienpi, an eastern Tartar tribe, which had formerly experienced all the weight of the Hunish yoke. We are led to believe that about 100,000 Huns have been absorbed into the mass of their opponents, for all trace of their name seems to have disappeared from the annals of Tartar history. Twenty thousand families retreated to the south, entered the service of the Chinese Emperor, and were placed in the province of Chansi for the purpose of protecting the frontiers.

The remaining tribes of the Huns contained no doubt the largest part of the fighting population, for we find that they determined to preserve their independence, and for this purpose migrated from those regions where the Chinese and Tartar rule predominated. After leaving the frontiers of China, they divided themselves into two hordes, directing their course towards the Oxus and the Volga. One of the divisions settled on the eastern shores of the Caspian Sea, and received the name of Enthalite and Nephthalite Huns. The country was inhabited by a peaceful and industrious people, and the land itself was rich and productive. This, together with the climate, had a most beneficial effect on the Huns. They not only became civilised, but, as it is stated, probably from their intermarrying with the former inhabitants, their features, colour, and complexion underwent great changes. They were afterwards known as the

White Huns. Their capital was Gorgo, and they were ruled by one of their hereditary leaders, who exercised a well-regulated sovereignty over the whole people.

The neighbourhood of these settlers seems to have excited the jealousy of the Persians, and the consequence was that they took every opportunity of interfering in the affairs of the Hunish kingdom. In their memorable victory over the Persian King Firuz, in the year 484, the Huns proved that they still possessed the determined bravery of their forefathers, although they had given up their barbarous customs.

The progress of the second division of the Huns appears to have been far slower. In the warm climate of China, ancient historians tell us, the Huns wore garments of silk. They were unaccustomed to the severity of the climate, and totally unprepared for it. This, together with the obstinate resistance of the savage tribes that inhabited those parts, rendered their advance very difficult. Arrived on the banks of the Volga, they seemed to have changed their former government, for they did away with the power of the Fandschus, and established a kind of republican confederation, the chief of each tribe managing the affairs of the people under his rule, while the important questions of the nation were settled by a council of the chiefs. They appear to have retained their nomadic habits, for we are told that in summer they wandered with their flocks and herds as far as Sarathon, and even as far as the point where the Kama falls into the Volga. In winter they passed their time amongst the fruitful pasturages which are situated to the mouth of that river.

History gives us little or no information with reference to the condition of this race, until we find them again, under their leaders Balamir, Charaton, and Huldin, advancing towards the west. It is highly probable that their ancient enemies, the Sienpi, had been gradually extending their dominions in the direction of the route which the Huns had taken in their retreat. Be this as it may, they now seem to have taken up their abode on the western bank of the Volga, and pushed forward into Scythia, where it appears they effected their junction with another body of their race, consisting of the best warriors of the southern tribes, who had refused to acknowledge the rule of the Chinese, and had migrated in search of their northern companions. Thus strengthened, under the leadership of Balamir, they again began to advance. On the banks of the Don, in the year 375, they encountered the warriors of the Alani, a Germanic tribe, who had subjugated a part of that country, though their original abode was between the Don and the Volga. These hardy warriors had already extended their excursions as far as the North Sea and the frontiers of India and China. A most desperate and bloody contest now ensued, for the Alani were quite equal to their opponents in bravery and military skill. Fortune, however, favoured the Huns, who defeated the Alani in a great battle, in which the king of the latter fell mortally wounded. The Huns seem to have acted with great prudence, for they formed an alliance with their former opponents, and undertook in common with them the invasion of the dominions of the Goths.[1]

[1] The origin of the Goths in general is very uncertain; there are many fabulous traditions, but all of them more or less obscure. One of these says that the Goths are of Scandinavian origin, and that on account of over-population they embarked in three large ships and landed upon the Prussian shore. In one of these ships, it is stated, were the Ostrogoths, in the other the Visigoths, and in the third the Gepides; the ship of the latter being a very slow and heavy one, they were on that account called the *Gepantas*, or lazy ones. The first great apparition which stepped from fabulous tradition into history was King Ostrogotha, a powerful monarch of the whole people. In the year 247 this monarch crossed the Danube and devastated the provinces of Mœsia and Thracia. The history of the Goths

The terror and dismay spread by the rapid advance of the Huns and Alani, as well as their great number, was aggravated by the astonishment and disgust produced by the screeching voices, uncouth manners, and repugnant ugliness of the Huns, to whom a fabulous descent was attributed; they were compared to bears and to those ugly figures called termini, which were often to be met with on bridges. They differed from their companions by their large shoulders, flat noses, small black and deep-set eyes, and, as they were almost entirely deficient in beards, they were distinguished neither by the appearance of manly youth nor by that of respectable age. The King of the Ostrogoths, Ermanrich, who was then advanced in years, prepared to meet them with the whole of his people; but unfortunately for him he soon discovered that the tributary tribes, exasperated by the cruel exactions of his countrymen, were ready at the first opportunity to side with the invaders. Disunion soon spread itself amongst the ranks of his warriors, and the brave but unfortunate old man, in a fit of despair, is said to have committed suicide. Withimer, his successor, nothing daunted by the alarming state of affairs, seems to have inspired his followers with fresh courage, and, headed by him, they commenced a deadly struggle against tremendous odds. After a short but brilliant resistance the Ostrogoths were totally defeated, and their heroic king fell mortally wounded, fighting at the head of his warriors. The Huns now became masters of the country, and the Ostrogoths had no option left but to acknowledge the Hunish authority, and thus the Amalians, their royal family, appeared in after-years as vassals of Attila. Athanaric,

---

was first written by Cassiodorus, the Prime Minister of Theodoric the Great; this work consisted of twelve volumes, but unfortunately for the world they were lost, and all that remains of them are a few extracts by Jornandes. Procopius has also given a good description of the history of the Goths.

chief of the Visigoths, caring more for the safety of his own tribe than for the welfare of the entire Gothic nation, had taken up on the banks of the Danube a position which offered great facilities of defence, and which he strongly fortified. The warlike astuteness of the Huns, however, deceived the watchfulness of Athanaric's warriors. The Huns had led their adversaries to believe that they would attack them on the bank of the river; but, instead of doing so, a powerful division of horsemen forded the Danube by moonlight and took the Visigoths in rear. It was with the greatest difficulty that their leader cut his way through his enemies and managed to retreat to the mountains. Here the undaunted Athanaric had already devised a fresh and skilful mode of defensive warfare, and would probably have prevented the devastating invasions of the Huns had he not been forced to give up its execution by the cowardly impatience of his people, who did not think themselves safe till they had passed to the other bank of the Danube. His plan seems to have been to carry on a sort of mountain warfare, and it would have been next to impossible for the Huns to operate against him with any chance of success, on account of their want of knowledge of the country, coupled with the fact that the greater and best part of their army consisted of horsemen, who would have here been perfectly useless. A separation of the Visigoths now took place. Athanaric, at the head of a few of his most devoted followers, retired into the mountainous districts of Transylvania, whilst the greater part, under the command of Fritiger and Alavius, hastened to implore the protection of the Byzantine Emperor Valens.[1] The immense extent of country over

[1] In 376 we find those two leaders proceeding to Adrianopol in quest of the assistance which the Roman Emperor had promised them. But it seems that they not only did not receive any help in men or money, but the Roman commissioners did not give them sufficient provisions to supply their daily

which the Huns and the Alani held sway, the distance of
the tribes from each other, and the power which each of
the chiefs possessed, joined with their mutual jealousy,
prevented their coming to any settled plan with reference
to a united advance into Europe.   Some of the tribes,
induced by the promises of Fritiger, fought together with
the Visigoths against the Romans, and their excellent
cavalry successfully supported the efforts of the Gothic
infantry.   The part which they now played was a very
inferior one.   Their victorious hordes ruled over that vast
extent of land which lies between the Volga and the
Danube, but their power was split in two by the quarrels
of their independent leaders.   Their valour was spent in
insignificant   predatory   excursions,   and   their   national
dignity was greatly diminished by the fact that from mere
desire for booty they often joined the standards of their
conquered enemies.   Thus, as we have before said, several
tribes, under Huldin, joined Alaric, King of the Visigoths, and forced the Romans to abandon to their possession certain territories, whilst others became mercenaries
of the Romans, and obtained, about the year 384, permission to settle in Pannonia (at present Hungary).
Several of their tribes traversed Asia Minor, robbing and
sacking both town and country, and the Eastern Roman
Empire was forced to purchase their forbearance.   In the
year 408 about 10,000 Huns entered the service of the
Eastern Romans as mercenary troops; the remainder
seem to have settled down amongst the Germans and
Sarmatians, occupying that territory which extends from

wants; and, in order to preserve themselves from starving, they attacked
the Romans, traversed the country, pillaging and laying waste all the
towns, and defeated the Emperor Valens in a pitched battle near Adrianopol
in August 378.   They then advanced into the Peloponesus, and overran
the East Roman Empire, but were at last induced, by money and promises,
to discontinue plundering the inhabitants.

the northern shores of the Black and Caspian Seas, and from the Volga to the Oural, probably Moldavia, Transylvania, and Wallachia, and were broken up into a number of semi-independent tribes, the names of which only became known after the death of Attila.

The Hungarians state that Attila was one of their kings, and that the tribes which were under the sway of his uncle Roas or Rugilas had established their camps in the precincts of the present Hungarian kingdom, which possessed everything that could be required by a nation of hunters and shepherds. Rugilas, through his skill and bravery, in a short time became so formidable that he held the balance of power between the Roman Empires of the East and West. His connexion with the latter was rendered still stronger by his personal friendship with the Roman general Aëtius.[1]

Rugilas appears to have rendered himself the terror of the East Roman Empire, for he not only invaded their territory, but threatened their capital. The Emperor Theodosius, to induce the King of the Huns to retire, was obliged to pay him a yearly tribute of 350 pounds

---

[1] Aëtius, a Roman patrician and general under the Emperors Honorius and Valentinian III., may be considered the last hero of the West Roman Empire. He was the son of Gaudentius, who held the chief command of the cavalry. Aëtius, when yet a boy, was enrolled among the imperial body guards. In his youth he was given as hostage, first to the Goths and then to the Huns. In time he became commander-in-chief of the army, and the real sovereign of the empire. On the death of the Emperor Honorius, the privy secretary of the empire, John the Usurper, relying upon the support of 60,000 Huns, whom Aëtius had induced to join his standards, seized the throne. But at a later period, when the Emperor of Byzantium, Theodosius, had conquered and executed John, and caused the infant son of Honorius to be made Emperor under the guardianship of his mother Placida, Aëtius took office under the new Power, after having obtained large sums of money for the Huns, to induce them to return to their country. It seems that Pannonia was made over to them. Aëtius rendered his name celebrated by the great defeat which he inflicted on Attila in 451, near Châlons-sur-Marne.

of gold. In order to save his dignity, this tribute was paid to Rugilas as the pay of a Roman general, the Emperor having conferred this title upon him ; but this did not preserve the Empire from constant molestation on the part of the Hunish tribes. Four independent nations, the chief being the Bavarians, instigated by the intrigues of the Roman Court, refused to submit to the rule of Rugilas ; but the instructions which this daring leader gave to his ambassador Estaw were of so threatening a character that the Court of Rome considered it advisable to induce their friends to obey the dictates of Rugilas. The Roman Senate, in common with the Emperor, knew but too well the character of the man against whom they had intrigued, and, fearing the effects of his revenge, they determined if possible to conclude a lasting treaty with him. While the negotiations were going on Rugilas died, and was succeeded by his two nephews Attila and Bleda, sons of his brother Mundzac, who concluded a treaty on horseback, in a plain near the town of Margus, with the Byzantine ambassador, who, to induce them to sign that treaty, had to double the tribute which had been paid to Rugilas. Attila, whose ambition was unbounded, saw that the first step to power was the death of his brother, whom he unhesitatingly murdered, for he knew that as long as Bleda lived he could never reckon upon the union of the tribes owing allegiance to the Huns. It was not only the East Roman Empire which trembled before this ferocious leader, but, under his rule, the Huns became the terror of the whole Western world. It was his great genius and undaunted spirit which alone kept together the machinery of that conglomeration of tribes and countries which he brought under his sway.

Attila was born in the year 406. To give a true picture of his character would be, owing to the many and evident misrepresentations of the authors who wrote shortly after his time, a matter of impossibility. The following, however, may be taken as a pretty true delineation of his character. He was by nature endowed with those manners which have enabled great men like Cæsar and Napoleon to inspire all those with whom they came in contact with feelings of unbounded fear and admiration, and who have, as if compelled by destiny, exercised their power for destruction only. He was adored by his own people, leading them invariably to victory, and was, in a word, the long-wished chief so ardently desired by all those warlike nations who hated peace and delighted in war. As to his person, his walk was proud, his looks terrifying, while his eyes glowed with that peculiar fire indicative of an immense superiority, to which we instinctively and invincibly feel bound to yield. He was without doubt far superior to any other leader of the Huns ; his three great animal attributes were obstinacy, cunning, and bulldog-like ferocity. He did not for one moment scruple as to the means to be employed for obtaining his object, and the lives of human beings were no bar to his ambition, although cruelty was by no means a predominant feature in his character ; but he considered it a good policy to strike terror into his people, though he fully understood the necessity of acknowledging civilisation, for towards the Romans and the Greeks he displayed a degree of moderation which seems unaccountable, when compared with his conduct towards his own subjects. Although the possessor of a large number of wives, and the father of a multitude of children (for it is said his children formed a small army), he preserved his mental capacity and bodily strength to the day of his death, nor was he in the least jealous. Attila was no doubt looked upon by his subjects with love and awe, simply because his justice was regulated by the social condition of his people. The

conquered nations preferred his sway to that of Rome or
Byzantium, for, unlike these empires, Attila allowed the
vanquished to retain their own laws and customs; and
the protection which he afforded to foreigners induced
Greek workmen, merchants, and artists to live in his
dominions.   We are told that he had at his court many
distinguished and learned foreigners, such as Onegisius,
Orestes, Constantius, Edeko, and others.   His army was
always ready to take the field, and he could at any
moment assemble a force of half a million of men.

Attila's march towards the West was occasioned by
circumstances over which he had perhaps but little control.   Complications which were not originated by himself
showed him the way he had to take.   His empire he had
based upon his success; each fresh success contributed to
increase the terror of his name, with increased powers,
his plans grew bolder.   He could as little stop in his onward
march as he could at the beginning have calculated the
way he should go.   There can however be no doubt that
the destruction of both the Roman Empires was the first
object he had in view.

At the death of Attila's uncle, Rugilas, both the East
and West Roman Empires were ruled by women : Pul-
cheria governed the West Roman Empire for her brother
Theodosius II., and Placida the East Roman Empire for
her son Valentinian.   The Emperor Honorius had already
given up Britannia and Armorica (Brittany), and Illyricum
had been ceded to the West Roman Empire for services
which it had rendered.   The Franks, the Burgundians,
and Visigoths had established a firm footing in Spain and
Gaul; on the borders of the Loire the Alani were the
masters, and it was only in that part of the province
round about Arles that the Roman supremacy was acknowledged.   Africa was lost to the Vandals through a
court cabal of the ambitious Aëtius, and since the year

439 Geiserich, a ruler of the Visigoths, had founded a new kingdom, of which Carthago was capital. The East Roman Empire was about this time threatened by three enemies—the Huns and the Bulgares on the northern frontier, and the Persians on the eastern boundaries—while its internal commotions were still more dangerous to itself than its external enemies. What resistance could these two empires, ruled by women and their eunuchs, offer to a powerful prince whom nature seemed to have destined for a conqueror, who was born with the talents of a ruler, and could enforce his powerful will with 1,000,000 of warriors?

The first ruler who seems to have resisted the power of Attila was the Emperor Marcius, who refused to pay tribute to him. Attila determined in revenge to conquer the Eastern Empire, but before so doing, he seems to have formed a design of invading the Western Empire. It is stated that the King Geiserich had ill-treated his queen, a sister of the King of the Visigoths, and fearing that the Goths might seek the assistance of the Romans against him, he determined to be beforehand with them, and therefore instigated Attila to attack his enemies. A certain king of the Franks had also requested Attila's help against Merovæus, the other king of the same nationality, and the Romans; but probably the principal inducement for postponing his attack on Marcius was the offer of marriage which Honoria, sister of the Emperor of the West Romans, Valentinian III., had made to him, backed with the promise of the West Roman Empire as her marriage dowry. In the year 451 Attila, having massed his immense army, which consisted not only of his own people and the tribes who were under his sway, but also of numerous independent nationalities, began his onward march. Historians state that these were the principal tribes who followed his standards:

the Gepides, the Ostrogoths, the Sueves, and the He-
ruleans.   This vast force advanced towards Germany.
Thuringia seems to have been the point on which they
marched.   Attila overcame every obstacle.   The tribes
through which he passed were pressed into the ranks of
his army : Thuringians, Burgundians, and Franks served
to swell his forces in his advance on Gaul.   All the
towns which he entered were totally destroyed, and the
country entirely devastated.

Attila's army is stated to have numbered upwards of
700,000 men; but he found his opponents fully prepared
to meet him.   They were under the command of the
celebrated Roman general Aëtius, who, in addition to his
own forces, had under him King Theodoric with his Visigoths, the Franks under their ruler Merovæus, and the
Alani.   Their army was superior in numbers to that of
Attila.   The two opposing armies encountered each other
in the plains of Châlons-sur-Marne, which were favourable for the cavalry of the Huns ; and one of the most
dreadful battles which have ever been recorded ensued.
It was called the ' Battle of the Huns.'   The speech of
Attila to the kings and leaders under his command has
been preserved by Cassiodorus, and given by Jornandes.

Theodoric with the Visigoths formed the right wing,
Aëtius and the Romans the left, whilst King Sangibar
and the Alani, whom neither Theodoric nor Aëtius
entirely trusted, were in the centre.   Opposite to them was,
in the centre, Attila with his Huns.   The Ostrogoths,
led by their king, Wladimir, and his brothers Theodomir
and Widimir formed the left wing.   On the right wing
stood Ardaric, the faithful friend of Attila, commanding
his Gepides.   Theodoric was killed in the battle, but his
faithful Visigoths, reeking with vengeance, led by his son
Thorismund, threw themselves with such a force and such
desperate valour on the Huns that they were broken,

and, for the first time, Attila was compelled to retreat. Night only put an end to the carnage and saved the Huns from destruction. They left more than 150,000 men on the battle-field; the loss of the Francs was also terrific. Seeing that further advance had become impossible, Attila retraced his steps into Hungary. In 452 he invaded Italy, and plundered the towns of Aquila, Vicenza, Pavia, and Milan, and advanced on Rome; it was only through the tears and entreaties of the Bishop Leo that he was induced to give up the idea of sacking this city. He now returned to Hungary, where he died shortly after, during the festivals on the occasion of his marriage with a Burgundian princess called Hildico. There is, however, great mystery with reference to the real cause of his death. His body was placed in a golden coffin, which was then deposited in a silver one, and the latter again in one made of iron. A deep excavation was made, and the coffin, together with a large number of jewels and arms of different nations which Attila had acquired in his different campaigns, was lowered into it. This last duty to the deceased leader performed, the prisoners and slaves who had dug the grave were all put to death, so that the place of the burial of Attila should never be divulged.

After the death of Attila, the most daring leaders attempted to become sovereigns. The numerous sons of Attila divided between themselves the sovereignty over the Germanic and Scythian tribes, but were constantly contending against each other. The brave Ardaric, king of the Gepides, felt the disgrace of such a division under foreign sway, and his people, who had reaped the bitter fruits of disunion and disloyalty, rallied round him to a man. The Ostrogoths, who had thrown off the Hunish yoke, also assisted him. The latter were led by three valiant brothers. The Sueves, the Herulians, and the

Alani, profiting by this revolt, also joined the standards of Ardaric. The Huns encountered their opponents on the banks of the Netad in Pannonia, where a decisive battle was fought, in which the Huns were totally defeated. They lost 30,000 men, amongst whom was the eldest son of Attila. Dengesish, another son of Attila, retreated with his followers to the borders of the Danube, where, although beaten and surrounded by enemies, he managed to render his name terrible to them for the space of fifteen years, but finding his ground untenable, he threw himself on the Western Empire. Having been defeated and captured, he was decapitated, and his head was exposed in the Hippodrome of Constantinople. The youngest and favourite son of Attila, Ernach, retreated with some of the hordes into Asia. The country of Attila, ancient Dacia, from the Carpathian mountains to the Black Sea, became the seat of a new State and Power, founded by Ardaric, King of the Gepides. From this period all further trace of the Huns as a nation appears to have been lost.

CHAPTER III.

ARPÁD, FIRST DUKE OF HUNGARY.

WE have in the preceding pages, through the means of ancient writers, attempted to describe the history of the Magyars up to the election of Arpád as their common ruler, but we cannot relinquish the idea that the Magyars were a high caste from which the rulers of the Hunic nationalities were chosen, and that they possessed a far greater affinity to the Turkestan race than their followers.

At this time there is no doubt that they had profited by the civilisation of their Persian neighbours. Arpád himself seems to have been a man who fully understood the art of ruling; and although he originated all the great plans of conquest, he wisely allowed his counsellors to believe that they were entitled to the credit of them. This is proved by the fact that before undertaking anything of importance he held a council, in which he was apparently guided by the voice of the majority. In the gradual decay of the Greek Empire, Arpád saw a chance of reconquering the vast kingdom of Attila, whose victories and history were deeply cherished in the bosoms of his followers. At length the long-wished-for opportunity arrived. The Emperor Leo VI., unable to subdue the powerful Simeon, ruler of the Bulgarians, sent his general Niketas as envoy to negotiate an offensive alliance with Arpád. To this the Magyar duke readily agreed; and in the year 888 the campaign commenced. Liuntika, a son of Arpád, assisted by the Greek fleet, which had advanced up the Danube, crossed that river and defeated the Bulgarians in three consecutive battles. These defeats compelled Simeon to conclude peace, and the Magyars returned to their country loaded with the spoils of the campaign.

The following extract from the writings of Leo VI. will give our readers a tolerably good idea of the social condition and military efficiency of the Magyars:

'The Turks' (as he always styled the Hungarians) 'are a numerous people, who love a wild independence, and prefer conquering their enemies to living in luxury. They are ruled by a king who is a most severe disciplinarian, and they are at all times ready to undergo the greatest hardships. They are excessively cautious, and preserve the greatest secrecy with reference to their plans; they are very avaricious and insatiable in their desire for plunder, and very apt to break their treaties. They prefer surprising their enemy either by a subterfuge or skilful manœuvre, rather than attacking him and giving him a fair chance of defence.

' Their weapons consist of a shield, a sword, a bow and arrows, a lance, or a javelin; in battle, they have two weapons, a spear and a bow; if they are pursued they generally defend themselves with arrows. The forepart of their horses is protected by a kind of iron shield. They are also first-rate shots when on horseback. In their trains they have a large number of horses and other animals for the purpose of deceiving their enemies with reference to their numerical strength, and also to make use of their milk as a means of subsistence on their march. They never conceal themselves behind entrenchments. They are divided into tribes or families, and leave their horses exposed to the elements during winter and summer. In times of war their horses are picketed close to their tents; they generally commence their attacks with them in the night.

' Their pickets or sentinels stand at some distance from
their tents in order to prevent their being surprised by the
enemy.   On the field of battle their legions are so close
to each other that they appear as one.   They also have
a reserve, which they use either for outmanœuvring the
enemy, or supporting any part of the army which
requires its assistance.   Their baggage stands generally
with a sufficient guard in rear of the order of battle.
Their favourite tactic is to commence the battle at a
distance, and by a series of skilful manœuvres suddenly
throw themselves in the middle of their opponents; these
manœuvres consist generally either in feigned retreats or
flank movements.   They also fully understand the art of
fighting in detached bodies.   If they defeat their opponent they do not pursue the tactic of the Romans and
other people, of following the defeated enemy for a
certain time only: they pursue him until they have
entirely annihilated the retreating force. As they possess
large flocks, they do not like their pasturage grounds to
be too near each other.

' They do all in their power to prevent their being
engaged in a hand-to-hand fight with the heavy infantry.
They are greatly opposed to any of their soldiers closing
with the enemy, as most of the legions being composed
of a tribe, they are afraid that the remaining part would
follow their example.'

The feelings of revenge which the Bulgarians and
their king felt towards the Magyars were doubly increased by the knowledge that their victors were a
kindred race.   Inspired by the thirst for retaliation,
they waited for the moment when they could safely
indulge it, and for this purpose concluded a treaty with
the Patzenaci, the ancient and irreconcilable enemies
of the Magyars.   In 889, whilst Arpád, at the head of

his warriors, had left his country for the purpose of
subduing the Sclavonic tribes of the north, Simeon
crossed the Danube, and the Patzenaci advancing at the
same time from the east, seem to have effected a junction
in the heart of the Magyar country, overcoming all
resistance and laying everything waste. We are told
that Atelköz, the capital, was entirely destroyed, and
that Liuntika and his venerable grandfather Almos
fell whilst vainly attempting to defend their homes. The
Patzenaci now took permanent occupation of the greater
part of the dominions of Arpád, who, on hearing of the
disasters which had taken place, was convinced, from the
strength of his two enemies, that it would be impossible
for him to reconquer his country, and determined to
acquire a new abode. For this purpose he advanced
against the Rugians, who, assisted by the Russians and
another warlike tribe, whose name and origin are doubtful,
defended their dominions with the most obstinate resistance. Their bravery, however, was no match against
the military skill of Arpád, who overcame them and took
possession of their country. The unfortunate Rugians
and their allies retreated to Kiew, but the difficulty of
their position was so great that they perceived further
resistance would be futile, and therefore sent messengers
of peace to Arpád, begging of him to allow them to
remain in peaceful possession of their new homes, and
pointing out to him that he had far better cross the
Alps and enter Pannonia than disturb them, as that
country was watered by two magnificent rivers—the
Theiss and the Danube—and the land, which was sin-
gularly fertile, was inhabited by Sclaves, Bulgarians,
Wallachians, who could offer him no resistance. The
information of the Rugian envoys was received with eager-
ness by Arpád and his warriors, who were nothing loth
again to enrich themselves at the expense of the Bulgarians,

for probably there were many of them who had been engaged in the expedition against Simeon, and knew the correctness of the statements of the Rugians. Arpád informed the envoys that he was ready to conclude peace with them on condition of their paying 10,000 marks in silver, together with a large number of weasel, martin, and sable skins. By a series of skilful negotiations the Magyar ruler also induced the principal leaders of the Cumanians and Rugians—Ede, Edömér, Ete, Bönger, Acháд, Vojta, and Ketel—to join his standards. Their alliance was considered of such importance that they were placed on an equal footing with the rest of the woiwodes, and they in return acknowledged Arpád as their ruler. The first great service which these new allies rendered the Magyars was the skilful way in which they conducted the entire army in safety to the neighbourhood of the town of Ladomer, whose prince came to meet his unwelcome guests. Here the Magyars and their allies remained three weeks. On their departure, the prince presented them with 2,000 marks in silver, 1,000 in gold, 300 chargers with martial trappings, a great number of valuable skins, and 1,000 head of cattle for the purpose of conveying their baggage. Arpád now directed his march to Galicia, and here again the ruler seems to have purchased his friendship at the price of 3,000 silver and 200 gold marks. The Hungarian forces remained in this place for the space of a month. Horwáth, in his ' History of Hungary,' supposes that this is the place where the envoys of the Secklers welcomed Arpád as the successor of Attila, and acknowledged him as their lord and master. Before going further with our narrative of the subjugation of Hungary by the Magyars, it seems to us advisable to give a slight sketch of its history.

The situation of Hungary in the southern parts of Europe, the splendid climate of the country, the fertility of the soil and abundance of its natural produce, have in all ages attracted the peoples of Asia and of Western Europe. Thus Dacians, Bastarnians, Getes, Illyrians, Iaconians, Sarmatians, Jazyges, Vandals, Bulgarians, Alani, Avarians, Huns, Sueves, Quades, Marcomanes, Gepides, Longobardes, Goths, and others, have invaded the country one after another, and either wholly or partially expelled the former inhabitants. From the above-named nations, there still remained a considerable number of Bulgarians, and different tribes of Sclaves, Wallachians, and Sarmates, when, lastly, the Magyars invaded the country and entirely conquered it. The history of the country before the Romans is not known; most likely it was inhabited by Celts. When the Romans spread their dominion over Rhætia and Illyria, and extended their northern frontier to the very Danube, they found to the north of Illyria the Pannonians, who were but hordes of robbers, and whom they then began to subjugate. It was under Augustus that they were entirely subdued, and Segatia, now Sissek, their capital, was taken in the year 35 B.C. The Pannonians often revolted, and it was only by erecting castles on the Danube, selling part of the inhabitants as slaves, and colonising the country that the Romans were enabled to effect its complete reduction. Speaking on this subject, Gibbon says: ' The country of Pannonia and Dalmatia, which occupied the space between the Danube and the head of the Adriatic, was one of the last and most difficult conquests of the Romans. In the defence of national freedom 200,000 of these barbarians had once appeared in the field, alarmed the declining age of Augustus, and exercised the vigilant prudence of Tiberius at the head of the collected forces of the Empire. The Pannonians yielded at last to the arms and institutions of Rome. Their recent subjection, however, the neighbourhood, and even mixture of unconquered tribes, and perhaps the climate, adapted, as it has been observed, to the production of great bodies and slow minds, all contributed to preserve some remains of their original ferocity, and under the tame semblance of Roman provincials the hardy features of the natives were still to be discerned. Their warlike youth afforded an inexhaustible supply of recruits to the legions stationed on the banks of the Danube, which, from a perpetual warfare against the Germans and Sarmatians, were deservedly esteemed the best troops in the service.'

Towards the middle of the third century the Emperor Probus introduced the cultivation of the vine. Under Constantine the Great, four bishoprics and two archbishoprics were established in the country, but after him Christianity soon lost ground again, as soon after that event the migration of nations began.

In the year 374 the Quades and Jazyges invaded Pannonia, laying everything waste. Then came the Huns, whom in 383 the Emperor Honorius tried in vain to expel. Not having succeeded, he left the country to them, and the Huns remained in possession till the death of Attila in 453, when they retired again to the Don. Pannonia was then successively occupied by the Gepides, the Skyrres, the Herulians, and the Rugians. The three former soon disappeared again, but the Rugians founded a kingdom composed of the upper part of present Hungary and the archduchy of Austria; the new kingdom was, however, again destroyed in 488 by Odomer.

The Ostrogoths under Theodoric took possession of the country, and kept it till the year 525. Already some time before this, the Avari, a Hunic tribe driven out of its steppes by the Turks, had settled in Dacia (the present Transylvania and upper part of Hungary). They now took possession of abandoned Pannonia, called it

Avaria (568), and made successful war from thence upon the Wendes and Serbi in Bohemia, Moravia, and Lusatia. Their dominion lasted 200 years, and its downfall seems to have been brought about by the constant inroads which they were in the habit of making into the dominions of Charlemagne.   In 791 this ruler assembled an army at Regensburg, together with an armed flotilla, which descended the Danube and defeated the Avari. Their final subjugation occurred in 796, when Pepin and the Duke of Frioul, Gerhold, stormed their great stronghold, which had formerly been considered impregnable.   The country then became a province of the great empire of the Francs, and the inhabitants for a short time professed to have become Christians.   During his stay in Galicia, Arpád seems to have busied himself in collecting a minute description of the races, and of the state of the country which he was about to subdue.

Horwath gives us the result of his inquiries.   The country to the west of the Danube was then inhabited by Germanic and Sclavonic tribes.   That part of the territory which extends between the Danube and the Theiss, as far as the foot of the Alps, was ruled by Zalau, a descendant of the Bulgarian prince Kean.   The northwest was under the sway of the Moravian prince Swatopluk.   On the opposite side of the Theiss the prince of the Chazaren, Marót, ruled over the territory which is bounded by the Maros, the Samos, and the forest of Ingvány.   The Bulgarian prince Glads held sway over the territory lying between the Maros and the Danube; and the present Transylvania was under the rule of Gyula, a Wallachian prince.   In order to expedite the departure of Arpád and his followers, the Galician prince placed at their disposal 2,000 bowmen and 3,000 peasants to assist them in overcoming the difficulties in their march through the Alpine forests.   Towards the end of the year 889 the Magyar forces crossed the Verezker pass, and followed the course of the river Latorcza in the present Beregher Comitat. Here they encamped forty days, during which they fortified their position, to which they gave the name of Munkács. The Sclavonians who inhabited that part of the country flocked in large numbers to do homage to Arpád, who, profiting by the influence which his army inspired, demanded that Zalau's lieutenant, who was governor of Ungvár, the capital of this district, should also do homage to him. This the Sclavonic general declined to do, and, not being sufficiently strong, he retreated before the Magyar forces. He was overtaken by some of Arpád's followers, and hung upon a tree near a rivulet, which up to the present day is called Laborcza, by which name the unfortunate man was styled by the Magyars. The town of Ungvár shortly after capitulated. The Magyars and their allies, to celebrate the fall of this fortified town, which was in fact their first victory on Hungarian territory, feasted four days. Before making an onward movement with the mass of his forces, Arpád seems to have sent out a number of expeditions for the purpose of subjugating the surrounding country. In this his generals met with no opposition on the part of the Sclavonic population, who, from what they had most probably heard of Arpád's policy, considered that his rule would be beneficial to them. Zalau, although not in a position, at that time, to withstand the Magyars, attempted to work on the fears of Arpád through the means of an envoy whom he had ordered forcibly to point out to the descendant of Almós the dangers which he would have to encounter should he attempt to subjugate his country. The envoy stated that Arpád must be prepared not only to overcome his master, but also his allies, the Greeks and the Bulgarians. The Magyar chief answered that, ' although that country

which extended from the Theiss and the Danube to
Bulgary had formerly belonged to his forefather Attila,
yet for the sake of preserving peace he would be contented if Zalau would allow him to extend his rule as far
as the Sajó, and at the same time send him a pitcher
of water from the Danube and a bundle of hay from the
fields of Alpár, in order that he might ascertain whether
the water of the Danube was as pure as that of the Don,
and the hay as sweet as that which was growing in his
former home.'   Arpád also despatched the woiwodes
Ond and Ketel with twelve thoroughbred white stallions,
together with the same number of camels and Cumanian
oxen, for Zalau, and twelve Ruthenian maidens, with an
equal number of rich dresses embroidered with gold, for
his wife.   Zalau, no doubt, flattered himself that he had
deceived his opponent, and as he knew that it would require
some time before Arpád could get peaceable possession of
the territory which he desired, he consented to its occupation, trusting that the interval would enable him to
bring about an offensive alliance with the Bulgarians and
the Greeks.   In order to lull still more completely any
suspicion which the Magyar ruler might entertain towards
him, he sent the bundle of hay and pitcher of water and
several rich presents to Arpád, though he must have
fully understood the signification of the former present.
Arpád now seems to have pushed forward into the country
with a select band of his warriors and counsellors, for the
purpose of ascertaining its state.   The spot from which
this reconnaissance took place was called by the Magyars
Szerencs, and the magnificent panorama which their
future homes presented from this point so excited their
imagination that they held a feast, which lasted three
days, after which they took possession of the country, and
pushed on two armed expeditions, one under the Cumanian
woiwodes Ede and Edömer, who advanced through the

Sajothál to Matra; the other under Bars, beyond the Hermadthan to Tatro, which they occupied.

Arpád, on finding there was little chance of his being disturbed by Zalau, despatched an envoy to Bihar, the residence of Prince Marót, for the purpose of demanding the cession of the Samos and the Nyirség districts, under threat of a declaration of war. When the prince declined to acquiesce in his demands, Arpád ordered Tas, the father of Lels, Zsabolcs son of Elöd, and Töhötön to advance with their followers against the unfortunate Marót. This prince, not being sufficiently strong to act on the offensive, retreated, and took up a position on the banks of the Korös. Zsabolcs, in order to get a permanent footing in that part of the country which he had subjugated, built, with the assistance of the population, a fortification, which he called after his own name. In conjunction with Tas, he took possession of Nyirség for the Magyars, and laid siege to Szamár, which fell into his hands after three days ; he then advanced as far as the mountain of Meszes. In the meantime Töhötön and his son Horka occupied the district of Ermellek. Before we proceed further, it may be well to relate how this leader got possession of a large part of Transylvania.

Arpád was most probably convinced that in order to obtain peaceful possession of Hungary he must stretch his dominions to their natural frontiers. He therefore now ordered Töhötön to advance through the passes of the Meszes mountains into Transylvania, and get if possible a permanent footing in that country. This order the hardy lieutenant seems to have executed, for we find that he advanced to the banks of the Almos, where he defeated the prince of that country, Gyula, who lost his life in the defence of his independence. The inhabitants of the country, now without a ruler, acknowledged the authority of the Magyars ; and the place where they did homage bears up to the present day the name of Esküllö, which means the oath. In recompense for the service which Töhötön had rendered, Arpád nominated him woiwode of the conquered territory.

The generals Zsabolcs and Tas do not seem to have been so successful, for they were obliged to content themselves with the occupation of that portion of the territory of the Chazaren which lies between the Samos and the Körös, as the Prince Marót could not be driven from the position which he occupied on this last river. Arpád now despatched another envoy to Zalau, again demanding a slice of this unlucky ruler's dominions, namely, that part of his country between the Zagyon and his own territory. Zalau, who had not yet succeeded in bringing about the wished-for alliance, was obliged to accede to the request of his powerful opponent.

The Magyar ruler now began to divide into districts all the territory which had fallen into his possession since he had first entered Hungary. He gave to the Cumanian chiefs Ede and Edömer that part of his dominions bordering on the Matra which is at present inhabited by the Paloczen. The woiwodes Desád and Bönger received the districts on the Sajó (now the Borsoder comitat, so called from Bors, son of Bönger). These appointments, everyone will admit, display a great sagacity on the part of Arpád. He knew that, as his own race was small in numbers, it was of the highest importance to him that their effective strength should not be diminished. He therefore, as we have before seen, wisely employed his allies in extending his dominions, and, in order to secure their fidelity, he generously rewarded them for their services. The state of Europe at that time afforded great facilities for a man of his talents and genius, not only to increase his power and extend his territory, but also to become a sovereign in Europe.

Arnulf had ascended the throne of the East Francs under the greatest difficulties; Italy and France had elected their own kings, and the Normans were renewing their inroads into his territory; Germany was also in a very unsettled state. Already Thuringia, Saxony, and Lorraine had their dukes; Count Rudolph had founded the kingdom of Burgundy, which included Savoy and Switzerland. Arnulf's greatest opponent was a Sclavonic prince, Swatopluk, who had extended his dominion over Bohemia and Poland to the banks of the Drave, and now threatened the dismemberment of Germany, by the unification of all the Sclavonic nationalities into one great empire. In this extremity, Arnulf was obliged to look about for a powerful ally, and finding in Arpád a willing instrument, he concluded with him an offensive alliance. The Magyar ruler was to advance against Swatopluk from the east, whilst Arnulf himself should come from the west. Arpád, however, seems to have been at this time aware of Zalau's intentions, and, believing that this prince would seize the opportunity of the advance of his troops against the Sclavonic king, he did not accompany his army, but ordered the woiwodes Huba and Bors, and Szovard and Radocsa the two sons of his uncle, to advance from the Matra in a westerly direction, whilst he himself, with the remainder of his forces, took up a position in the district of Zagyva. The Magyar expedition pushed along the Grau without meeting any resistance, and divided their forces into two bodies. Bors took possession of the valley of the Grau, and erected on the banks of that river the fortresses of Zohl and Bars. The remaining body encountered Zobor, the general of Swatopluk, who, instead of massing his troops in rear of the important fortress of Neutra, had advanced to meet his foes. The Sclavonic army was defeated, and its leader hung on the top of a promontory which still bears his name. The cause of his execution was his manfully declining to break his oath of allegiance to his sovereign. The remnants of Zobor's army sought refuge behind the walls of the fortifications of Neutra, which must have been of considerable strength, for this fortress seems to have been able to hold out for some time against the victorious army. After the fall of Neutra, the strongholds of Galgocz, Sempto, Trenecsin, and others fell into the hands of Arpád's generals, who then crossed the Neutra and subjugated the country as far as the Danube and the Carpathian mountains, capturing the principal chiefs of the country. Here Arpád again displayed the talents of a great conqueror, for, by means of arguments and promises, he induced his prisoners to swear allegiance to him, and forthwith gave them their freedom and allowed them to occupy the different positions which they had held formerly. The woiwode Huba was made commander of the important fortress of Neutra. Swatopluk had in the meantime been defeated by Arnulf, and retired to end his days in a cloister. He was succeeded by his two sons, whose fratricidal disputes soon brought about the downfall of the Sclavonic kingdom, so that the Magyars remained undisturbed possessors of their newly acquired demesnes.

In the meantime Zalau, who had at last formed an alliance with the Greeks and Bulgarians, resolved not to lose so favourable an opportunity as that which this expedition gave him to recover those provinces which he had been forced to cede. He therefore sent an envoy to Arpád demanding the restoration of his territory. Arpád declined to do so, stating that when Zalau sent him the bundle of hay and pitcher of water it was a ratification of the cession of his country to him, which he paid for by the twelve stallions which Zalau had received. War now ensued. Zalau, with his allies, advanced as far as the plains of Alpár, where he encountered the Hungarian forces. Arpád directed Lil, son of Tas, to begin the attack, and if possible to throw himself on the Bulgarians, who composed the main strength of Zalau's army, and defeat them. The soldiers of Arpád were burning with impatience to inflict upon the Bulgarians those injuries which the latter had committed against their countrymen in their inroad into Atelköz ; the Bulgarians, on their side, not forgetful of the past victory of Liuntika and the immense booty which that leader had taken from their country, were not better disposed towards the Magyars. The signal for onslaught was the blowing of a horn by Tas. The Bulgarians, nothing loth to meet their former opponents, whom they considered as their natural enemies, rushed forward with the greatest bravery. A most terrible and bloodthirsty hand-to-hand fight now took place. The Bulgarians, defending the ground inch by inch with the greatest determination and bravery, retreated, leaving the battle-field covered with corpses. Their overthrow compelled Zalau to seek safety in flight, in which he did not pause till he reached Weissenburg in Bulgaria. After this victory Arpád took up a position near the Lake of Kórtvel, in the forest of Gyümölcsös. Here, we are told, was assembled a great council, which lasted for thirty-four days. The result of the deliberations of Arpád and his counsellors was a classification of all the grades of society which should exist amongst his people, and all the rights appertaining thereto, together with the code of laws by which they should be ruled. Horwáth is of opinion that this council had for its purpose the division of the country into certain royal domains, of which the different strongholds which had fallen into the hands of Arpád should form the centre or capital, and of which the chiefs of the different tribes should be governors. Two-thirds of the people who lived near one of these castles had to

defend it, and were to receive for their services a certain
portion of the land as an hereditary fief. The remaining
parts of the population were intended for military purposes, such as making inroads in the neighbouring
countries. Hungarians call this meeting Puszta Szer.

Arpád now busied himself in the internal affairs of his
State, and became complete master of the entire territory
which lies between the Theiss and the Danube. He then
despatched a strong expedition against Belgrad. This
force crossed the Danube where the Drave effects its
junction with that river. Simeon and his brave Bulgarians were again defeated, and in order to prevent further
molestation, and be left in peaceful occupation of his kingdom, this ruler was compelled to pay a yearly tribute to
the Magyars. The victorious Hungarians now overran
Croatia, defeating and killing its ruler. Spalatro, on the
Adriatic, also fell into their hands; but they do not seem
to have permanently occupied the country, for we are
told that they took with them the sons of the principal
chiefs, and returned loaded with booty to Arpád, who
was then encamped on the Bodrog. Another expedition,
under the command of Szovard and Kadocsa, crossed the
Theiss, defeated the Prince Glad, and forced him to
swear allegiance to Arpád. In his ‘History of Hungary,’
Horwáth says that the victorious leaders advanced as far
as Durazzo, on the Adriatic. Here Szovard married,
and seems to have taken up his abode, for the people of
that country were afterwards called Stuben Magyars, or
Door Magyars. Arpád, having now got his kingdom in
order, determined to erect the capital, and for this purpose he selected one of the islands in the Danube, which
was called by the Cumanians Csepel. Here he built a
palace for himself and family. His example was followed
by his counsellors, and by degrees traders, to whom
Arpád always ensured every species of protection, were

induced to settle in those parts. Hungarian writers
seem to believe that this town contained a large number
of palaces. In this opinion we cannot coincide, for the
few remains of old buildings which are still to be seen in
Hungary give a very poor idea of the architectural
talents of the Magyars. In fact, their nomadic habits
must, we think, have rendered them greatly averse to
becoming inhabitants of cities.

The continued unsettled state of Europe again enabled
Arpád to increase his territory, for we find him leading
in person a large number of troops in search of conquests.
It is stated that he first marched to the stream of Rakós,
where he crossed the Danube and took possession of
Etzelburg (Buda or Ofen), which offered him no resistance—in fact, seems to have received him as a friend. A
slight historical sketch of that town may not be without
interest for some of our readers.

As early as A.D. 256, Alt Ofen, or, as it was then
called, Sicambria, was colonised by the Romans. History, however, furnishes us with but very few facts relative to this ancient city. In 454 a great battle was
fought near that town, in which the Huns, under the son
of Attila, were entirely defeated; and towards the end of
the ninth century it fell, as we have before said, into the
hands of the Magyars. Stephen built a church and introduced Christianity into Buda in 1022. In 1261 the
town was almost entirely destroyed by the Tartars, who
again, in 1285, made a second descent into Hungary, but
were this time repulsed. In was in the plains of Rakós,
near Pesth, as it was called at the end of the eleventh
century, that the public assembly of the States was accustomed to be held. In 1514, Thomas, the Archbishop of
Gran, having obtained from the Pope, Leo X., permission
to preach a crusade, the plains near Pesth were designated
as the point from which the expedition should proceed. An

immense number of peasants, glad to escape in that way from the oppression of the nobles, assembled, and, under the command of Droscha, soon took a threatening attitude. The nobles having resorted to strong measures to restrain their serfs from joining the standards of the Cross, Droscha gave up the suburbs of Pesth to the rage of his followers. A bloody strife now ensued, and it was not till the leader of the insurgents and more than 70,000 peasants had lost their lives that the insurrection was completely quelled. In 1526, Pesth fell into the hands of the Turks, and their Sultan, Soliman, suffered his soldiers to pillage the town and put to death a great number of the inhabitants. When the Turks retired, John Zapolyay, woiwode of Transylvania, caused himself to be acknowledged King of Hungary, but, being attacked by Ferdinand of Austria in 1527, he called the Turks to his assistance. Soliman, at the head of an army of 300,000 men, entered Hungary in 1529 and established his authority over the town, converting the churches into mosques, and forming arsenals and a harbour for his fleet. For a period of nearly sixty years the town remained in the possession of the Turks. The fortifications were almost entirely destroyed in the many attempts which were made to drive them out, and when, in 1686, the town fell into the hands of the Duke of Lorraine, it was in a most miserable state. Under the domination of the Turks the greatest part of the Christian population had taken to flight, and the few inhabitants who remained were poor and miserable. On account of the different changes which had taken place in its government, and the constant sieges which it had sustained, all the suburbs of the town had been long demolished, the fortifications almost entirely destroyed, and the town itself was a mass of ruins. From that time however the picture brightened. Its privilege of a royal free town was restored to it, and the Emperor Leopold took it under his special care. It was adorned with public buildings. In 1724 the two High Courts of Justice were fixed at Pesth; in 1727 the University was transferred from Ofen to Pesth; the population rapidly increased; foreign traders, seeing the protection which was given to the town, were again induced to settle in it; and Pesth soon regained its former prosperity.

We return to Arpád and his followers. Horwáth says that the Magyars were greatly struck by the sight of the stone buildings which they found in this town. This fully confirms the opinion already expressed that the Magyars knew little or nothing of the fine arts. The Magyar duke and his forces seem to have passed a very pleasant time with their hospitable friends, for we hear a great deal of the gold and silver vessels, which clearly proves that they were as fond of the juice of the generous grape as their descendants are at the present day. Arpád completely gained the affection of the people of this neighbourhood, and induced many of them to join his standard. After twenty days of festivities, he again put his army in motion, but before so doing he divided it into three bodies. The first corps advanced against the stronghold of Baranya, which was taken after a siege of three days, and subjugated the surrounding neighbourhood as far as the Drave; a second body pushed into Corynthia, and extended the frontier line to the river Lapincs; whilst the third division, led by Arpád in person, marched against the Moravian Sclaves. The Magyar duke first directed his march to the foot of the Vertes Gebergs, and defeated these Sclaves at Banhida; he then pitched his camp on the St. Martin's mountain. From this point Arpád in a short time overran the country lying on the banks of the Raab and Babcza.

The Magyars and their allies do not seem to have

retained permanent possession of the mountainous country, but domiciled themselves in the immense plains extending between the Theiss and the Danube, together with the rich and undulating country which extends along its opposite bank. Arpád took possession of Stuhlweissenburg and the surrounding territory as his private property, which was to remain perpetually in his own family. According to Horwáth, the woiwode Elöd and his son Zsabolcs, with their followers, settled in Vértesalja; Bulcs in Zala, in the neighbourhood of the Platten See; Vojta occupied the low grounds of Sárviz; Ede and his people the district of Barranya; Örs remained in his former possession between the Sajó and the Zagywa; and Ond in the Nyírség. We are informed that about this time Arpád's wife gave birth to a son, who was called Zsolt. This great event was hailed with the highest satisfaction, and celebrated by the Magyars with a continued round of festivities; for it seems that Arpád was at that time childless, as all his male descendants had either perished on the field of battle or died from natural causes. This leads us to the supposition that Arpád had married twice, for Greek writers mention besides Liuntika the names of three other sons who must have reached the age of manhood before their death, and Liuntika himself could not have been less than thirty years of age when he fell in the defence of his country, or else his father would never have allowed him to take the command of so important an expedition as that which he led against Simeon. The geographical position of the dominions of the ruler of the Chazaren, on account of their interrupting the communication with Transylvania, rendered it extremely desirable that they should be incorporated into the dominions of the Magyars; but Arpád, as we have before stated, had acknowledged its independence on condition that the ruler, Marót, should pay him a yearly tribute, which in those days was generally considered as a sign of subjugation.   Nevertheless, up to the time of which we are writing both parties seem to have kept faithfully their agreement.   From what the great Hungarian historian states, it would seem that Arpád despatched an armed force, under the command of the woiwodes Velek and Ö   b, to conquer that country. The brave Marót, unable to resist, fled from Bihar, and took refuge in the forest of Ingvány.   After Bihar had fallen, and the inhabitants had taken the oath of allegiance, Marót sent envoys to Arpád, entreating him to be allowed to remain in peaceful possession of his kingdom during his life, and, as he had no male descendants, his young daughter should be married to Arpád's son, and on his (Marót's) demise the kingdom of the Chazaren would come into the possession of Arpád's family without bloodshed.   The Magyar ruler agreed to this proposal on condition that the young princess should be at once sent to his court.   From what history tells us of the character and former acts of Arpád, we should be rather inclined to think that the talented Magyar leader would have at first attempted to get peaceful possession of the country, for he must have known that Marót was then totally unprepared to meet the large forces which the Magyars could bring against him; and, moreover, as the King of the Chazaren had no male issue, the princess was one of the most eligible matches for his son, for such a union would give him a firm hold on the affections of a people whose warlike character rendered it highly desirable that they should become the supporters of his dynasty.

The great number of nationalities over which Arpád ruled, and the small number of his own race, rendered it far from unlikely that at his death a catastrophe similar to that which destroyed the Huns might befall his empire. He knew that his talents and genius were the only real

E

tie which held together this mass of races, and in order to ensure a peaceful possession to his son he married him when he was a mere child. He then induced all the different leaders to acknowledge his heir and legitimate successor as their sovereign duke, and, in order to increase the validity of this transaction, Szolt took the constitutional oath. About two years after this ceremony Marót died, leaving his son-in-law as his successor. From this period up to his own death, Arpád gave his whole attention to the development of his kingdom, and was obliged for many years to allow his followers to exercise their warlike and barbaric propensities on the inhabitants of the surrounding countries. The records of history are full of interesting anecdotes of these raids, in which the Magyars and their allies proved that when not under the immediate surveillance of Arpád they were not inferior to the Huns in bravery, perhaps superior in barbaric ferocity. Their constant success and the immense amount of booty which they obtained induced them to flock together in large numbers, and advance into Italy. Here they defeated King Berenger in 899 on the Brenta, the Italians losing upwards of 20,000 men. The lawless horde took and sacked the towns of Milan, Pavia, and Brescia, crossed the Po, and pushed on as far as Parma and Nonantula. In order to prevent their further advance, and to obtain the evacuation of Italy, the King was obliged to pay them a large sum of money. This last expedition seems to have aroused the fears of Arpád that unless he put a stop to these depredations all Europe might fall on him and his people, and drive them back to their original homes. He therefore, in conjunction with the principal chiefs, forbade his subjects to make war against the people of neighbouring countries without his permission. Unfortunately for Hungary, he died in 907. There is no doubt that had his life been prolonged

Hungary would never have been distracted by the constant feuds between the nobles and their kings. Arpád's death created a most profound impression, not only upon his own race, but also on the various nationalities over whom he extended his sway. His body was burnt, according to the Eastern custom, and the ashes buried on the banks of a rivulet which flowed in the direction of Etzelsburg. When Christianity was introduced into Hungary a church called the White Church of the Holy Virgin was built in the place where his ashes had been deposited,

CHAPTER IV.

STEPHEN.

CHRISTIANITY had already made considerable progress in Pannonia when its advance was retarded by the Magyars; but it seems certain, from the forbearance which the Hungarians exercised towards the religious opinions of those whom they had subjugated, that they did not exterminate the true faith. The constant terror with which the predominance of the Magyars inspired the Greek Government induced the latter to try if they could possibly obtain some permanent influence by religious conversion in the councils of their powerful neighbours. The crushing defeat which the Magyars had experienced at Wels in the year 994 emboldened the Byzantine Emperor to refuse his yearly tribute. The Magyars thereupon entered his dominions and forced him to come to terms. The Greek Government, in order to carry out the idea which we have just mentioned, requested the ruler of Hungary to send hostages to Byzantium as guarantee that they would not molest the Greek Empire. The Magyars readily agreed, and sent at first Bulcs, and subsequently the woiwode Gyula. These chiefs the Greek court loaded with honours, and, for the purpose of converting them to the Greek faith, raised them to the rank of patrician. Bulcs remained faithful to the creed of his fathers, but Gyula became a zealous convert, and on his return, after having persuaded his daughter to embrace his new religion, he married her to

Geiza. We are also informed that Gyula brought with him a monk, named Hierotheus, who induced many of his patron's friends to become Christians. The constant warfare in which the Hungarians were engaged left them little or no time to think of religion, but the terrible defeat which they experienced at Augsburg at the hands of Otto I. on August 10, 955, when they left on the field of battle 40,000 men (a great part of whom were drowned in the river Loch), had a most beneficial effect on their warlike proclivities. Hungarian writers state that of this army only seven men returned to their native country. The Duke of Hungary, Taksony, and his chiefs, saw the necessity of putting an end to this war, as the nation was not in a condition to stake everything in another battle. They therefore resolved in future to pursue a peaceful policy, and be on good terms with the, neighbouring countries, but Taksony did not live long enough to carry out his wishes.

Geiza, who succeeded him, renewed the attempts to bring about a treaty of peace with the Emperor Otto. This the monarch declined to accede to unless the Hungarians would undertake for ever to discontinue their attacks on the German Empire, and he stated that the only means of ensuring this arrangement was the conversion of the Hungarians to the Catholic creed. In order to carry out his views, he despatched the Bishop of Verdun to the Hungarian court, where he knew that the friends of the late princess would assist the bishop in gaining over the Duke to his views. This seems to have been the case, for Geiza sent envoys to the Emperor for the purpose of concluding a permanent peace, which was agreed to, and Geiza undertook, not only to allow priests to enter and preach the new doctrines in his dominions, but also made himself responsible for their protection, and married a Catholic princess, Adelaide, sister of Micislaus,

King of Poland. A priest from Swabia, named Wolf-gang, was the first missionary who openly preached the Roman Catholic faith in Hungary. His example was shortly after followed by many others. Bishop Pelegrin, who then occupied a very high position in the ecclesiastical world, was the chief instrument in the propagation of his religion in Geiza's dominions. In a letter which he wrote to the Pope this prelate stated that not only did the nobles allow their Christian slaves to exercise their re-ligion (at that time the latter were superior in numbers to the former), but were themselves inclined to embrace the new doctrines.

The rapid progress of Christianity was arrested by the ambition of Geiza, who, wishing to profit by the un-settled state of Germany, had concluded an alliance with Henry of Bavaria, then in open rebellion against Otto II. Pelegrin, who remained faithful to the King, concluded a treaty with Luitpold of Bamberg for the purpose of protecting his bishopric against the devasta-tions of these two enemies. These missionaries, fearing that they would have themselves to bear the brunt of Geiza's anger, fled from Hungary. Their example was followed by many other priests, but in the year 993 the Gospel was again preached by St. Adalbert, Bishop of Prague, who came in person to assist in this glorious undertaking. During the time of his sojourn in Hungary, his eloquence had a most marvellous effect on the dif-ferent nationalities who flocked in thousands around him. This worthy bishop is stated, not only to have converted Geiza, his brother Michael, and his two sons Szárlász and Vazul, but also to have baptised the son of Sarolta, Geiza's first wife, who received the name of Stephen, and induced the Duke of Hungary to found the convent of St. Martinsberg for the Benedicts. Prior to his depar-ture from Hungary, Adalbert nominated as his successor a Saxon called Astrik. The immense success which the Bishop of Prague's endeavours had obtained induced Geiza, at the instigation of his wife Adelaide, to adopt stringent measures against those of his subjects who still remained heathens. This arbitrary act, instead of producing the desired effect, caused so much discontent that, inspired by the fear of rebellion, Geiza partly returned to the belief of his fathers, and in answer to Astrik's reproach on his idolatry he proudly replied that he was rich enough to support two religions.

This sacrifice, however, did not satisfy his subjects, and in order to prevent any outbreak, Geiza concluded an alliance with Henry of Bavaria and the Emperor Otto III.

Stephen ascended the throne in his twenty-sixth or twenty-seventh year, and may be considered as one of the most intelligent sovereigns of his time. He was married to Gisela, the daughter of King Henry the Holy. This marriage was contracted under the condition of his introducing, and, in fact, establishing the Christian religion in Hungary. His father, through the protection which he afforded to foreigners, had induced a considerable number of military leaders and their followers, with some ecclesiastics, to live at his court. With the assistance of these Stephen considered himself strong enough to force his subjects to forsake the religion of their forefathers. This process of conversion does not appear to have agreed with the Hungarians, for a large number, under the command of Kulpa, the woiwode of Sümegh, flew to arms and unfurled the banner of revolt. They assigned two reasons for disaffection—namely, the influence which foreigners exercised, and Stephen's attempt to introduce the Catholic religion. Stephen well knew that if this revolt was not immediately subdued, it would probably spread over the greater part of his dominions, as it was generally known that even some members of the ducal family were opposed to the Catholic religion.   He at once thereupon called to his aid the remaining woiwodes who were faithful to him, together with the foreigners, and advanced against Kulpa.   His army seems to have been under the command of Wenzellin, Count of Wasserburg. The battle raged for some time with varying success, until at length Stephen's general encountered the rival chief in a hand-to-hand conflict, and slew him.   Here, we are sorry to say, Stephen did not display any feeling of Christianity, for he ordered the body of the fallen woiwode to be quartered, and the mutilated parts to be hung up in the four quarters of his kingdom.   Stephen, it is stated, had sworn that if he was successful he would finish building the convent of St. Martinsberg.   The military skill which the foreigners displayed proved to the mass of the Hungarians that as long as Stephen could rely upon them armed resistance was useless.   Stephen had on a former occasion set an example to his subjects of giving freedom to all Christians whom he held as bondsmen.   He now demanded of them that they should do the same, and we are told that he himself instructed his chiefs in the truths of the Christian religion.   As there was in those days a great scarcity of priests in Hungary, he sent messengers to all parts of Germany and Italy, begging of them to come and assist him in establishing the doctrines of Christianity.   He divided Hungary into ten bishoprics, which he richly endowed, and built monasteries for the order of St. Benedict in Pécsvárad, Szalavár, Bakonybél, and on the mountain of Zobor.   One of his greatest acts of charity was the founding of the abbey of St. Lazarus as a place of refuge for the unfortunate descendants of the seven men who escaped from the battle of Augsburg, and who, on account of their having fled, had been made slaves.   Their children themselves, despised by the whole nation, were forced to wander about as beggars.

In order to be classed amongst the European sovereigns, Stephen sent one of his favourite churchmen, to whom he promised the bishopric of Kalocsa, to the Pope, Sylvester II., with a request that his Apostolic Holiness should send him a crown, and at the same time ratify all the acts of Stephen regarding the Roman Catholic religion. The Pope joyfully acceded to Stephen's prayer. He not only sent him the crown, with the title of Apostolic King of Hungary, but he also presented him with a patriarch's crosier, and gave him permission to regulate the religious affairs of his kingdom, and at the same time stated that it was his wish that Stephen should order all Christian serfs to be set free.

During the time that Stephen had ruled as Duke it was apparent to him that the code of laws imposed on Hungary was not adapted to the necessities of the times. The chiefs, as we have seen, were constantly increasing their power, which was incompatible with the executive authority of the sovereign. The introduction of the foreign nobles and other strangers, together with the bishops, left a large body of his subjects without a voice in the affairs of the nation. He therefore determined to do away with the constitution of Atelköz, and introduce a new one similar to that which existed in Germany, as it appears that Germans and their priests were the persons who assisted him in its formation. His first step in this direction was to define the right of succession and the attributes which appertained to the Crown, such as declaring war and making peace, the supreme authority over all the affairs of the Church, bestowing and confiscating estates, and the option of accepting the advice of his counsellors.

The whole nation was under his reign divided into two

classes—the Servientes, who served the State in person;
and the Contribuentes, who gave supplies in money and
produce.   The former were again subdivided into:
1. Populi castrorum, a sort of royal guard, who were
entrusted with the defence of the fortresses; 2. Condi-
tionarii servientes, who gave certain services to the State,
and for the rest bore a share in the contributions; 3. The
servientes puræ ac meræ nobilitatis, who devoted themselves entirely to the service of the State as officers of
the Crown. From this latter class, we are told, the nobility
took its origin. Such was still the state of things in 1222,
when the nobles, profiting by the factions which disturbed
the country whilst their King, Andreas II., was occupied
with the Crusades, framed for themselves a system of
privileges and immunities, which on his return they
forced him to ratify and confirm in their celebrated
Golden Bull.   Many Hungarians refer to the Golden
Bull as the Magna Charta of their rights; but when they
compare it with our Magna Charta they forget that the
most important feature of the latter was that it secured
the liberty of the people, whilst the Golden Bull, far
from assuring their liberty to the people, threw every
burden upon them, and raised the nobility above the
control of the Crown itself.

Stephen also instituted an Assembly of State, which
consisted of three classes: 1. The clergy, who by his
munificence had become the richest of the land; 2. The
high nobility; 3. The inferior nobility, who consisted of
the offsprings or descendants of the high nobility and the
chiefs of the different races.   All questions which were
submitted to this Assembly were to receive, before becoming the law of the land, the assent of the majority of
the three classes, but the King, if he thought fit, could
refuse his own ratification.   Stephen declared hereditary
all the property which was held by the Church dignitaries

and nobility, and the right of possession could only be lost by acts of disloyalty. The powers which the King granted to these two classes gave them uncontrolled authority in their estates, and they were responsible to no one but himself and the Palatine, who was the first dignitary in the State after the King. Next to him came the court lawyer, or legal adviser of the King, who in afteryears occupied the post of supreme judge. And here it may not be thought out of place to give a slight sketch of the different dignitaries in the kingdom of Hungary, their functions and attributes. The first office in the State is that of Palatine. This functionary is chosen by the States from candidates presented by the King, and holds his office for life. He is protector of the throne in the minority of the King, and president of the Chamber of Magnats in the Diet, of the Statthaltery, Septemviral Council, and Obergespann, or chief executive magistrate of the Comitate of Pesth. He is very often also invested with the dignity of Locum-tenens regius or Viceroy.

Next in rank follows the judex curiæ regiæ, who has much influence in the Statthalterey and in the juridical proceedings in the Septemviral Council, and who presides both in the Diet and Septemviral Council in the absence of the Palatine.

Next in order of precedence come the Bannus or Governors of Croatia, of Dalmatia, and of Sclavonia, whose powers are at present much more limited than formerly.

The reichs barons and magnats acquire their superiority from office or inheritance.

The obergespann, or chief executive magistrate of the county, presides over the public meetings of the Comitate; these functions are fulfilled in his absence by the vice-gespann.

No one can fail to see what the King intended to effect by this new constitution—namely, the increase of the exe-

cutive power; for from the composition of the three
States he had always a casting vote.

The present comitate system had, as we have before
seen, been commenced by Arpád. Stephen now declared
the royal demesnes unalienable, and nominated a number
of chiefs as the commanders of the fortresses. In order to
provide a regular garrison for these places, he instituted
a class of soldiers, or, as one might say, military retainers, selected, it is stated, mostly from the early
Christian population, and whom he raised to the rank of
inferior nobility. The rents of the estates were the source
from which they derived their pay, but the service
descended from father to son. These retainers were divided into companies of a hundred and ten men, and in
all civil and military matters were dependent upon the
burgrave and judge. These two ranks are, in fact, similar
to those of over- and vice-gespann. The vassals who occupied the domains belonging to the strongholds, which
then consisted of the former inhabitants and prisoners of
war, were also under the sole control of the two above-
named officers. The remaining part of the royal demesnes
seems to have been cultivated by a class of persons such
as counts, chamberlains, stewards, or treasurers, hunts-
men, grooms, inspectors of vineyards, &c., &c., who were
under the control of officers appointed by the obergespann.
The intention was that these servants of the State should
always be in attendance on the court when it was in their
neighbourhood, and supply it with all that it might need.
The nobles seem to have done the same in miniature in
their feudal estates, over which the obergespann had at
the time not the slightest authority. We now come to a
class of men who were the founders of trade and cities,
and which was chiefly composed of foreign mechanics and
men who had gained their freedom from the hands of
their lords. To the credit of Stephen, this class could

become landed proprietors, and were responsible only to the Crown, to which they paid a regular tax. Unfortunately for Hungary, her nobles have always been adverse to the rise of the middle class, and have preferred dealing with a Jew than with a foreign trader. The consequence is that at the present day the middle class is not represented, while the nobles have their estates embarrassed by the mortgages of the Jews.

In order to see that no injustice was committed by those in power, the King undertook that he and his successors would from time to time visit the different comitates and assemble courts of justice, composed of the nobility, the clergy, and the obergespann, when the King would act as judge, for the purpose of settling all disputes, and hearing any appeals for justice which the inhabitants might wish to make to him. He also appointed two judges to decide in trivial matters; and as he and the Palatine could not visit each comitate every year, on the approach of royalty these two judges were to meet the King or his representative, and explain to him the details of each case on which he had to give judgment. Guilt was proved either by witnesses or by oath; but only a free man could give evidence against another free man, and such was also the case as regards priests. In the most difficult cases, it is supposed that the accused was allowed to prove his innocence by the ordeal of hot iron or boiling water. The judge of a comitate was held responsible for his verdict for the space of one year, during which time the parties had the right of appeal to the Crown. This right was also extended to the retainers of a burgrave, with a proviso that if the King confirmed the judgment, the appellant had to pay ten gold florins. Few crimes were expiated by death. Amongst these were high treason, and incorrigible dishonesty or theft on the third offence. The greatest number of crimes were punished either by a fine or severe clerical penance. One of the most important political acts of Stephen was the formation of a standing army, in which the superior officers consisted of foreigners or soldiers of Hungarian descent, to whom he had given fiefs on condition of their being ready to do service whenever required. The inferior officers consisted of the military retainers of the obergespann and freemen, while the army itself was composed of Christians who had formerly been slaves, and men who were supplied to the King by the holders of fiefs or certain royal grants and privileges. The whole force was under the sole command of the King, and the revenues derived from vassals who occupied royal demesnes were employed in paying it. Hungarian writers state that this army was formed by the King when he was called upon by the States to raise this force in order to be able to protect the frontiers, and maintain good order in the country.

Stephen also instituted a national army, which consisted of the whole nobility and clergy, who were bound to join the army when led by the King in person, and on this account were never called upon to pay taxes, but, if required, had to furnish for the King's army a contingent, the strength of which depended on the extent of the territory which they occupied.

Stephen's enthusiastic endeavours for promulgating the Christian religion appear to have again met with severe opposition on the part of his people. This was occasioned by the erection of a large number of churches at the expense of his subjects. It is true that the King had provided for the adornment of the interior, and the bishops paid for the priests and educational books; but the veneration which the Hungarians felt for their ancient religion, and their forcible conversion, had excited their hatred of the clergy and the King himself. The

greatest opponent to the Christian religion and the new
innovations was the Duke of Transylvania, Gyula II.
This prince appears not only to have refused to accept
the new constitution, but also to have afforded every
protection to the heathen Hungarians who fled from
Christian persecution; and about two years after the
coronation of Stephen, the Transylvanian prince threw
off his allegiance, and entered Hungary at the head of a
large body of malcontents, together with some Patzenaci
with whom he had effected an alliance, and Stephen
marched against his former vassal. The superiority of
the King's army in skill and discipline soon put the Transylvanians and their allies to flight, and the heathen duke
and his two brothers were taken prisoners. Stephen
made the woiwode Zoltan governor of Transylvania, and
created a bishopric at Karlsburg. The Patzenaci, however, though defeated, were not conquered, and they continued the war under their King Kean. Stephen was
compelled to march into their own country, Moldavia,
probably for the purpose of forcing them to withdraw
from Transylvania. On his approach, Kean and his warriors retired into the mountains. Stephen, however, with
great difficulty compelled the Patzenaci to accept a battle
in the open country, in which fortune again smiled on
the banners of the Hungarians. Kean was mortally
wounded, and the Patzenaci were compelled to fly, leaving behind them immense treasures which they had accu-
mulated, and which were the fruits of their constant inroads
into Greece. With the proceeds of this booty Stephen
erected a Catholic church at Ofen, and one at Stuhlweissemburg. This victory restored complete order in Hungary, and the King was now able to devote all his talents
to the cause of civilisation; and there can be no doubt
that the doctrines of the Christian religion greatly con-

duced to soften the turbulent disposition of the Hungarians. Stephen also founded several schools.

Stephen's Queen was not backward in assisting her liege and lord in his arduous duties. She and her ladies busied themselves in making vestments for the Church; and the coronation cloak worn by the kings of Hungary was made by her industrious hands. The domestic life of this good and great King and Queen was embittered by the loss of all their children, with the exception of one, whose name was Emerich. The growing beauty and talents of this, their only child, appeared as if he had been sent to console them for the severe afflictions which they had endured; the young prince was beloved by all who surrounded him, and under the care of the Bishop Gerhard grew into manhood. When Emerich reached his 24th year, Stephen determined to have him crowned King of Hungary. For this purpose he called the States together, and the coronation was to take place on the 8th September 1031; but six days before that fixed for the event, this promising prince was swept from the midst of his family and future people by the hand of death. The demise of his royal son placed Stephen in a most unfortunate position with reference to his successor, as amongst Arpád's descendants there were none capable of filling his place. The next in succession to the crown was his cousin Vazul, who on account of the disorderly life which he led had been several times in prison. Next to him were Andreas, Bela, and Levente, nephews of Vazul, who were known to be opposed to the Christian religion. Another heir was Peter, son of one of Stephen's sisters, who had married the Doge of Venice, Otto Urseolo. After his father's downfall, Peter had sought refuge at the court of his uncle, and Stephen had made him lieutenant in his body guard. The Queen appears to have taken a great fancy to him, and advised her husband to designate the young lieutenant as his successor; but to do this was out of Stephen's power, as he would have to break the oath which his great ancestor had so solemnly sworn to keep, and had ratified by his own blood. He declined to accede to her entreaties, and hearing better accounts of the mode of life of his cousin Vazul, the good King forgave him, and sent messengers to Neutra bidding him to appear at court. Hungarian writers would lead their readers to believe that Gisela joined in a conspiracy for the purpose of preventing the nomination of Vazul, who was on his way attacked by the friends of Peter: his eyes were put out, and molten lead poured into his ears. With regard to the criminality of the Queen, her former life, and the affectionate terms on which she lived with her husband, lead us to discredit the above statement.

The news of this barbarous tragedy seems to have been a death-blow to the health of the rapidly sinking King, who, enfeebled by years and illness, had not sufficient strength of mind to have the abettors and perpetrators of this shameful crime brought to trial and punished. All that he seems to have done was to advise Vazul's nephews to seek safety in flight. It is also related that shortly before the King closed his eyes in his last sleep a conspirator attempted to assassinate him. This wretch, favoured by the coming darkness of night, crept stealthily to the couch of the dying benefactor of Hungary; but that all-seeing Providence which protects the lowest to the highest prevented Hungary being the executioner of the man whose name will remain dear to the memory of every Hungarian as long as there exists one of that nation; for the moment the cowardly assassin was about to commit this hideous crime, he started back as if struck by the lightning of the Almighty, threw away his dagger, and, falling on his knees, called aloud for mercy. This last shock was too much for the venerable Stephen:

he died a few days after, on August 15, 1038.   He was
buried in a marble sarcophagus, on which rested a crown
of gold, in the church of Stuhlweissemburg.   Thus passed
away from the world the spirit of a man who can be
rightly classed amongst the first sovereigns of the middle
ages.   He possessed all the brilliant qualities of his great
ancestor Arpád, and had but one failing, if it can be so
called, which was his zeal for the Catholic religion ; but
those who can understand the state of the people over
whom he ruled, and the time in which he lived, will agree
with us when we say that the introduction of Christianity
into Hungary was a case of life or death as regards its
existence as an independent kingdom.

    Religion brought into Stephen's dominions industry,
learning, and unity.

CHAPTER V.

JOHN HUNYADY.

IT is indeed a pleasure to relate the life of this founder of the celebrated family of Hunyady. John Hunyady, a descendant of the lower class of nobility, was one of the bravest and most patriotic sons of Hungary. In his boyish days he displayed all those qualities which in after-years rendered him the darling of the people, and already, as a youth, he showed great military abilities. We find him at a very early age commanding a considerable force against the Hussites, and protecting the frontiers from the inroads of the Turks. In his engagements with the former he displayed great moderation, and always did his best to prevent fanatical zeal interfering with the treatment of his prisoners. It is stated that night or day he was always ready to assist the humblest peasant in rescuing his small flock from the hands of the Turkish freebooter. In a short time Hunyady became known as one of the first military leaders. As a reward for his services, Albrecht made him bannus of Serbia, and in the year 1441 Vladislaus I., as a mark of his special favour, made him lord-lieutenant of Temese, and commandant of the important town and citadel of Belgrade, at the same time raising him to the high position of woiwode of Transylvania, and confiding into his hands by this promotion the defence of the entire Hungarian frontier. In this post Hunyady so repeatedly defeated the Turkish bands, who were constantly in the habit of entering the country and spreading terror and devastation, that they for a short time altogether ceased; but in the year 1442 a large body, who had managed to escape his vigilance, broke into Transylvania, under the command of Medschid Bey, and at once set about plundering and sacking all the houses and villages through which they passed. The brave Bishop of Transylvania, George Lepes, put himself at the head of all the available forces he could collect, and led them valiantly against their inveterate enemies; but the Crescent triumphed over the Cross, and the worthy bishop and his forces were nearly all killed or taken prisoners. The Mahomedan leader now advanced without opposition to the walls of Hermannstadt, which he expected would fall into his hands before Hunyady could come to its aid. Although the place and garrison were not in any way prepared to hold out, yet such was the influence of the name of their woiwode, who they knew would hasten to their relief, that the inhabitants resolved to hold the town to the last; and they were right, for that valiant soldier, as soon as he had discovered the way which the Turks had taken, followed it as a bloodhound tracks the scent of blood. The victory which the Turkish leader had gained induced him to believe that he could measure his forces with those of Hunyady; and raising the siege of Hermannstadt, he courageously fronted his opponent. He instructed his soldiers to capture, if possible, the Hungarian commander, dead or alive, and gave a minute description of Hunyady's personal appearance, and that of his horse and trappings. The Hungarians having become acquainted with the enemy's design, Simon Kemeny adroitly persuaded his general to exchange horse and armour. The fight was a desperate one; poor Kemeny and five hundred picked Hungarian horsemen were cut to pieces by the Turkish cavalry, who thought they were attacking Hunyady and his body guard. While the mass of the Turkish cavalry were directing their onslaught on the point which Kemeny occupied, Hunyady threw himself on the opposite flank of the Turks, who were at the same time attacked in their rear by the garrison of Hermannstadt. This brought about a general flight of the Turks, who were hotly pursued by the Hungarian cavalry to the rise of the Wallachian moun- tains, leaving the battle-field and the road which they had taken in their flight strewn with the dead and wounded. Medschid Bey and his son, at the head of the celebrated Turkish cavalry corps, were completely over- thrown and routed. Hunyady was too well acquainted with the revengeful disposition of his opponent not to believe that he would again appear on the scene of his former disgrace. He therefore set about organising his corps, and setting the country in a state of defence. In a very short time he had assembled under his banner a select body of men, a large number of whom were veterans who had from their childhood been accustomed to the peculiarities of Turkish warfare. With this army, con- sisting of about 15,000 men, he took up a position facing the frontier, which offered every facility for massing his whole force on any of the threatened points of attack. His attention was directed chiefly to the defence of Bel- grade, which was in fact the key of the Hungarian frontier, and the events proved that he was perfectly right. Medschid Bey returned with an army of 80,000 men. The Turks were under the command of one of their best generals, who, unfortunately for his country- men, so undervalued the Hungarian army that he boasted that the mere sight of his turban would scare them for miles from the frontier. Hunyady advanced as far as the Iron Gates, and there waited his opponent's attack. The Hungarian leader's victory was more decisive than that which he had formerly gained, for he not only captured an immense booty, consisting of 200 flags, 5,000 prisoners, together with a large amount of specie and articles of Eastern luxury, but also practically demonstrated that the Hungarians, if properly commanded, could, with inferior numbers, safely reckon upon the victory. The Turkish leader, together with some of his principal officers, was amongst the killed. No sooner had the news of this glorious feat of arms reached Rome than the Pope, Eugenius IV., believing that the moment had arrived for driving the Turks from Europe, gave orders for the organisation of a crusade for this purpose, and despatched Cardinal Julian into Germany and Bohemia in order to superintend the formation of this army of Christians. The result was that Hungary had never since the battle of Nicopolis seen such a collection of foreigners in its camps.[1] The King commanded in person. This miscellaneous army amounted to 40,000 men, composed chiefly of Hungarians, Germans, Bohemians, Servians, Wallachians, and a sprinkling of what may be termed the fighting knights of Europe. The Hungarian monarch advanced to the banks of the Danube by Vegh-Szendro, where the whole army crossed. Here Hunyady pushed

---

[1] The unsettled state of Hungary during the reign of Sigismund determined that monarch, for the purpose of withdrawing the attention of the Hungarians from their own country, to declare war against the Turks. For this purpose he organised a species of crusade. A large number of Germans joined his standards, and several bodies of crusaders. The King of France sent 12,000 men, making a total of 60,000 men. With this force Sigismund advanced through Servia to the walls of Nicopolis, where, shortly after, the Sultan Bajazet came to meet him at the head of 200,000 men. The Hungarians were totally defeated, and fled in the most disorderly manner, the King himself escaping with the greatest difficulty. It appears that he embarked on board a ship on the Danube and proceeded by sea to Constantinople, whence he eventually returned to his own country. The Sultan successfully overran Sclavonia and took possession of the neighbouring country.

forward at the head of 12,000 followers, the flower of the
Hungarian fighting population, whilst the King, with the
main force, remained two days' march in the rear of this
advanced body, and proceeded as far as the rise of
the Balkans.   In his rapid advance Hunyady captured
several important fortresses, amongst which were Nizza
and Sophia, and defeated four Turkish armies which
opposed his progress.   He then effected a junction with
the royal army in the plain of Jalovacz, where, on the
last day of the old year (1443), he inflicted a severe
defeat on the Turks, who had attempted to drive him and
the King from their position.   Unfortunately, we are
unable to give an account of this fight, in which the
Hungarian hero proved that he fully understood the art
of manœuvring in close proximity to his enemy, and the
principle of acting on the interior lines of the enemy's
communications, for we are told that it was by these
movements that he enabled the King to gain a decisive
victory.   Mahmud Cselebi, brother-in-law of the Sultan, and several other pashas, were amongst the prisoners.   In February 1444 the King made his triumphal
entry into Pesth, accompanied by his prisoners.   Ancient
chronicles give a lively description of the immense excitement which the appearance of these prisoners created
amongst the population, who flocked together from all
parts, at the different halting places through which the
royal *cortége* passed on its way to the capital, where a
tremendous ovation awaited the King.   In this triumph
the Hungarians fondly believed that the first step towards
the expulsion of the Turks from Europe had been made.
The enthusiasm of the people, and the offers of men and
money for the purpose of continuing the war which were
made by the envoys of the different foreign States who
had come to Pesth for the purpose of congratulating the
King on the discomfiture of the Turks, induced Cardinal

Julian to urge the assembling of a Diet for the purpose
of making arrangements for renewing the campaign.
The worthy cardinal supposed that the power of the
Turks had been broken, and that in order to drive them
into Asia the Hungarian success should be immediately
followed up.   The Hungarian members of the Reichstag
were not so sanguine, and Hunyady himself advised that
no further step should be taken until the different fortifications held by the Turks in Servia had been captured.
But the eloquence of the King's adviser gained the day,
and the cardinal's project was put in execution.   A considerable Hungarian force was assembled about the middle
of the summer at Szegedin, but the foreign Powers sent
neither men nor money.   During the time that the Hungarian army was awaiting those subsidies, envoys of the
Sultan Mahmud arrived at the camp.   Their proposals
proved that the cardinal was right in his conjectures as
regards the Turks not being in a position to meet the
Hungarian army, for the Sultan, who had at that time
his hands full with the difficulties which had broken out
in Asia, alarmed at the news of the probable invasion of
his European provinces, sent envoys to offer to the King
of Hungary the provinces of Wallachia and Servia as
the price of a ten years' peace, which he was prepared
to ratify by oath ; and he offered, at the same time, the
sum of 70,000 ducats as ransom for his brother-in-law.
Hunyady, and some of the chief counsellors, advised the
King to accept so profitable a peace, and it was accordingly ratified.   Shortly afterwards came letters from
the Italian admiral, who was cruising in the Hellespont,
and the Greek Emperor Palæologus, describing in the
most glowing terms the embarrassment of the Sultan,
and backed by the offer of a contingent of 30,000
men from the Prince of Epirus, George Castriota, surnamed Skander Bey.   This news greatly strengthened

the war party in the King's camp. In a great council
which was held with reference to the future actions of
the King, John Hunyady, true to his noble and knightly
character, vehemently protested against his royal master
breaking his oath, at the same time pointing out the
great danger which the King ran in advancing into the
Turkish territory at the head of so small a force as he
then had under his command. He added that there was
not the slightest doubt that, however great might be the
difficulties with which the Sultan had to contend in Asia,
the fanaticism of the Turks would induce them to fight
with the greatest desperation, knowing, as they did, that
if defeated they would perhaps never again set their feet
on European soil. Moreover, their numerical strength
was in every respect superior to that of the Hungarians,
and in all probability Murad, the Turkish leader, a man
of great military ability, would force the King to fight
in an unfavourable position; if the Hungarians were
defeated, the Turks would at once advance into the
heart of Hungary, as there would be nothing to stop
their victorious progress; and before a foreign army
could come to their aid, the capital would have fallen
into their hands. Unfortunately for the King of Hungary, the fiery eloquence of the Cardinal Julian had
gained complete sway over his better judgment, and,
heedless of this practical argument and of the loss of
honour, he violated his oath. Hunyady was not the
man to forsake his sovereign in the hour of danger. He
knew that this campaign would in all probability destroy
his military prestige, and lead to the subjugation of the
greater part of his native country. Yet we find him not for
one moment exhibiting the slightest want of obedience, but
on the contrary straining every nerve to render his master's army as efficient as possible. In the month of September, Vladislaus, with his army of 20,000 men, crossed

the Danube at Orsowa, where he expected that the Prince of Epirus would have effected a junction with him. We are told that in an interview which the King had with the woiwode of Wallachia, that great dignitary repeated substantially the arguments of Hunyady against the Turkish campaign; but here the Hungarian patriot proved how well he knew the position which he then occupied. As leader of the King's army he had to see that his master's will was obeyed; and in an interview his words so excited the wrath of the woiwode Drakul that the latter drew his sword against Hunyady, who seems to have turned this to good account by advising the King to pardon his turbulent vassal on condition of his giving him a contingent of 4,000 men, under the command of his son. The Turkish generals offered little or no opposition to the rapid advance of the King's army, which, after the capture of Varna, directed its march towards Gallipoli. The Ottoman general Murad, who appears to have driven off the Italian fleet, embarked his troops, and crossed the sea. After having effected his landing, he pushed up in order to occupy a favourable position before the Hungarians could come up to him; but the vastly superior numbers of the Turks induced Hunyady to retrace his steps, and take up a position in the neighbourhood of Varna, which afforded him great facilities for manoeuvring. In order to excite the passions of his soldiers, Murad had placed on a high pole the broken treaty. Hunyady, who had placed his army in a masterly position, had entrusted the King with the reserve, and solemnly entreated his sovereign, if he wished to be victorious, on no account to move from the spot which he then occupied until he (Hunyady) should give him the signal to do so. Hunyady now began the battle with his usual tactics, and in a short time threw himself with such violence on the opposing wings of the Turkish army that the latter were driven back, and some of his most daring horsemen had planted their flags on the fortified tents of Murad, when, unfortunately, the King, in the excitement of the moment, unable any longer to control his desire for sharing in the victory of his great leader, rushed with the whole reserve against Murad's tents, which were defended by a picked body of veteran janissaries whom constant victory had rendered invincible. The small band which followed the King was totally annihilated. Vladislaus' horse, which had been wounded, fell to the ground with its rider, and a grey-haired janissary, with one sweep from his scimitar, severed the King's head from the body. This gory trophy was afterwards placed on the top of the pole, beside the above-mentioned treaty. Hunyady, seeing that the movement made by the King had destroyed every chance of success, did his utmost to arrange an orderly retreat, but no sooner was the terrible news of their King's fate known to the Hungarians than the whole army fled in disorder, and after the most daring feats of valour, Hunyady had to leave that scene of disaster, where, had the King only followed the advice of his general, the Hungarians would have gained for Hunyady and his master a victory which would have saved the lives of thousands of beings, and their homes from the devastating inroads of the Ottoman. Amongst the killed was the unfortunate instigator of the campaign, together with the Bishops of Erlau and Grosswardein, Stefan Bathory, and several other important personages. Hunyady had to pass through the districts of Wallachia, where the power of the woiwode was all supreme, and in revenge for Hunyady's former conduct Drakul made him prisoner, but he was shortly after obliged to release him.

The Palatine of Hungary, Hedervary, a very ambitious man, in order to retain the supreme power in his own hands, spread the report that the King had not fallen in the battle of Varna, but had fled to Poland. In this he seems to have been successful, but, at the instigation of Hunyady, agents were sent to Poland, to ascertain the truth of the statement as to Vladislaus being alive. The information which they gained, together with the news which had been received from the East, proved but too clearly that the King was dead. Hunyady then demanded that the young King should be at once put on the throne. The Landtag supported him in this proposition, and ordered that a suitable embassy should at once proceed to the court of Frederic at Vienna, and bring back the prince, with the crown of Hungary; it was also resolved that during the prince's minority a regent should be selected to carry on the government, and that Hunyady should retain his rank of commander-in-chief. In the course of these transactions the Hungarian patriot led an expedition against the woiwode of Wallachia, who it appears was in correspondence with the Turks, and who, not being able to rely on Turkish assistance, fled from the seat of his government. Hunyady, having appointed Dáu as his successor, proceeded to Croatia, where Ulrich Cilley, taking advantage of the unsettled state of Hungary, produced by the intrigues of the Palatine, had taken possession of several Hungarian forts. These Hunyady at once recaptured, and began levying contributions in the possessions of Cilley, which he did not discontinue until that proud chieftain had again sworn allegiance to the crown of Hungary. A great Landtag which had assembled for the purpose of electing a regent, came to the unanimous conclusion that John Hunyady was the only person who was competent to hold this high post. The unsettled state of Hungary (partly caused by the minority of the prince and the conduct of Frederic), and still more the fear of the invasion of Hungary, required that the executive power of the State should be placed in the hands of a man whose character was a guarantee that the rights of the King and nation would be maintained. The power which was given to Hunyady was nearly the same as that of a king of Hungary, and if we take into account the influence which his name gave him amongst the turbulent nobles, we should say that he had more authority than many kings of Hungary. Scarcely had he accepted the reins of government, when his old enemy Drakul, assisted by the Turks, appeared in Wallachia, and displaced Hunyady's nominee. Before setting out on this expedition, the Regent explained to the Assembly the impossibility of his carrying on a war without the necessary funds, as the system of living ' from hand to mouth '—that is, compelling the inhabitants of the country through which they passed to furnish the troops with pay and provisions—would only excite a bad feeling, as by acting thus the whole burden of the war would be cast on the shoulders of one, and that the poorest, part of the population. The deputies, acknowledging the soundness of his argument, supplied him with the necessary funds. It was also agreed that another deputation should be sent to Frederic to demand the delivery of the young King.

Hunyady saw the necessity of at once crushing the Wallachian rebellion. Fearing that any temporary success which Drakul and the Turks might gain would bring others to the standard of revolt, he advanced with rapidity into Wallachia, where he totally defeated Drakul and his Ottoman allies, and again placed the province under the Crown of Hungary. Scarcely had he finished this work than the alarming news arrived that Frederic had refused to liberate the Hungarian King. Hunyady thereupon demanded that the Government should declare war against Frederic unless he at once released Vladislaus. In conformity with orders from his Government, he began

his march upon Vienna. This had the effect of forcing
Frederic, who was totally unprepared, to ask for an
armistice, to which Hunyady agreed, on condition that
arrangements should at once be entered into for the purpose of restoring the young King to his subjects. Although
it is stated that the Pope acted as a mediator, the Hungarians, instead of receiving their King, for some unaccountable reason, agreed to an armistice for two years ;
but Hunyady was not to be circumvented, and in the
following Landtag had Vladislaus again solemnly acknowledged as the legitimate King of Hungary, and it was
enacted that anyone who did not acknowledge him as
such should be guilty of high treason.   These acts were
in fact the crowning proofs of John Hunyady's disinterested loyalty ; but, to the disgrace of Hungary, there
were men in those days in whose bosom not a spark of
patriotic feeling existed, who were not only ready to be
traitors to the country, but longed for the opportunity to
sell the land of their birth to the Mussulman.   In the
campaign in which Vladislaus had lost his life we mentioned that the promises of the Prince of Epirus, Skander
Beg, had contributed in a great degree to the violation of
the Turkish treaty.   This ruler had now become entangled in another war with the Turks, and Hunyady,
reckoning on the loyalty of his countrymen, considered
that this circumstance would afford him a glorious opportunity of revenging the death of his King and comrades who fell in the disastrous battle of Varna.   Ulrich
Cilley—who, on account of his not having been elected
Bannus of Sclavonia instead of Szekely, together with the
humiliation which he had experienced at the hands of
Hunyady, had become the Regent's most deadly enemy—
had so excited the ruling classes by means of bribes and
promises that Demetrius, who had been appointed by
Hunyady Bishop of Agram, was not allowed to enter

his see. A considerable number of Croatian and Sclavonian nobles, together with George Brankovics, ruler of Servia, joined Cilley in his conspiracy against Hunyady. The first step which these malcontents made was the refusal of George Brankovics to furnish Hunyady's army with his contingent, and, not content with this, he disclosed to Murad, who was then besieging the capital of Epirus, the plans of Hunyady, upon which the Turkish leader raised the siege, and concluded an armistice with Skander Bey. Hunyady's emissaries soon brought him tidings of this perfidious act of one of the first nobles of Hungary, and, for the first time in his life, the Hungarian patriot seems to have acted without consideration, for he immediately sequestrated the Hungarian estates of Brankovics, and entered Servia, for the purpose of bringing its ruler to obedience, at the head of his army of 24,000 men, with which he had intended falling upon the Turks while the greater part of their army was engaged in besieging the capital of Epirus. In the midst of his operations, he received the news that the Turkish army, numbering 150,000 men, was rapidly advancing against him. No other option was then left him but to collect his forces and take up the most favourable position he could reach, and we accordingly find him taking post in the plains of Amsel, on the frontiers of Bulgaria and Servia. Here he awaited the Turkish general, and on the morning of October 17 placed his army in order of battle. Let us for a moment consider the object and mutual position of these two armies. Murad, who was then esteemed one of the most able leaders in the Turkish army, had in all probability been for some time in correspondence with the malcontents, and knew that, should Hunyady receive the slightest check, many of the nobles who now supported him would seek to obtain the command of the army, while there were others who would

gladly avail themselves of the ill-fortune of the great
Hungarian in order to bring forward their individual
claims to the regency. But this was not all. The
Turkish leader knew that Frederic, for his own selfish
ends, was opposed to the continuance of Hunyady's rule,
and that if he wished to obtain a permanent footing in
Hungary, the only way of doing it was by grasping the
hand of traitors, and defeating Hunyady as soon as possible. And now for the Hungarian leader. The fruits
of his promised victory had been destroyed by his perfidious countrymen, while the chances of outmanœuvring
and defeating in detail the vastly superior forces of his
opponent had been lost by allowing his feelings as a
patriot to get the better of his judgment as a general.
He knew that if he retreated, his enemies would insinuate
that he was playing the part of a poltroon, and had
lost the favourable chance of gaining a decisive victory,
and that he was no longer competent to hold that post
which his country had generously confided to him. He
therefore determined to fight a decisive battle, being fully
aware that any partial success would inevitably have the
same effect as his complete discomfiture. Hunyady seems,
by a series of skilful movements, followed by rapid onslaughts of his cavalry, to have overthrown that of the
Turks, who were most ably supported by the janissaries; up to midnight, though superior in numbers, these
brave veteran troops had not been able to retrieve the
discomfiture of their cavalry, and everything seemed to
promise a great victory to the skilful Hungarian general.
At the first dawn of light, the frightful carnage again
began with the same ferocity on both sides. Unfortunately for Hunyady, his generals did not possess the
knowledge of handling troops in the steady method of
their commander, for they seem to have allowed the
Turkish light cavalry to outflank them, and thus placed

the Hungarian army between two fires. But here Hunyady again proved how superior he was to all those who surrounded him. In a short time he formed front towards his antagonists, and completely defeated them. He now rushed to his right wing, with which he intended to crown his victory. But, alas for Hunyady! and alas for Hungary! disunion was again the cause of misfortune. Dan, who had been raised by Hunyady himself to the powerful dignity which he then occupied, had deserted his friend and general in the very moment of victory, and gone over with his whole force to the Turkish general. The Hungarian soldiery, not knowing what fresh treachery awaited them, fled in wild confusion from the spot whence their gallant leader was about to lead them on to victory. The German and Bohemian contingents, which served with the Hungarian army, did not join the fugitives, but retreated to Hunyady's camp, which they defended to the last man, proving how well they understood the duty of a soldier—fidelity and obedience to the commanding officer. This victory was bought by the Turks with the lives of 40,000 men; the Hungarians lost 17,000. Hunyady, we are told, having become separated from his followers, in attempting to rejoin them was so suddenly set upon by two robbers that it was impossible for him to draw his sword. In attempting to get possession of a valuable cross which was suspended from his neck, they however allowed him to grasp one of their swords, with which he immediately cut one in two, and put the other to flight. Shortly afterwards the defeated general again nearly lost his life. Fatigued and weary in mind and body, he determined to sleep one night at a Servian peasant's cottage, and in the morning his host offered to show him the way to Belgrade. Instead of so doing, the treacherous peasant led him to the neighbourhood of Szendrö, where Brankovics resided, and the Hungarian leader was suddenly surrounded by a large number of his enemy's followers, and made prisoner. Brankovics at once offered to deliver him to Murad, who indignantly declined the offer of the traitor; and, finding there was nothing to be done with the Turks, Brankovics thought it more prudent for his own safety to come to terms with the Hungarian Assembly, then sitting at Szegedin. To this he was no doubt greatly impelled by the conduct of the ruler of Bosnia, Maravics, who was then making preparations for the purpose of forcibly delivering Hun- yady. By means of skilful intrigues, Brankovics in- duced his illustrious prisoner to agree to the following arrangement before he liberated him—namely, he (Bran- kovics) was to receive back his Hungarian property, and Hunyady's youngest son Mathias was to be affianced to Cilley's daughter, whilst Vladislaus, the eldest, should be sent to Szendrö as hostage for the ratification of the above conditions. Hunyady now returned to Hungary, where he was welcomed by the mass of the people; and when he presented himself to the Landtag of 1450, to request the annulling of the arrangement extorted from him by Brankovics, there was a universal shout in the affirma- tive. It was unanimously agreed that the latter should be proclaimed a traitor to his country for having been in correspondence with the Turks, that all his estates should be confiscated, and he himself forcibly reduced to obedience. Hunyady accordingly marched at the head of an expedi- tion against Brankovics; but the latter had powerful friends in the persons of Cilley and Zaray, who were Hunyady's most deadly enemies. These men, by means of skilful intrigues, forced Hunyady to give up his plan, on condition that his son should be released, and that Brankovics should undertake to bring about an armistice with the Turks, in return for which a part of his estates was also to be restored to him.

Hunyady must have, indeed, bitterly felt this humiliation, yet his noble heart beat with but one impulse—the love of his country. He knew that to revenge himself on his opponents he must have recourse to arms, and that meant civil war. Actuated by his noble sentiments, he agreed to these proposals, and concluded a three years' armistice with the Turks. This peace enabled him to turn his attention to Upper Hungary, which had been disturbed by Giskra, a Bohemian soldier whom Elizabeth had called into the country with the title of commander-in-chief. This leader maintained that his rank was superior to that of Hunyady, with whose opponents he was in correspondence. Giskra, who appears to have been a man of considerable ability, had taken possession of the greater part of the strong places in Upper Hungary, from which his Bohemian followers were in the habit of levying contributions on the inhabitants of the surrounding districts.

On the approach of Hunyady, as he had no wish to encounter the great Hungarian in the open field, Giskra retreated with his followers to his castles. No option was therefore left to the Regent but to drive him from his retreat. He soon got possession of one of the chief strongholds; and, finding that his army was not sufficiently strong to lay siege to the rest, he concluded an armistice with Giskra, on condition that his Bohemians should cease their depredations. Hunyady also trusted by these means to put an end to the intrigues of Elizabeth. Hardly, however, had he retired when the Bohemians again renewed their attacks, and in a very short time overran a large part of the country, and got complete command over the district of Neoyra, which they strongly fortified. Giskra, relying on the support of the malcontents, now began to make preparations for the subjugation of the whole of Upper Hungary. Hunyady, at the head of several contingents furnished by the counties and the nobles, returned to the

field of action. In an engagement which took place
shortly after, a large number of his forces passed over to
the enemy, and Hunyady was compelled to retreat; but
having collected a body of his own veteran soldiers, he
drove the insurgents back into their castles, took by storm
Rosenau, Sohl, Derecseny, and several other strongholds.
His enemies, however, were intriguing against him, and,
as a reward for his services, the Ministry not only concluded without his consent a treaty of peace with Giskra,
but actually refunded to him his war expenses, thus paying him as a rebel, and for levying contributions on their
own countrymen. This last blow seems to have determined Hunyady to withdraw from a position which had
brought upon him so many indignities; but before so
doing he considered it his duty to restore to Hungary the
young sovereign. Frederic, who was on the eve of his
departure for Rome, for the purpose of receiving the
imperial crown from the hands of the Pope, could, Hunyady thought, be induced to give up the King, who was
still in his custody, if a powerful combination were formed
against him. In order to effect this, the Hungarian
Government entered into arrangements with some of the
chief Bohemian, Moravian, and Austrian nobles, who
being strongly adverse to the illegal detention of the
infant King, were ready, if required, to effect his liberation by force of arms. To the astonishment of every
one, Ulrich Cilley, the uncle of the King, who had formerly been known as an adherent of Frederic, now appeared as his opponent, and brought all his influence to
the aid of Hunyady, who, in his generous nature, forgot
the character of the man with whom he was dealing.
Frederic refused the request of the deputies who had
been sent to him by the several parties, and took the
young King to Rome; but on his return to Vienna the
Hungarians and their friends surrounded him at Wiener

Neustadt, where he was forced to deliver up his prisoner. The reason why Cilley had broken with Frederic now became apparent. In his capacity as uncle of the King he claimed the right of guardianship over him until he reached his majority, and by the help of his creatures his appointment was ratified. Hunyady, sick at heart and disgusted, resolved to delay no longer the execution of his intention of resigning his post as Regent; but, probably fearing that some catastrophe might occur which would deprive Hungary of its King, and cause the destruction of his friends and himself, he determined, with all who sided with him, to hold all the fortresses and strongholds which were in their possession until the King had reached his majority. The shameless artifices by which Cilley sought to ruin the strength of mind and bodily health of his unfortunate nephew are of too disgusting a nature to be described. Having rendered his ward Vladislaus his docile instrument, he led him to believe that Hunyady sought his destruction for the purpose of seizing the crown. The great Hungarian patriot possessed the right of holding the regency until the majority of the King; but, as we have before said, he was sick of State intrigues, and he convoked a Landtag at Presburg in the beginning of the year 1453, with the intention of carrying out his purpose. The deputation which proceeded to Vienna to escort the young King to Presburg appears to have been unable to bring the crown with them (as it still remained in Frederic's possession), so that the King could only take his coronation oath. Hunyady, who headed this deputation, on his arrival in Vienna, solemnly resigned his office. The majority of the deputies assembled at Pressburg called upon the King to acknowledge the great services which Hunyady had rendered to the country; and, disregarding the threats of his uncle, Vladislaus made Hunyady Count of Bistritz, gave him the castles of Görgeny and Deva, and raised his eldest son, Vladislaus, to the dignity of Bannus of Scla-vonia and Croatia. The Duchess of Presburg and the arguments of Cilley soon induced the young King to break his promise of remaining amongst his subjects, and he returned to Vienna, there to renew his life of dissipa-tion. As King of Hungary and Bohemia, he was able to keep up a large court, composed of Germans, Bohemians, and Hungarians.

Cilley, who, as we have before said, was in fact the ruler, had by his arrogance made himself many enemies. Amongst these was one of the principal Austrian noblemen, named Eitzinger, whose feelings Cilley had on several occasions wantonly outraged, and to revenge himself, aided by several other nobles, Eitzinger brought about Cilley's overthrow. Under his management, Vladislaus began a new life, and the most disreputable creatures of the late favourite were banished from his presence.

After the capture of Constantinople by the Turks, great alarm was felt in Hungary as to whether the country was able to defend itself from their invasions. This was perfectly natural, for the quarrels of the differ-ent political parties had destroyed the power of unity, and the people felt and knew that there was but one man capable of bringing Hungary out of the chaos into which it had fallen. This was Hunyady, the great patriot whom persecutions had compelled to retire from political life. Their worst fears were soon verified. Foreign traders returning from Constantinople brought the tidings that the Sultan was making immense preparations for the subjugation of Hungary. Hunyady, who after resigning his office, had retired to his estates in Transylvania to find in the society of his wife and his children that con-solation which he so much needed, was called from his retreat, and appointed commander-in-chief of the forces.

The most stringent orders were issued by the Landtag for the formation of a large army, and for providing the necessary funds for its support. The first whom Hunyady had to assist was his old enemy Brankovics, for Firus Bey, at the head of 30,000 men, had suddenly advanced and laid siege to Vegh-Szendrö. The Hungarian patriot forced the Turkish general to raise the siege, took him prisoner, and nearly annihilated his forces. As hard fate would have it, Cilley at this time regained his former predominance over the King, and for the purpose of retaining him in Vienna he induced him to appoint a certain number of commissioners to carry on the government. By his misrepresentations, he also induced the King to believe that the only way of saving his life was by imprisoning Hunyady. Vladislaus therefore ordered the Hungarian general, on his return from Servia, to come to Vienna, as he wished to ask his advice. Cilley had, in the meantime, plotted with Garay and Ujlaky for the purpose of waylaying Hunyady on the road. The Hungarian patriot, apprised of his danger by the bishop John Vitez, who had heard of Cilley's doings, in reply to the King's summons said he was perfectly willing to meet his royal master in any part of Hungary, but respectfully declined to proceed to Vienna, which was not in his (the King's) dominions. This refusal, the unworthy favourite turned to his own advantage, and Vladislaus, more convinced than ever that Hunyady sought his life, at Cilley's advice sent him another message, requesting him to meet his crafty Minister in the frontier town of Kittsee. With this order Hunyady complied, but, to the discomfiture of the King's uncle, he appeared at the head of 2,000 well-armed followers; and finding it impossible to capture him in the presence of his retinue, Cilley resolved to do so by stratagem. He sent a message ordering the Hungarian hero to meet him in the neighbouring castle, on the plea that he represented the King, that he was, moreover, of higher birth than Hunyady, and it was therefore the duty of the latter to pay his respects to him. Hunyady answered that he had not been sent to meet Cilley, but Cilley had been sent to meet him, that paltry knaves alone reckoned their nobility by their quarterings, and not by their deeds, and thereupon retired with his followers. Cilley's vexation at being thus foiled in his design, and his insatiable thirst for revenge, excited him to make another attempt against the life of his enemy. Hunyady was again summoned to the presence of his King, with the promise that he should receive a letter of protection on crossing the frontier. The Hungarian noble this time nearly fell a victim through his own heedlessness. Many of his enemies had accused him of being wanting in obedience by not going to Vienna on a former occasion, and on the second by appearing at the head of so large a body of retainers; others accused him of cowardice. The patriot's manly nature could not endure these goading insults. He therefore proceeded to Vienna with a few followers. Near the capital he was met by Cilley, who had an armed retinue, and now made certain of securing his prey. On Hunyady's asking for the letter of protection, the traitor said he had forgotten to bring it with him. The Hungarian general saw at once the trap that had been laid for him; but the man who had faced so many thousands in deadly strife was not likely to lose his presence of mind before so contemptible a wretch as Cilley. His retainers, seeing the danger of their master, contrived to place themselves between Cilley and his retinue; the great warrior then told his adversary what he thought of him. So thunderstruck were the traitor and his band that they allowed Hunyady to retire unmolested. The great patriot took no further notice of this perfidious conduct, but a large number of Hungarian nobles were so indignant at this shameful treatment that Hunyady with great difficulty prevented them from breaking out in open revolt. In order to appease the wounded feelings of his nobility, the King convoked a Landtag in 1455. Here Hunyady, in order to prove his loyalty to his sovereign, and leave to the courtiers no grounds of envy on account of the position he held, resigned all his posts and honours, with the exception of his title as Count of Bistritz. This was the signal for fresh outbreaks of clamours against the King and the opponents of Hunyady. In the midst of this excitement news was received that the Turks intended to attempt again the conquest of Hungary. Hunyady, again called upon, gave a most noble proof of his disinterested patriotism and generous and Christian character. He not only offered to equip and place in the field an army of 10,000 men, but became reconciled with Garay and many of his inveterate enemies. As a mark of favour, the King summoned his son Mathias to court. This, however, Horwáth tells us, was nothing more or less than a specious pretext for the court party to get him into their power, and thus have a strong hold over Hunyady.

Messengers were now despatched to the Pope to request his help, and accordingly a crusade against the Turks was preached in all parts of Europe. Cardinal Carvajal was sent to Hungary for the purpose of organising the united forces of the Crusaders, and by his advice a Landtag was convoked for the year 1456. The representatives of the country ordered the calling out of the whole military force of Hungary, and despatched messengers to the different foreign courts who had promised support to hasten the arrival of their subsidies. Hunyady repeated his former offer, which was accepted, and a regular plan for the ensuing campaign was drawn up. The Italian fleet was to attack Constantinople, while Hunyady and the King undertook to deal with the Turkish forces on the Danube. Towards the close of the deliberations news reached the Landtag that Sultan Muhamed was advancing on Belgrade for the purpose of capturing that important stronghold. At the moment when his presence was most required at the camp, and after having solemnly pledged himself to accompany Hunyady, caring more for his own pleasure than his duty as a sovereign, the King, instead of at once putting himself at the head of his army, and by his presence inducing the nobles to join his standards, yielded to the persuasions of Cilley, and went to Vienna for the purpose of amusing himself with hunting parties. The absence of the King from the camp facilitated Cilley's endeavours to prevent the magnates from sending their contingents. These treacherous manœuvres Hunyady could easily perceive, but they did not in any way cause him to relax in his efforts to bring the army together. By unheard-of exertions he at last managed to assemble a small fleet on the Theiss, the Save, and the Danube, and his son Vladislaus, with his brother-in-law Szilagyi, conveyed a large quantity of provisions to Belgrade. Another man, actuated by that peculiar religious zeal of those days, not only played a most prominent part in healing the discords which were then eating their way into the vitals of Hungarian prosperity, but persuaded the Hungarians to join the army in large numbers. This was the monk John Capistran. His fiery eloquence had brought around him upwards of 60,000 men of all classes. This force was, however, but indifferently armed. In fact, the greater part of them had nothing but agricultural implements, similar to those used by the Hussites, and had taken up a position at Szegedin, whence they could distinctly hear the bombardment of Belgrade by the Sultan at the head of a force of 150,000 men, with 300 pieces of artillery. The siege of this fortress began about the middle of July. Hunyady, at this time, had been waiting for several contingents of nobles who had been ordered to join his standard; but, following the advice of Cilley, they were in no hurry to increase his forces. They wished, on the contrary, to decrease them, in order to enable the vastly superior forces of the Turks to obtain a decisive victory over Hunyady. But the latter, acknowledging the importance of Belgrade, saw that it was loss of time to wait for further reinforcements. He therefore, in conjunction with the fleet, pushed on to the scene of action.

On July 14 his fleet, availing itself of a favourable wind and strong current, advanced under full sail against their opponents, whom they utterly defeated in a very short time. The Sultan was compelled to order the total destruction of a large number of his ships for fear of their falling into the hands of the enemy. This victory enabled Hunyady to throw reinforcements into Belgrade, and he accordingly entered the town with the Crusaders and the greater part of his army, the remaining portion of his forces being stationed in a fortified camp at Semlin. As the tremendous fire which had been kept up by the Turks for several days had effected several breaches in the fortifications, the Sultan ordered a general attack on July 21 for the purpose of storming the place. Hunyady, knowing the weakness of the fortifications, determined to break the force of the assaulting party before it reached him. In order to do this, he ordered his troops to divide into two bodies and advance from the outworks into the plain, and there to meet the Turks. One column, consisting of the Crusaders, was under the command of Capistran, whilst the other, composed of picked troops, was led by Hunyady in person. On his side his presence and his inspiring words electrified those around him with ardour for the coming fight. His scarred and hardy veterans felt that the time was at hand when they would have revenge for past misfortunes. The banner of the Cross, carried by a man whom they believed inspired, hatred of the Crescent, which stood as a mockery in the distance, had raised the excitement of the Crusaders, who formed the second column, to such a pitch that they waited with impatience for the moment when they would be brought face to face in a deadly combat with their opponents. The fight was long and desperate, and for some time victory appeared uncertain. The large reserves of the Turks enabled them constantly to bring fresh troops into the field and push forward their storming parties, who twice penetrated into the town, but were each time driven back by the valiant defenders of the citadel. Nothing daunted by ill success, the Turks manfully and bravely rushed on with loud cries for a third time, and effected a footing in the town, driving a large number of the defenders into the outer works, and began storming the citadel and remaining fortifications. During this sanguinary struggle the brave Capistran had taken his post on a bastion of the outer works, from which by voice and action he inflamed his followers to defend the holy symbol which he held in his hands; but it was on the bridge leading from the town to the citadel that the greatest carnage was now taking place. Some of the Turks, who had already effected their passage, aided by others who had managed to scramble through the ditch, now began to scale the walls of the citadel. One of them was about to plant the flag of the Crescent on the battlements, when a certain Dugovics rushed forward to meet him, and a mortal struggle then ensued. Both were equally matched as regards strength; both were excited by the tumultuous shouts of thousands of their comrades. The Hungarian, unable to make successful use of his

weapons, entwined his arms round the body of his antagonist, and, with a desperate effort, sprang with him from
the battlements into the moat below.   Everything now
seemed to indicate that the Turks, through their superior
numbers, would ultimately gain possession of the citadel,
when a lucky idea of the Crusaders turned the fortune of
the day.

The constant fresh attacks of the Turks had driven
the Crusaders in rear of the outer walls of the citadel,
and, in order to prevent the ingress of their enemies,
they had filled up the breach with faggots; they now
sprinkled these with sulphur and pitch, and, taking them
separately, they lighted them and threw them amongst
the Turks.   The light and inflammable garments of the
Ottoman soldiers soon caught fire, and they presented the
most awful scene that perhaps has ever been witnessed.
The whole mass of them seemed one sea of fire, and, nearly
driven mad with pain, they rushed like lunatics into the
open plains, hotly pursued by Hunyady and the Crusaders.
The victory, however, was not yet gained, for a great number of the enemy still remained in the outer works, and
their reserve and fortified camp had not been molested.
In defiance of the orders of Hunyady, the Crusaders,
unable to restrain their ardour, now rushed on the camp.
Luckily they had Hunyady to support them, for that
great leader had kept his troops so well in hand that he
was prepared when the decisive moment arrived to give
the final blow.   He now came to the assistance of the
Crusaders.   The Turks nobly defended their position,
but were unable to withstand the impetuous attack of
Hunyady's veterans, and began to retreat.   This enabled
a body of Crusaders to throw themselves on the Turkish
artillery, and Muhamed, in rallying his troops to their
defence, was wounded.   In vain did he run from point to
point, attempting to restore order amongst the broken

masses of his troops. He was at last himself swept away with them in a tumultuous flight, and was unable to restore anything like order in the shipwreck of his once magnificent army until he had reached the walls of Sophia. We are told that in the battle and in their flight the Turks lost upwards of 30,000 men. The details and exact amount of booty which fell into the hands of the Hungarians are unknown. Whatever reward he would have received at the hands of his King and countrymen, fate had decreed that Hunyady should not live to see it, for twenty days after his victory he died from an epidemic which had broken out amongst the troops, in the fifty-sixth year of his age.

It would be needless for us to describe the character and qualities of this great man, for they appear in every action of his life. He was a poor man's friend, and a saviour of his country's honour, and we trust that the time will come when we shall see his majestic features handed down to posterity by the sculptor's hand. Capistran did not long survive Hunyady; he was called to a better world two months later, and thus was spared the pain of seeing the sufferings and grief of the widow of his companion in arms.

CHAPTER VI.

RAKÓCZY II.

THIS celebrated Hungarian was the son of Rakóczy I.,
who, through his diplomatic skill and bravery, had not
only obtained the rank of Sovereign Prince for his son,
but at the treaty of Linz had also induced the Emperor
to grant full freedom of worship and ratify the arrangements of the year 1608, by which the followers of the
evangelical faith were allowed to build churches and
establish places for the burial of their dead, and which
declared the Protestants capable of holding any office.
George Rakóczy was therefore not only considered as a
champion of the Hungarian Protestants, but as the
opponent of Austrian predominance in Hungary. He
had already, during his father's life, displayed all those
qualities which are attributed to a knightly character, and
which naturally made him popular with a martial people
like the Transylvanians. In 1648 he succeeded his
father in the government of Transylvania, and shortly
after, yielding to the specious arguments of the King of
Sweden, who must have led him to believe that the
Poles were in a discontented state, he entered Casimir's
territory at the head of a large army, with the King
of Sweden, for the purpose of depriving Casimir of his
dominions. In this transaction Rakóczy displayed an
utter want of foresight, for he knew that the Sultan, the
Emperor Ferdinand, and the King of Denmark would
oppose his project; but with his usual impetuous and

headstrong bravery, he seems to have overlooked the
dangers of this undertaking. He effected his junction
with his ally at Cracow, but Charles Gustav shortly received news of such a nature from his own country that
he was compelled to give up all idea of taking any active
part in the campaign, and retired to Sweden to defend it
against the attacks of the Danish King. The dangers of
Rakóczy's position became every day more evident to
him, for the Emperor Leopold had formed an alliance
with the King of Poland, and sent 16,000 men to his
assistance. The Sultan had also despatched the Khan of
the Tartars to operate against the Transylvanian army,
and the Cossack contingent of Rakóczy, foreseeing the
ultimate fate of his army, deserted him in the hour of
need, and, still worse, a Polish army was already in Transylvania. Rakóczy knew that if his enemies effected a
junction, there was little chance, with the mass of their
cavalry, of a single man of his own troops reaching
his native home. He therefore retreated, leaving a
small garrison in Cracow. A great part of his army
lost their lives in the Vistula, and thousands were either
trampled to death by the enemy's cavalry or perished by
the sword, and Rakóczy was obliged to purchase peace by
the payment of the sum of 1,200,000 guldens. Kemeny,
one of his generals, was entirely surrounded by the
Tartars and taken prisoner with all his forces, who after
several months of serfdom received their liberty in consideration of a considerable ransom. Scarcely had the
unfortunate Rakóczy arrived in his dominions than an
envoy of the Sultan appeared calling upon the States of
Transylvania to elect another ruler. The unfortunate
prince entreated Leopold to assist him, but to no purpose,
for that monarch had at that time no wish to engage in
another war with the Turks, who on a former occasion
had done such good service in preventing Rakóczy's

father seizing the greater part of Hungary. Nor is there much doubt that some of the Transylvanian nobles were in league with the Turks, who gladly seized this opportunity of squeezing more money out of this unfortunate country.

Köprili Mustapha advanced into Transylvania at the head of 80,000 men, and called upon the inhabitants, if they required peace, not only to elect his tool Achatius Barcsay as their prince, but also to pay a tribute of 40,000 ducats a year, instead of the usual sum of 10,000, and a sum of 500,000 thalers for the expenses of the war. The people had no option but to submit. They elected Barcsay as their ruler ; but it was secretly agreed that if Rakóczy could either come to terms with the Turks or be enabled to bid them defiance, Barcsay should be compelled to resign, for, whatever might be the faults of the unfortunate Rakóczy, his manly character and daring bravery, together with the deeds of his great father, had too strong a hold on the hearts of the Transylvanians to allow them to relinquish the hope of his again being their sovereign. Rakóczy, in accordance with the above, first attempted through the medium of the Emperor of Austria to come to some compromise with the Turks ; but his enemies feared his return to power, as they too well knew that, if he obtained his rights, they would be the victims of his just vengeance for having called the Turks into his native country, and thereby enabled them to reduce the mass of his countrymen to beggary. They therefore did their utmost to excite the Sultan against him and destroy all his influence in Transylvania, and they were but too successful in both their designs. The Porte not only demanded that Rakóczy should be delivered into its hands, but also entertained the idea of plundering him of all that he possessed. Rakóczy's opponents not only confiscated all his property in Tran-

H

sylvania, but threatened to do the same with all those who
should support him.   But a man of Rakóczy's character
was not to be so easily intimidated.   Danger rendered him
ten times more desperate, and he issued a proclamation
vividly describing the perjury which his people had committed, and calling upon them to save their honour and
be ready to assist him on his return from his estates,
where he was collecting all his feudal retainers.   The
miserable Barcsay, at the first approach of danger, resigned and fled in dismay to Dava, where he fully proved
his real character by resuming his title and proceeding to
Temesvár for the purpose of entreating the assistance of
the Pasha.   In the meantime Rakóczy had entered his
former dominions and marched in triumph to Maros-
Vasarhely, where, in order to render his position more
legitimate, he allowed himself again to be elected as a
ruling prince amidst the joyous shouts of the people, who
had assembled in vast numbers from the most distant
parts of the country to welcome back their sovereign,
His first act was now to prepare himself for coming
events, and for this purpose he concluded an alliance
with the woiwodes of Wallachia and Moldavia, and sent
deputies to Leopold and the Landtag at Pressburg, requesting their good offices between himself and the
Sultan; and adding that, in the case of failure, he and
his people would rather die sword in hand than pay an
enormous tribute which must eventually reduce them to
starvation.   But the Hungarians and Leopold were not
in a position to assist him, and the Sultan, perceiving
that Rakóczy could not rely on the help of Austria,
ordered the Pasha of Ofen to reinstate Barcsay in his
former government.

The advance of the Turks was again aided by Count
Bethlen, who had put himself at the head of Rakóczy's
opponents.   Nothing daunted by the numerical inferiority

of his army, the intrepid Transylvanian ruler léd his soldiers against the forces of his opponents, and accepted a pitched battle.   In this bloody and desperate struggle Rakóczy proved himself worthy of his name, and his personal prowess produced terror and dismay amongst the Turks.   But their superior numbers enabled them to capture his artillery, and he was compelled to retreat with a loss of 3,000 men.   Barcsay was again imposed as ruler upon the Transylvanians; but as soon as the Turks had retired from the country, Rakóczy resumed active operations, and advanced to besiege Hermanstadt, which was then the seat of the Turkish nominee's government.   In order to spare bloodshed, he now attempted to persuade Barcsay to come to a compromise, and thus prevent the reappearance of the Turks.   This the usurper, in order to gain time and enable the Turks to join Bethlen and his forces, pretended he was willing to do.   This delay was fatal to the interests of Rakóczy, for it prevented him from annihilating Bethlen and his followers before they could be joined by the Turks, who were already in the country.   He had no option but at once to meet them, and stop their further progress.   The two armies encountered each other in the neighbourhood of Klausenburg.   It was but too natural that the patriot's army should fight with the most stubborn courage, for they knew it was their only chance of throwing off the galling yoke of the Mahomedan.   Although greatly inferior in numbers, Rakóczy's troops would have gained the battle had not their leader, with his usual impetuous bravery, in one of the final charges, rushed headlong into the midst of his enemies.   In a few minutes he killed seventeen, but in the exultation of victory he became surrounded by thousands of his foes.   The terror of his war-cry, his personal skill in the use of arms, made his enemies pause; but only for a few minutes. . . . . They bore upon him, and he fell wounded from his horse, fighting sword in hand, till at last, exhausted by the loss of blood, he sank to the earth. His soldiers, terrified at the loss of their leader, fled in wild dismay from the battle-field where everything seemed to have promised them such a brilliant victory. Rakóczy was carried by his faithful squires to Grosswardein, where, in a few days, he died from his wounds.

Thus departed the spirit of one of the most valiant princes of Transylvania. His qualities rendered him beloved by all who knew him, and he was himself his greatest enemy.

CHAPTER VII.

TÖKÖLYI.

EMERICH TÖKÖLYI, son of Stephen Tökölyi, who had already made his name famous in the history of his country by his constant opposition to the Austrian Government, was, as we might say, born on the field of battle. From his childhood up to the death of his father, always either in the turmoil of warfare or the council chamber, he became a skilful politician and a great military leader. The discovery having been made that he was engaged in a conspiracy with his father, just before the latter's death, he had to fly to Transylvania for protection, accompanied by his friend Petróczy. He did not, however, remain long in his retreat, for the revolution again broke forth with fresh fury, and the French Government gave pecuniary assistance to his party. The Turks also seem to have instigated Apafy, through his minister Teleki, to give armed assistance to Tökölyi and the refugees, and a French general, Boham, at the head of a force of 6,000 men, composed principally of Poles, joined the insurgents. In the ensuing short but decisive campaign, the talents and military abilities of Tökölyi became so apparent that he was unanimously elected commander-in-chief of the forces. Immediately on receiving this appointment he issued a proclamation to the inhabitants of the different counties calling upon their nobles to join his standard. His name and fame had such an effect that he was in a very short time joined by 20,000 noblemen. His first victory was over the Austrian general Leslie; and in order to get possession of the important lands near the districts of the Bergstädte he despatched a brigade of refugees, under the command of Stephen Josza, priest of Talga and abbot of Erlau, to the above district. They had instructions to proceed thence to Zips for the purpose of revolutionising the country. Tökölyi himself took Murany, Arva, and the Bergstädte, but three months after was driven back from these towns by the Imperialists. About this time the French general received the news that his King had concluded a treaty of peace with the Emperor. This compelled him to retire with his contingent. It soon also became evident to Tökölyi that the Turks did not intend offering him any effectual assistance; and knowing that if his army met with the slightest reverse a diminution in his forces would most probably follow, he concluded an armistice with the Emperor through the archbishop Zelepcsenyi. The negotiations which were then commenced led to no satisfactory arrangement, and the war was renewed in 1670. Hungary was, during that year, visited by a frightful scourge, the pest, which swept away thousands. It seemed as if the Almighty intended showering His wrath on the unfortunate Hungarians, for we must remember that this splendid country had for years been the scene of bloodshed. Both parties seem to have contented themselves with carrying on a species of guerilla warfare during these dreadful times, as large masses of men were afraid to congregate together. Thus nothing of importance took place, and in the latter part of the year both parties again agreed to an armistice which was to last to the end of the spring of the year 1680. The miserable state of the country led Leopold to believe that he should be able to come to a friendly settlement with his discontented subjects. He therefore assembled a council of the principal nobles for the purpose of advising him how to bring about this happy result. The counties were called upon to state their grievances in writing and forward them to the council, but alas, no satisfactory arrangement was come to, and Tökölyi, again subsidised by France, resumed hostilities. Unfortunately for him, his companion in arms, Petróczy, whom he had despatched to Silesia for the purpose of devastating that country, was totally defeated, and although already in possession of several towns, Tökölyi found that he was no longer in a position to continue active operations, and therefore accepted an armistice which Zelepcsenyi had again negotiated with the Emperor. The intrigues which were then going on between the Hungarian leaders and the Turks excited the fears of Leopold, and, in order to counteract their influence, he sent envoys to Constantinople to induce the Sultan to ratify a prolongation of the treaty of peace which existed between Austria and Turkey, and in the meantime he assembled, in the year 1681, a Landtag, which Tökölyi was personally invited to attend. Instead of doing so, Tökölyi, in his name and that of his followers, sent a document which contained the following demands: That the freedom of religion and the constitutional rights of the nation should be put in force; and as a guarantee that this should take place, a friendly understanding should at once be come to with the Turks. No notice seems to have been taken of these demands, and Count Paul Esterhazy was elected as Palatine. Hereupon Tökölyi solemnly protested, not only against this election, but also against all that had been agreed to in the Landtag, and again unfurled the banner of revolt. The Turks induced Apafy to reinforce his army with a body of 10,000 men, but in consequence of some misunderstanding between the Transylvanian prince and the Protestant leader, the former left Tökölyi's army and retired to his own country.

Tökölyi now concluded an armistice with the Austrians, for the purpose of obtaining the hand of the celebrated Helen Zrinyi. In the Landtag, which was convoked shortly after, the Catholics at first protested against the discussion of matters involving religious controversy; but the Protestants, backed by Tökölyi's troops, forced their opponents to allow this question to come on for debate. After several months of great excitement, on the 9th of November, they came to the following arrangement, viz. : That those rights which were guaranteed to the Protestants by the Treaty of Vienna should be made the law of the land, and that no more churches should be taken from them ; but those of which they had been deprived prior to 1670 were to be left to their present proprietors. To this latter clause, however, the Protestants would not agree, and they formally protested against its enactment. The Government further agreed to give force again to all the old laws of Hungary, and no longer to entrust official posts to foreigners; foreign troops were to be withdrawn, and a better discipline introduced amongst the soldiers. After having referred the remaining grievances to the consideration of a new Diet, the present one was dissolved.

Tökölyi concluded a treaty with the Sultan, who undertook to protect the independence of Hungary, to acknowledge him as Regent of Upper Hungary, and, if required, to send him armed assistance, on condition that he and his successors should pay to the Porte a tribute of 40,000 thalers. The King of France at this period also sent him a large sum of money ; and the Protestant leader issued one of those inspiring proclamations which he knew so well how to pen, calling upon his countrymen to rally round him in defence of their rights and religion. His glowing language had the usual effect, for large numbers joined his camp. Finding himself sufficiently strong, he proclaimed open war against the Emperor of Austria, and took in rapid succession the towns of Kaschau and Eperies. The possession of these two places gave him the command of the greater part of Upper Hungary, and he now advanced and laid siege to Fülek, where he was joined by a Turkish auxiliary corps, under the command of the celebrated Ibrahim, Pasha of Ofen, who acknowledged him, in the name of his sublime lord and master, as King of Upper Hungary, and as insignia thereof presented him with a sword, flag, and head-dress. Tökölyi, however, declined this rank, and accepted the more humble one of Prince. After the installation of the Protestant leader, the Turkish Pasha retraced his steps to his own country, leaving a considerable body of his army with Tökölyi, who now advanced and took possession of the Bergstädte, in which he found 100,000 newly-coined ducats. This booty was most welcome to Tökölyi, as it enabled him to increase the magnificence of his court. He now went into winter quarters, and convoked the Landtag at Kaschau. As soon as the Deputies met, they took the oath of allegiance to Tökölyi, and acknowledged him as their ruler. In order to increase the good understanding which existed between him and the Sultan, they despatched to the Porte an extraordinary mission, consisting of four of their principal members, who were charged to present a sum of 20,000 ducats to the Sultan, and to request him not to increase the yearly tribute, and not to conclude a treaty of peace with the Emperor of Austria without their cognisance. This latter request they needed not to express, as the celebrated Rosscheif was already fluttering in the wind, and the Sultan Muhamed, believing that the long-wished-for opportunity had arrived for realising the dream of every devout Mussulman—that, with the help of revolted Hungary, the flag of the Prophet would in a few weeks float from the lofty spire of St. Stephen, and that that venerable edifice would be turned into a mosque—had already put in motion an immense army, with which he expected to conquer Christian Europe.

Arrived at Belgrade, he gave over the supreme command to his Grand Vizier, Kara Mustapha, solemnly entrusting him at the same time with the precious flag of the Prophet, that flag which had several times made the world tremble, and which, such at least was the impression of the faithful followers of Mahomet, rendered those over whom it floated invincible. Here, in the midst of these great ceremonies, the Prince of Hungary arrived. The splendour of his retinue is said to have equalled that of his sublime host. Did the great Protestant leader, in the moment of his exultation, think of the terrible part which he was about to play? Did not his foresight tell him that those very rights, for the defence of which he and his forefathers had so often shed their blood, would be trampled under feet and utterly destroyed, should the Crescent triumph and Vienna fall? We fear not. Tökölyi was a strong-headed man, and when once he had made up his mind nothing could shake his resolution. He undertook to lead the Grand Vizier to the walls of Vienna, even as John Szapolyai had led Soliman.

Through the skill of his diplomatic agents, the Emperor Leopold had received timely information of the intentions of the Sultan, who was strongly supported by the King of France. Louis XIV. had already seized Strasburg, and he trusted that the advance of the Turks would compel the Emperor to withdraw his troops to oppose this new inroad, and thus enable him to extend his frontiers; but Leopold, who knew but too well what he could expect from France, came to an arrangement with the German princes, by the terms of which they undertook to give him their armed assistance. A treaty was also concluded with the King of Poland, Sobiesky, who placed 40,000 troops at the disposal of Leopold, receiving in return 12,000,000 gulden to defray the expenses of their equipment.

Kara Mustapha arrived before Vienna on July 14, 1683, and at once vigorously attacked it; but Count Rudiger von Stahremberg, who had been entrusted with the defence of the town, completely defied all the skilful attempts of the Ottoman troops. His trust, however, seemed doomed; Vienna, nearly reduced to ashes, could have held out but a few hours longer when, from the dome of St. Stephen, the Poles were seen advancing. It was a long time, however, before the Viennese could believe that their allies were actually in sight, for the watchmen had often deceived them, taking, in the dawn of morning, a distant herd for the Polish troops. The news spread like wildfire, and the delirium of joy of the defenders was tenfold increased by the appearance of the Imperial troops, numbering 50,000 men, under Charles of Lorraine, who at once effected his junction with the Polish troops. This happy event was brought about by the defeat of Tökölyi at Bisamberg in the end of August. At the beginning of the campaign his task, in the general plan of the Turkish leader, seems to have been to harass the troops of the Duke of Lorraine and prevent his junction with Sobiesky's army; he was also to cut off the supplies of men and provisions in Hungary and Moravia, as well for the fortresses as for the troops in the field. In order to carry out his instructions, Tökölyi established in the beginning of July a camp at Tyrnau, where he was soon joined by a body of Turkish troops. Thus reinforced, he advanced on Pressburg, occupied the town, and attacked the castle on July 20; but the Duke of Lorraine, coming up to its rescue, completely defeated Tökölyi and his allies. The Protestant leader, in a despatch to Kara Mustapha, attributed the defeat to the Turkish general, who it appears had allowed himself to be surprised, having previously refused to follow Tökölyi's advice and take up a more favourable position to check the advance of the Austrians. Shortly afterwards a body of 10,000 Tartars was sent to reinforce Tökölyi.

The Duke of Lorraine having taken up a position at Marshegg, Tökölyi pushed forward a large number of his followers towards Moravia, levying large contributions, and devastating the surrounding districts. It is stated that their progress was discerned from Vienna by the burning villages through which they passed, but in all their encounters they seem to have been worsted, and Tökölyi was forced to turn towards the mining towns for the purpose of raising contributions and forcing them to forsake the Austrian alliance. The Duke of Lorraine having left his position at Stillfried and Auyern, in order to unite his forces with those of Sobiesky, Tökölyi was compelled to retrace his steps, and detach a portion of his troops into Moravia for the purpose of obtaining information of the march of the Polish troops, and of delaying their advance.

On August 20 the Grand Vizier despatched a body of Tartars to Tökölyi's assistance. The Duke of Lorraine sent part of the corps of Lubomicrsky after them. The Tartars were defeated in several skirmishes. The Protestant leader also shared the same fate in Moravia at the hands of Colonel Fittweiss. Tökölyi and the Pasha of Grosswardein advanced along the left bank of the Danube, and effected their junction with a body of troops who had traversed the river in two boats. In their progress they destroyed the chief villages which lay on their line of

march. On August 27 the Duke of Lorraine reached
Bisamberg, and at two o'clock in the afternoon a furious
engagement took place. Tökölyi and his allies were
totally defeated, and as the bridges had been broken, and
they had only two vessels with which to recross the
Danube, the greater part of their troops perished in the
floods. After this defeat the partisan leader had no
option but to join the Turks before Vienna. In the great
battle which followed, Tökölyi, according to a plan found
among the papers of the Duke of Lorraine, occupied with
his contingent the rear rank of the Turkish army, by the
side of the Moldavians and Wallachians.

On the day which followed the junction of the Imperial
and Polish troops the opposing armies faced each other.
Historians state that it was one of those mornings on
which Nature assumes her brightest smiles, as if intending
that it should be a day of peaceful festivity.

The sun, as it rose from its eastern couch, shone forth
with resplendent majesty, and was hailed by the opposing
armies as a token of success. One of the most dreadful
and bloody battles to be found in history now began.
Both armies fought with the most determined valour,
but the steady and stubborn advance of the Germans
was not to be arrested by the fiery onslaughts of the
Turks. The Polish cavalry also committed fearful
havoc. At about four o'clock the Turks and their allies
were driven back to their camp in the suburb. Here the
Polish King followed them up with his usual impetuosity,
and the Vizier defended his position with the ferocity of a
wounded tiger. But at last he was driven out; and the
whole Turkish army sought safety in flight, leaving to
their victors 300 cannons, 15,000 tents, and 600 bags of
specie. The Turks, it is stated, lost in this battle 60,000
men; and the Tartars returned to their country with
90,000 captives, the greater part of whom were in chains.

Kara Mustapha did not stop in his flight till he had reached the walls of Raab, where he had the Pasha of Ofen at once executed, alleging that he was the cause of their defeat. It seems also that Tökölyi was accused of having corresponded with the Emperor, but the testimony of the general of the Janissaries and the widow of the Pasha enabled him to prove, to the satisfaction of the Sultan, that these charges were false, and that the Grand Vizier was the chief cause of the disasters.

Sobiesky and Charles of Lorraine now advanced into Hungary, following up the retreating Turks, whom they again defeated at Parkany. After this success they laid siege to Gran. Tökölyi here made overtures to the King of Poland, and besought him to bring about a peace between himself and the Emperor; but his terms were so exorbitant that the Duke of Lorraine declined forwarding them to Leopold, and added that if Tökölyi sincerely wished to come to an understanding, he must resign his estates and person to the grace of his Sovereign, and be ready to turn his sword against his former allies. These terms were not acceptable to Tökölyi. After the fall of Gran he again sent envoys to the King of Poland, imploring him to render his name immortal by using his influence with the Emperor to induce him to grant to his Hungarian subjects those rights for the recovery of which they had sacrificed so much. Sobiesky received these envoys, trusting to be able to bring about an understanding between the different political parties, and thus have free hands to drive the Turks across the frontier. In the presence of a council of war, presided over by Sobiesky and Charles of Lorraine, the envoys of the Protestant leader demanded for their master that he should be acknowledged ruler of Upper Hungary. As this was tantamount to placing himself on terms of equality with Leopold, this demand was declared inadmissible. In fact, it was generally believed that Tökölyi was negotiating merely in order to gain time, and this was soon after proved by a despatch of the Hungarian party leader which was intercepted. In this he informed the Porte that his design was to bring about an armistice which would prevent a winter campaign; but as he feared Leopold would not accept his terms, he entreated his allies to put at his disposal the troops under the Pashas of Wardein and Erlau, which would enable him to resume hostilities in the early spring with every chance of success. The despatch concluded with assurances of the most cordial good-will to the Porte. Negotiations were thereupon broken off; and it was agreed between the King of Poland and the Austrian leader that the former on his return homewards should capture Kaschau and Eperies. Sobiesky before setting out is stated to have again entreated Tökölyi to become a loyal subject, and warned him not to molest the Polish troops then stationed in winter quarters along the banks of the Theiss.

The Protestant leader reinforced the garrisons of Kaschau, Eperies, and Bartfeld, and did his utmost to excite his countrymen to join him in defying the authority of Leopold; but the indifference which the nobles displayed in Upper Hungary so enraged him, that he seized several of the chief Magnates and had them executed. This favourable opportunity was not lost sight of by the Emperor, and he immediately granted a general amnesty to all those who would renounce their allegiance to Tökölyi. This measure greatly thinned the ranks of the malcontents, and their leader again attempted to bring about a mediation. For this purpose he applied to the German princes, especially the Elector of Saxony; he also made ineffectual overtures to the Pope. Seeing how little he could depend upon external assistance, except from the Turks, he redoubled his energies to collect a force suffi-

cient to enable him to maintain his position until he could
induce them again to advance into Hungary. The nature
of the country and the important strongholds which he
occupied greatly strengthened his position.

In the spring, General Schulz, at the head of 6,000
men, was ordered to march into the Zips and drive
Tökölyi from his position. Upper Hungary and the
surrounding districts were a scene of constant bloodshed
and conflagration. Schulz, with the stubborn energy of
the German, followed his adversary step by step, never
allowing himself to be deceived by his system of guerilla
warfare, and waited patiently until he could come at
close quarters with the main body of his troops. At last
his efforts were rewarded, for, having ascertained from
spies the position of the main body of the malcontents,
he suddenly left his camp, and, by a rapid night march,
totally misled the light troops of Tökölyi as to his line of
march, and in the morning was able to surprise the
Protestant leader in his camp. Veterani, who commanded the Austrian vanguard, drove all before him.
It is stated that so complete was the surprise that Tökölyi
had barely time to throw himself, half dressed, on the
first horse he could find, and saved his life only by a
rapid flight. Schulz now prepared to go into winter
quarters near Eperies, where he had obtained this advantage, and allowed Tökölyi to cut off several convoys
of provisions without hindrance, till at last, rendered
bolder and less prudent by this apparent inactivity, the
Protestant leader was again surprised and utterly routed.
The Austrians were, however, unable to take Eperies.
Tökölyi, unfortunately, in this campaign soiled his hands
with the blood of Hungarians who had made their submission to Leopold.

In the ensuing year he undertook to revictual the
important fortress of Neuhensiel, on the frontier, where

the Turks had collected a large body of troops, as well as the fortress of Neograd, which two places were invested, the first by Schulz, the other by Heisser; but he was unsuccessful. The greatest part of his convoys were intercepted, and his own followers began to display great discontent. Tökölyi repressed it, informing them, with his usual determination, that he would exercise the most fearful revenge on any of them whom he might meet in the ranks of the Austrians.

The delay in the arrival of the Turkish reinforcements compelled him to remain inactive, while Schulz was vigorously besieging Eperies; and, fearing at last that the courageous defenders would be compelled to surrender, he offered to deliver up all the strongholds in his power and make his submission, if he could thereby secure reasonable terms, but no answer was made to his overtures. Eperies fell on September 11; Neuhensiel had already capitulated; and Tokay, not being reinforced, soon after surrendered, as well as several smaller places. Kashau was invested on October 13. This stronghold being one of the strongest and garrisoned by Tökölyi's most determined adherents, doubts were at first entertained as to the possibility of its capture; but the Turks had gradually become more and more suspicious owing to their long run of ill-success, and offered to conclude peace with Austria. The Duke of Lorraine demanded that Tökölyi should be at once delivered into his hands. Ibrahim Pasha, fearing to arrest him in the middle of his troops, effected his capture as follows:—The Pasha of Grosswardein, to whom the Hungarian leader had applied for reinforcements, was instructed to request his presence at a council of war, and Tökölyi, not suspecting the treacherous intentions of the Pasha, at once repaired to his presence; but he was seized, loaded with chains, and sent to Adrianople, charged with having betrayed the

Turks to the Austrians. This treachery had such a dis-
heartening effect upon Tökölyi's adherents that Kashau,
several other fortresses, and the greatest part of his followers, at their head his most trusted friend Petnchazy,
made their submission, and Apafy's crafty minister, perceiving that there was little chance of the Turks being able
to retrieve their disasters, concluded a treaty with the
Emperor. Munkács was the only town of Upper Hungary
which now held out against the Imperial standards, and
it was defended by the heroic wife of Tökölyi.[1] The
Turks, who had been in possession of the greater part of
Hungary for the space of 150 years, and during that time
had been guilty of fiendish cruelties against its unfortunate
inhabitants, had now been compelled to evacuate nearly all
the territory of Hungary. Anyone who studies the history
of that country will, I think, acknowledge that the real
cause of the Turkish success was the insubordination of
the Hungarian nobility. It is true that they called in the
aid of the Turks in order to maintain the existence of their
ancient constitutional right, but they must have known
that if Austrian influence disappeared in Hungary it
could not fail to be replaced by a yoke ten times more
galling and despotic; and the welcome which greeted the
Imperial colours in those places which knew from years of
experience what Turkish rule meant demonstrates the
correctness of the above opinion.

The success of the Duke of Lorraine and his generals
now rendered it possible for them to commence the siege
of Ofen, the great stronghold of the Turkish power.
Months before this great event took place the inhabitants
of Vienna saw with wonder and admiration Christian
soldiers from the most remote provinces of Germany,
England, France, Spain, Italy, Poland, and wherever the

---

[1] The history of the siege of Munkács will be found in the life of Helena
Zrinyi, in the Second Part of this work.

Cross held its sway, passing through their ancient town, to join the victorious standard of the great Austrian leader, whose army then numbered 25,000 Imperial troops, and 20,000 Hungarians, the remaining 45,000 consisting of the above-mentioned strangers. The Sultan saw that unless Ofen was relieved, the key of Hungary would be lost to him. Prayers were offered in all the mosques of the Empire, and Constantinople soon became the centre of the followers of Mahomed. Fortunately for Tökölyi his great enemy Ibrahim was disgraced and decapitated, and Soliman Pasha, one of the most determined and skilful generals of the Turks, was made Grand Vizier. His first act on receiving the supreme command was to liberate Tökölyi, whose influence in Hungary, and talents as a general, would greatly enhance his chances of success, as he trusted that the greatest part of the malcontents in Hungary would again fight under his banner.

Tökölyi therefore received the command of an army, was subsidised with funds, and ordered to incite Upper Hungary to revolt, as this step, the Grand Vizier knew, would compel the Austrians to divide their forces. Tökölyi at once attempted to relieve Munkács, but was unsuccessful.

The siege of Ofen cannot be said to belong to the life of Tökölyi, as he took no part whatever in it; yet as its fall brought about the coronation of Leopold's son, Joseph, as King of Hungary, we may be pardoned for introducing here the masterly description given by Horváth.

' About the middle of June the Austrians began their attack upon Ofen, the bulwark of Turkish strength in Hungary, and defended by one of the most skilful Turkish generals, Abdi Pasha, a soldier of fortune, who had embraced the Mussulman faith, relinquishing at the same time his name of Abdul Haman for that of Abdi.

' The garrison consisted of 16,000 veteran troops, with

abundant supplies of provisions and munitions of war. On June 24 the Austrians made the first assault, and after a terrific resistance, took the lower town. The Turks thereupon retired to the upper and strongest part. On July 12 the Imperials advanced in large masses for the purpose of overwhelming the garrison in one general attack. In this they were totally unsuccessful, and were driven back with tremendous loss. This induced the Austrian general to follow the advice of his engineers, to begin a regular bombardment of the town, and by means of several mines to destroy the outer fortifications of the citadel. His artillery was under the command of Antonio Gonzales and the priest Gabriel, the former being known as one of the most experienced artillerists of his day in the employment of red-hot shot. Gabriel, who appears to have been a very scientific man, and had made several important discoveries with reference to the explosive power of gunpowder, had invented a peculiar kind of shell which was used during the siege, and which from the strength of its composition destroyed all the outer stockades on the walls of the fortress, and on this account the inventor was afterwards called by the *sobriquet* of the fiery Gabriel.

'On July 22, one of Gonzales' red-hot shots struck the immense powder magazine of the Turks. Its effects were like those of an earthquake. The Danube overflowed its banks, and one part of the fortifications, which from its impregnable position could not be further sapped, had in it a breach of 60 paces. The Duke of Lorraine fondly fancied that this frightful catastrophe would subdue the courage of the Turks. He, therefore, again summoned them to capitulate; but for answer the Turkish leader exhibited on the ramparts the heads of 100 Christians whom he, without the slightest reason, had decapitated. Five days afterwards the Austrians

made another general assault; but that fanatical zeal
which renders a Mahomedan ten times more desperate
when he fights without hope, gave the Turks fresh
courage to meet the advancing foes. It was in vain
that the Austrian leaders, time after time, attempted to
make head against the solid mass of their opponents.
After a most bloody and desperate fight, the Imperials
were driven in the wildest flight to their camp, where,
had it not been for Prince Eugene, who through his
determined bearing rallied them, the whole army would
have been a flock of fugitives. After a short time, the
Austrians again renewed the attack, and although the
advancing party was nearly all swept away by the
murderous fire of the garrison, they managed to get
possession of an important bastion, and one of the former
supporters of Tökölyi successfully planted the royal
banner on its walls. That the position was purchased at
a tremendous sacrifice is seen by the fact that the Duke
of Lorraine, although aware of the rapid advance of the
Turks and the machinations of Tökölyi, did not follow up
his successes, but again called upon the Turks to capitulate.
This Abdi Pasha declined, as he knew that the Grand
Vizier was then within four hours' march of the town, with
an army of 80,000 men. But the Austrian general proved
by his precautions that he was master of the position.
He so strengthened his camp that it was impossible for
the Turkish general either to attack him or to throw reinforcements into the town. The Austrian leader was
thus enabled to organise a general attack, which took
place on September 2 at six o'clock, and was signalled by
six cannon-shots.

' A feeling of desperation existed among the Turks and
Austrians alike. Each knew that it was a final crisis,
and each determined to shed the last drop of their
very heart's blood in order to procure victory. Should

the Austrians fail, the Turks, led by the Grand Vizier,
would have been able again to appear before the walls of
Vienna, and the capital of the Hapsburg would have
been numbered among the things which have been.   The
Turks, on the other hand, knew that the fall of Ofen not
only meant the destruction of the Vizier's army, but the
annihilation of their power in Hungary, and their
military prestige in the rest of the world.   Those who
have read of the desperate resistance of the Jews in the
defence of their ancient city, or that of Tippoo Sahib in
his capital, may form some idea of the resistance of the
Turkish veteran.   For a time, it was impossible for the
Imperialists to gain ground, on account of the numbers of
the dead and wounded who covered their path.   At last
Tökölyi's former companion in arms, Petnehazy, at the
head of his Haiduks, by the most tremendous exertions
got over this bloody mass of lifeless corpses.   It is stated
that the Imperial troops were unable to make any
prisoners, as the whole garrison headed by their veteran
leader died sword in hand.   No one can describe the
exultation of the inhabitants when they beheld in the
morning the Imperial flag floating in the breeze, for we
must remember that for the space of 145 years Ofen had
been in the possession of the Turks.   Nothing now remained for the Turkish Vizier but to retire.   Tökölyi
during this time did his utmost to counterbalance the
terrible loss of the Turks, and it was only through his
endeavours and those of Apafy that they were enabled to
make a temporary stand.   In the spring of the year 1687,
the campaign was again renewed with redoubled fury.
Both sides had been strongly reinforced.   The Archduke
Charles first attempted to take Essegg, but he was foiled
in his object by the superior numbers of the Turks.   The
Imperial general then, by a series of skilful manœuvres,
enticed his opponents to follow him, and on August 12

he took a strong position at Mohács, where, 161 years before, the Hungarian army had been annihilated. But this time, the arms of Austria were successful, for after a sanguinary contest the Turks had to retreat, leaving 20,000 men on the field of battle. Tökölyi and his confederates had to seek safety in flight, and Apafy, compelled to accept the most humiliating terms from the Archduke Charles, retired to Fogaras, where he still kept up his court, although he could no longer be considered in the light of an independent ruler.'

We now come to a period of Tökölyi's career which demonstrates but too clearly the dreadful punishment which a party leader inflicts on his country by intriguing with the foreigner in order to restore himself to power. Karaffa, one of the leading officers of the Imperial troops, reported to the Emperor that there existed a vast conspiracy in Hungary, which had for its object his assassination, and that Tökölyi was at the head of it. So specious were the arguments of Karaffa, that Leopold believed that his life and authority were in jeopardy, and he unfortunately gave full power to Karaffa to punish according to the Hungarian law all those who were implicated in the said conspiracy. Karaffa at once introduced a reign of terror, and seems to have taken the most terrible vengeance, not only upon those who were supposed to have been connected with the plot, but also on all his personal enemies. Luckily for the Hungarians, the Palatine, whose loyalty no one could doubt, proved to the King that Tökölyi's intrigues had been greatly overrated; and from what we have read of this great party leader's character, we cannot for one moment entertain the idea that he countenanced the plan of assassinating the King. Tökölyi's power was at this time completely broken, for his heroic wife had been forced to surrender the fortress Munkács, and the Hungarian Landtag had declared that

the title of King of Hungary should be hereditary in the
family of Leopold, resigning the right of election and
that of opposing with armed force illegal and arbitrary
acts of their King.   To crown the triumphs of Leopold,
his eldest son Joseph, after taking the inaugural oath, was
solemnly crowned King.   From the year 1687 Tökölyi's
military talents were of the greatest assistance to the
Sultan ; but the jealousy of the Turkish leaders prevented
his receiving any large command, and he was chiefly
employed in revictualling their strongholds and devastating the country.   It is true that he once nearly subdued
Transylvania, where he forced himself to be acknowledged King of the country; but the victories of Louis
of Baden compelled him to retreat from his newly-
acquired dominions.   In 1691 he again renewed his
attempt to reconquer that province, but was foiled in his
object by General Veterani.   The greatest victory which
the Austrians and loyal Hungarians gained over the
Turks was on the banks of the Theiss.

It appears that Prince Eugene surprised them as they
were effecting the passage of that river.   We are told
that upwards of 10,000 Turks were drowned and 20,000
killed in their entrenchments   It is related that Tökölyi,
prior to this battle, had advised the Sultan to march upon
Szegedin, which was then totally undefended, and contained a great store of provisions, but the Sultan declined
to accept his advice, as also that of destroying the bridges
suggested by Tökölyi in order to increase the courage of
the Turks.

Unfortunately for the Austrians, their war with the
French prevented them from being able to reap the fruits
of this glorious victory.   Tökolyi, who had been subsidised
by France, was unremitting in his efforts to retrieve the
disasters of the Sultan, but was totally unsuccessful.   In
the year 1699 peace was concluded, through the interven-

tion of England and Holland, between Austria and Turkey. The Austrian Court knowing that as long as Tökölyi remained on the frontiers of Hungary, that country would be perpetually disturbed by his intrigues, demanded that he himself, and his companions should reside in the interior of the Sultan's dominions, whereupon Tökölyi, accompanied by his wife, took up his abode in the town of Nicomedia, where his health seems to have completely broken down. He died in the year 1705.

CHAPTER VIII.

GEORGE KLIMO, BISHOP OF FÜNFKIRCHEN.

THE life of George Klimo, whose name is still cherished
by many Hungarians, and claims a place in the gratitude
of all, exhibits a striking instance of the power of merit
and virtue in elevating its possessor, even under the
most unfavourable circumstances.   This great man was
born in 1710 at Lopessaw, in the Neutraer Comitat, of
humble Hungarian peasants, who however found the
means of procuring for him an education in the public
schools at Tyrnau, which were then highly esteemed.
George Klimo distinguished himself in his studies, and
early obtained some small church preferment at Vágujhely.
He became later a secretary in the archbishopric of Gran,
and was subsequently appointed to a prebend at Pressburg. He remained but a short time in this office, having
been soon after raised to a similar one in the chapter of
Gran.

Count Emerich Esterhazy, who was at that time
Primate of Hungary, knew well how to appreciate George
Klimo's merit and abilities.   His preferment advanced
therefore with unusual rapidity.   He obtained the united
dignities of abbot and archdeacon, was honoured with a
titular bishopric, and at the age of thirty already sat in
the council of the Hungarian Government.   In the year
1747 he was called to Vienna to fill an important office
in the Hungarian chancelry.   During four years he discharged the duties of his new situation with the greatest

honour, and received as a reward of his merit the bishopric of Fünfkirchen.[1] In this important station he conducted himself in a manner which secured him the heartfelt esteem of the whole diocese; and at the same time he had also to fill the office of obergespann in the two counties of Barany and Tolna, to which that of Veröcz was added in 1755. On an occasion of great difficulty, in a dispute between the magistrates of the comitats, he was called upon to act as arbitrator, and obtained great praise for the ability with which he discharged the duties of this difficult office ; and at a later period of his life he was again called by the Empress Maria Theresa to assist in the council of the State. His care to promote the interest of the bishopric and encourage learning was unceasing. The noblest monument of his liberality is a public library, which he had enriched with 20,000 volumes. At a large expense he also caused many valuable manuscripts to be carefully copied, added to all an extensive collection of ancient coins, and settled a considerable fund for the maintenance and increase of the library. Besides this, he built several churches and monasteries, and most liberally endowed many institutions for education. His laborious and useful life was closed in the year 1777. The encouragement which he gave to science collected in the diocese many men who have distinguished themselves in the paths of general literature and of *belles-lettres*, as well as in the severer pursuits of theological inquiry.

[1] Fünfkirchen is of no mean interest as connected with the ecclesiastical history and the literature of Hungary. It was erected into a bishopric by St. Stephen so early as 1009, and many of its bishops have truly been ornaments to their high stations. In the year 1364, Louis I. founded at this place an university, which was at one attended by above 2,000 students ; but it was entirely destroyed after the battle of Mohács in 1526, and it was not until 1694, when the Jesuits founded a college which grew into much repute, that Fünfkirchen was again known as a place of education.

CHAPTER IX.

STATESMEN OF THE PRESENT DAY.

FRANZ VON DEÀK.

FRANZ VON DEÀK was born on October 13, 1803, at the humble but ancient abode of his family, in the small village of Kihida, in the county (comitat) of Zala. He was educated for the bar, at the University of Raab, where he won a name for good humour and for the benevolence of his disposition. He was returned as member for the district of Zala, which his elder brother, Anton, had represented before his death. It is related that, when Anton Deàk had to retire from political life on account of ill-health, he told his friends that he would send to them, as his successor, a young man who had more knowledge and honourable feeling in his little finger than he himself possessed, although the latter was his younger brother.

Deàk was in his twenty-second year when he entered the Diet of 1825. This Diet was the commencement of the great reform movement in Hungary.[1] By an extraordinary coincidence, the great benefactor of Hungary, Count Stephan Szécsenyi, took his seat for the first time at the Magnaten table when Franz von Deàk became Deputy. Stephan Szécsenyi had as colleague Baron Nikolaus Wesselenyi. Deàk was also firmly supported by the celebrated orator Paul von Nagy, whose fiery eloquence, it is stated, overshadowed that of Kossuth. The reform

---

[1] See note on the State of Hungary, p. 70.

which these four men boldly declared that they intended
to attempt was considered by the mass of the people to be
the dream of madmen. They asked from the rich to give
up the greater part of their income, and those who possessed rights to be themselves the instruments of their
annihilation. It is stated that a venerable deputy, on
hearing Deàk say ' I am for an extreme radical reform,'
remarked ' Shall I then in my old age live to see my
beloved country commit suicide?' Yet in a space of
twenty-three years the demands of these great patriots
were acknowledged by their countrymen to be just, and
the Diet of 1847 unanimously confirmed them.

In the Diet of 1832–36, Deàk, who was then in his
twenty-ninth year, became the acknowledged leader of
the then rapidly-increasing reform party. He displayed
in his speeches in defence of the peasants, general taxation, and the state of Poland, a commanding eloquence
and facility of expression which had such an effect on his
hearers that they were afraid to attack his arguments,
although the unfortunate Szécsenyi was the target of the
political arrows of his opponents, and was considered by
many of his brother nobles to be a renegade to their
cause. The result of this Diet seems to have convinced
the Government that they must take active steps to prevent the increase of the reform movement; and in order
to intimidate the moderate reform party they unwisely
placed in confinement Louis Kossuth and Vladislaus
Lovassy, who, had they been left alone, would, through
their ungovernable folly, have induced many of the
moderate party to strengthen the ranks of Deàk's opponents.

The consequence of this and other acts on the part of
the Imperial Government was that it found its opponents
greatly increased in the Diet of 1839. Through his
masterly tact Deàk gained the entire leadership and con-

fidence of the Lower House; and he never pushed his
victory too far, but was always ready to effect any practical compromise with his opponents, and there is no
doubt he thereby gained their respect, for they perceived
that he wished to effect his object by constitutional means.
The result was that this Diet ended in bringing about a
good understanding between the King and his people.

Deák now became, as we may say, the first political
personage in Hungary—as Count Stephan Szécsenyi at
this time ceased to take an active part in the whirlpool
of political life—but he had worthy followers behind him
in the persons of Counts Louis Batthyany, Vladislaus
Teleki and Baron Eötvös. Amongst Deák's most celebrated colleagues, who occupied a high position in public
opinion, were B. von Szémere, G. von Klausal, E. von
Beöthy, M. von Perczel, F. von Pulszky, A. von Trefort,
L. von Szalay, and Ivon Ludvigh. The great platform
agitator of the day was Louis Kossuth, who no doubt,
through the violent language which he used in his journal
' Pesti Hirlap,' created a party whose policy will always
interfere with the gradual development of constitutional
reform in Hungary, and thereby assist blindly those
nationalities who wish to assert their own independence.
In the year 1843 Deák again stood as candidate for the
county of Zala, and in his address boldly proclaimed
himself the advocate of universal taxation. Zala at that
time contained 274,000 inhabitants. Amongst these were
24,000 peasants belonging to the inferior class of nobility,
together with a large number of richly-endowed clergy;
these two classes were in fact the voters. Deák's proclamation was tantamount to a declaration of war against
the rights of these voters, for they were at that time
exempt from taxation. One of the most severe elec-
tioneering contests now took place, both parties adopting

every possible means to effect the victory of their representative. Hungary had seldom seen such a scene of
unlimited bribery, corruption, and coercion; and blood
was shed in many cases. Deàk, on being acquainted
with the means by which his supporters intended placing
him at the head of the poll, stated that he would not be
a party to such transactions, and would rather resign.
None of his party would believe him, but, on his return
being announced to him, Deàk refused to accept his
nomination. Many of his friends who had spent considerable sums of money to purchase votes, were suffering under
great pecuniary embarrassment; they were naturally
greatly irritated at what they considered prudishness on
the part of Deàk, who, to his great honour, was proof
against all such specious arguments, and remained at
home. At the opening of the Diet, Eugen von Beöthy
moved that the question should be put at the opening of
every Diet whether Franz Deàk was there, and that the
chair which he usually occupied should be left vacant.
Deàk's honest conduct had the effect of gaining him the
respect of his bitterest opponents. Even the various
nationalities acknowledged the virtuous integrity of his
conduct, and his five years' retreat no doubt had the
most beneficial effect on the country at large. It was
generally expected that in the Diet of 1847 Deàk would
again represent the county of Zala, but, unfortunately,
he was at that time attacked by an illness which seems to
have baffled the skill of his physicians, for they advised
him to travel for the benefit of his health. During this
time he visited Italy, Switzerland, France, England, and
Germany, and was therefore unable to be present when
his ideas became the law of the land. But let us for a
moment consider what were his demands; 20,000 of the
most noble families of Hungary, six-sevenths of which

were of the Magyar race, and who possessed the most
absolute feudal rights, should give up their privileges and
make themselves equal to their former serfs!

Deák's place as a leader of the liberal party was now
occupied, we might say seized, by Louis Kossuth, who, it
is stated, was elected through the influence of Count
Louis Batthyany, whom it seems Kossuth, by his fiery
and wonderful eloquence, had gained over for a time to
his extreme views. In this Kossuth seems to have been
equally successful with the Deák party.

When Count Batthyany, in March 1848, was called
upon to form a Ministry, he consented to do so with the
reservation that Deák should be one of its members.
Deák, who had now returned, considered it his duty to
join the Batthyany Ministry, in which he received the
portfolio of Minister of Grace and Justice. This was
one of the most delicate posts in the cabinet, as the new
reforms had quite upset the old laws, especially as regards
the rights of the nobles over the peasants; and it is stated
that it is principally through Deák's great tact that the
most serious disturbances were prevented, for the seeds of
Louis Kossuth's policy were already developing socialistic
ideas among the peasants. Deák during his presence in
the cabinet, designed several legislative reforms with
reference to the common law of Hungary, which are now
being introduced into practice. He ceased to be a
member of the Batthyany Ministry in October 1848.
During the time he was in office, he always sided with
the more moderate party, who we are told consisted of
Batthyany, Eötvös, Klausal, and General Meszaros.
Deák was one of the deputation who went to Vienna
for the purpose of negotiating with the Reichstag in
September 1848. On his return he seems to have taken
little or no active part in the affairs of the day. Hungary
and its King now stood in armed opposition to each other.

On Christmas eve, the Imperial general Prince Windisch-grätz appeared with an army before Pesth. Both Houses of the Hungarian Parliament before dissolving deter-mined to send the following deputation: George von Majláth, Counts Louis Batthyany and Anton Majláth, the Archbishop of Erlau, Josef von Lunovics, and Franz von Deàk to the Imperial commander, for the purpose of coming, if possible, to some understanding with him in order to prevent the shedding of blood. This deputation the general declined to receive. The Hungarian Govern-ment thereupon hastily retreated to Debreczin ; Deàk for the time having retired into private life to his country residence at Kihida.

In January 1849, Prince Windischgrätz entered Pesth. It is not my intention to enter into the details of this unfortunate dispute. Many think that if Deàk had come forward in 1849 he could have brought about a compromise between the two contending parties; but it seems more likely that Deàk, from his intimate knowledge of the character of the men who were taking an active part in the conflict, was convinced that such an attempt on his part would have been perfectly fruitless; and there is little doubt that Deàk saw with a prophetic glance the events which have since taken place, and in order to be of service to his country he had for the time being deter-mined to remain an inactive spectator. During his retreat he held little or no personal intercourse with politicians. The Imperial Government seemed as if passively to ignore his existence. His well-known face was to be constantly seen at Pesth and even in Vienna. When the Viennese cabinet attempted a reorganisation in the unfortunate state of affairs in Hungary, they invited Deàk to come to Vienna and give them his assistance. Deàk wrote a letter to the Chevalier Schmerling modestly but firmly declining to accede to the invitation. He stated that his

K

reason for so doing was that the policy of the Viennese cabinet was in direct opposition to his own opinions, because that policy was illegal.   Had Deàk gone to Vienna, we think from what is now known of the political opinions of the unfortunate Baron von Bruck that he would have found in him a warm supporter, who had for his purpose the well-being of the Emperor-King and his Hungarian subjects.   The minister Bach seems to have cherished the idea that if he saw Deàk alone, he would be able to gain him over to his views.   He therefore invited him to a private audience; but Deàk was not to be convinced, and after several interviews, he took leave of the minister, uttering these remarkable words: ' Your excellency, I trust, will excuse me; I know of no other constitution but the Hungarian; and as long as it does not exist, which at present is the case, I also cease to exist.'

Deàk passed his winters in Pesth or Vienna, and the summers at his own country residence; but he seems now to have mixed more with some of his political friends belonging to the extreme moderate party: chiefly Baron Eötvös, A. von Esengery, and the journalist S. von Kemeny.

After the Italian war, the old conservative party attempted to open negotiations with the Emperor.   Encouraged by their reception, they sought the assistance of Deàk : the extreme national party also applied to the patriot to support their views ; but he declined to have anything to do with either of them.

Before following him further in his political career, we think we had better give our readers a slight description of his personal appearance and traits of character at this time.   Deàk is a strong and powerfully-built man, with broad shoulders, a fine Roman head, short hair, determined eyebrows and bushy moustaches, with ingenuous eyes and a good-natured expression; his voice is clear and manly but subdued. He is very frugal in his habits, but cannot for a moment be without his favourite cigar; and when not in society, he is always engaged in study. Yet this remarkable man, whose mind contains a mine of wealth, has never written a line in his life, although he has been President of the Academy of Science since 1839. He has only about 6,000 gulden a year, and yet his purse is always open to the poor and needy; and it is a well-known fact that his generosity is constantly imposed upon. Although a bachelor, Deàk is very fond of female society, where he makes himself thoroughly at home, and enraptures everybody with his witty and humorous conversation. So great a favourite is the old bachelor, that it is stated that the ladies are very fond of thronging around him and openly kissing him. To this process he does not at all object, and calls the ladies his sisters. He is considered to be the greatest favourite of his Empress-Queen; and if anyone wishes to pay a compliment to the old man, he has only to express his admiration and respect for the lovely Queen of Hungary. But what is most extraordinary is the effect which it produces on him; and this I noticed myself the last time I saw him at Pesth, when he had just recovered from a severe illness. His voice and manner became suddenly changed, his eyes flashed fire, and he spoke with all the enthusiasm and fiery impetuosity of a thorough young Hungarian. A fact worthy of notice is that he is one of those few politicians who will give you a direct and straightforward answer to any question with reference to his political life or that of his country; but he never introduces politics into conversation unless called upon to do so. He is without doubt one of the most agreeable and lively of companions, and his amusing anecdotes and genial conversation would dissipate any amount of spleen in the most hypochondriacal individual.

Deàk is also one of the most tender-hearted men ; from his lips, it is stated, have never fallen those withering sarcasms which men of great intellect are so prone to employ, and he was never heard to make an unkind remark.

He is moderate in all his opinions, and yet his remarks display such a strength of character that they leave behind a lasting impression on the minds of his hearer. Patriot without ambition, he never sought to be the leader of his party; and still there is no doubt nature intended him to be one, for from the commencement of his political career he has always been acknowledged to be chief of his party, not only by those who entertain opinions similar to his own, but also by his opponents. His talents as an orator are, no doubt, of the highest quality. It is true, he does not possess that fiery eloquence which produces shouts of applause from its hearers, and for the time being convinces them of the truthfulness of the arguments of the orator, nor can he speak when he has no real subject to speak upon, but what he does say can be read in print, and years afterwards appears as a fragment of history.

Deàk's first sign of recommencing his political life was the part he took in the celebrated interview which he and Baron Eötvös had with his Majesty the Emperor-King of Hungary. In all the deliberations in which he took part with reference to the compromise, there is no doubt that his influence and moderation greatly aided the Emperor in coming to a good understanding with his subjects. On March 11, 1861, he was elected Deputy by the central district of Pesth. Although he declared that it was unconstitutional that the Diet should be assembled at Ofen instead of Pesth, still, in the hopes of bringing about some peaceful arrangement, Deàk not only took his seat, but induced many others to follow his example.

In the great debate from May 13, to August 8, 1861, with reference to the answer to the speech delivered from the throne, the extreme party of action, which assumed the name of the 'Fatherland party,' had openly proposed to return no answer whatever, but have their reply published in the different Hungarian newspapers. Some of the moderate party remarked that the common laws of courtesy required that the royal speech should be answered. Deàk then rose, and read an address which he proposed should be sent as a reply to the speech from the throne, and which made his name from that time famous in Europe. The address was unanimously adopted by both parties, with the exception of the so-called 'Fatherland,' who adhered to their former resolution. Chevalier von Schmerling, who was in favour of the centralisation policy, was naturally strongly opposed to Deàk's opinions. He therefore advised his Imperial master to dissolve the Hungarian Diet, as he believed that the different nationalities would ultimately, one by one, come to an arrangement with him.

In 1865, the Emperor acknowledged the independence of Hungary as a constitutional State; but he reserved to himself certain rights as Emperor of Austria, which did not meet with the approval of his Hungarian subjects. Deàk again came forward as the spokesman of his country, and his celebrated answer to the Emperor's proclamation, on February 2, 1866, brought about the present compromise.

The first real step towards a practical solution of the Hungarian question was taken at the time when Baron Beust took the portfolio as Minister of Foreign Affairs. The Diets of Hungary and Croatia were convoked; on November 19, the Deputies were informed that it was the intention of their Emperor-King to form as soon as possible a Hungarian Ministry, but with the proviso that the unity of the army should exist, and also indirect taxation, customs duty, and a common national debt. The extreme left of the Diet refused to take any part in the debates on the address until the Hungarian ministry were in office. Deák, on the other hand, moved that a reply should be made to the Imperial speech, stating that the ministry should be nominated as soon as possible, but that the House did not object to enter into discussion on the affairs which were common to both parts of the empire. In the meantime Deák and the leaders of the different parties had constant interviews with Baron Beust. On February 18, 1867, it was announced, amidst the applauding shouts of the Deputies, that Count Andrássy was Prime Minister of Hungary, and that he should forthwith form a Hungarian ministry.

On the evening of that eventful day Pesth was a blaze of light. A tremendous ovation was paid to Deák, who was acknowledged by all parties to have been the instrument of bringing about this happy event.

On March 30, in the debate on the national debt, Deák made the following celebrated remark : That this question could not be dealt with in a statesmanlike point of view, because the geographical position of Hungary was such that, in case of any great danger arising from Russia or Germany, it was necessary that Hungary should have an ally on whom it could depend, and such an ally was to be found in Austria.

Their Majesties the Emperor Francis Joseph and the Empress of Austria were solemnly crowned legitimate and constitutional sovereigns of Hungary on June 8, 1867. All the transactions which were then going on between the Hungarian and Viennese cabinets were greatly assisted by Deák's moderate opinions ; and up to the present day, he has always steadfastly adhered to the same views and principles which he had for so many years advocated. It is true that nowadays many Hungarians consider him a clog on the wheel of reform, but they forget that reforms and a new code of laws are not made in a day.

Many have often asked the question why Deàk was not made Prime Minister of Hungary. The reason given is, that although he is one of the first politicians and jurists in Europe, the peculiar organisation of his mind renders him unable to take the initiative. With this opinion we do not agree. In our belief, Deàk considers that by maintaining his present position, he keeps together many political factions which, if he took office, becoming divided, would seriously impede, and probably frustrate the great reform which is now taking place in Hungary; and we are convinced that whenever his country stands in need of his services as a statesman, although far advanced in years, Deàk will prove by his moderate opinions and strength of character that he is perfectly competent to steer the helm of State.

COUNT EMERICH MIKÓ,

Minister of Communication and Public Works.

The Counts of Mikó are amongst the first of the Transylvanian noble families. The present minister was born in the year 1805. In his scholastic career as a boy, he was known for his talents and industry, and, like many of the Hungarian nobles, was educated for the bar. When he had completed his legal studies, he entered the service of the Government, and in the year 1841 we find him already President of the Transylvanian Gubernium.

At the commencement of the troubles of 1849, Count

Mikó resigned his official duties, and ceased to take any part in public affairs. During this period of his political inactivity, he devoted himself to literary labours, the results of which were some very interesting descriptions of the history of his small but picturesque country ; but he deserves to be more widely known for the large sums which he expended for educational purposes, and for his efforts to improve the social position of his countrymen. He entirely rebuilt and endowed at his own expense the school, Nagy-Enyed, which had been destroyed by the Wallachians during the revolutionary struggle, and as a Magyar naturally did his utmost for the predominancy of his nationality and language.

We now draw the attention of our readers to an act of munificence of this nobleman, which would alone shed a lustre on his name. Count Mikó not only made to his countrymen a present of a palace and the surrounding grounds, but he added to it the various collections of a splendid museum, one of the most interesting which Hungary possesses, for it contains specimens of everything that can be found in Transylvania, and we should strongly advise all those who pass through the hospitable town of Klausenburg to go and see it. When I last visited it, on my admiring the beauties of some stones in which this country abounds, I was informed, to my great astonishment, that there were only two lapidaries in the country.

Count Mikó is also known as a great supporter of agricultural societies, and has sacrificed time and money to bring about an improved system of farming. In the year 1860, he was elected to the rank of Gubernator of Transylvania, where, as a Magyar diplomatist, he laboured for the supremacy of his country, but he was obliged to yield to the influence of the Nadasdy-Schmerling Government. The Landtag of 1865 enabled him to continue his efforts to bring about the union of Transylvania with Hungary.

Count Mikó is a clear-sighted politician. His oratory is clear but telling. He is modest and retiring in his manners, and possesses a most humane character. If the intrigues of Foreign powers amongst those races which inhabit the land of his birth should end in disappointment, he will take rank among those who have done most to increase the resources of his country.

BARON JOSEPH EÖTVÖS,
Minister for Religion and Education.

Baron Joseph Eötvös was born in Buda in 1813. His father, through unfortunate speculations, lost nearly all his property. At his death his son nobly gave up the little he had to receive in order that his father's debts might be liquidated. Fortunately, nature had endowed him with sufficient abilities not only to hold his position of a nobleman, but also to acquire the means to keep up his rank.

He studied for the bar at the University at Pesth; after having passed his examination, he entered the service of the State. His duties seem to have been of a political as well as of a judicial nature. Baron Eötvös remained only four years in Government employment; but there is no doubt that in this short space he derived great benefit as regards a practical knowledge of departmental work.

Eötvös about this time commenced his career as a poet. His compositions proved that far greater things could be expected from his pen, and in this the public were perfectly correct, for in a short time he became one of the first novelists of the day. His earliest production in this sphere entitled ' A Carthansi,' a kind of sentimental novel, was entirely original; it contained masterly and philosophical ideas, and the language was brilliant. Eötvös did not confine himself to romance, he also wrote several pamphlets on political matters, such as the emancipation of the Jews, the improvement of the prison system, and on Irish pauperism. This latter work created a great sensation, for it proved that the young author was well versed in a subject which in those days was considered a most difficult question by our English statesmen. In one of his novels called 'The Village Notary,' Eötvös did his utmost to ridicule the county institutions of Hungary, especially the great power of the nobles over the peasants. In this he was fully successful, for the immense circulation which this work had prepared the minds of the mass for future radical reforms. A novel which he published, bearing the title of 'Hungary in the year 1514,' is, perhaps, one of his best productions. It consisted of an historical description of the peasant insurrection, and fully demonstrates the evils resulting from the serfdom of the peasants, clearly proving that, unless the nobles were prepared to give up their feudal rights, in the hour of danger, they would find themselves isolated, as they did ten years later in the Turkish war.[1]

---

[1] The peasant insurrection seems to have been brought about in the following way:—Cardinal Thomas Bakars had been sent to Rome to settle a difference which had arisen between the Pope and the Emperor Maximilian. Having ascertained that the Turks had again made inroads into the Hungarian territory, he obtained permission from the Pope to preach a crusade against them, but before he had reached Hungary, peace had already been concluded with them. The Cardinal, however, could not be induced to forego putting his plan into execution, and in the cabinet council of his Sovereign, he produced the permission of the Pope, and asked leave to preach the crusade, which was unanimously agreed to; the only person who seems to have opposed it was the chancellor, Telegdi, who boldly pointed out to his brother counsellors the danger of placing arms in the hands of those whom they oppressed. On the proclamation of the crusade, the peasants flocked in vast numbers to enrol themselves.

The year 1848 produced the harvest of the radical seeds which Eötvös had so carefully sown and reared; but, unfortunately, the harvest was too bountiful, and the Magyars thought that they could rule themselves the many incongruous elements which compose that which is called Hungary, and that the rule of the Hapsburg family could be dispensed with.

A young man, George Dózsa, a Szekler by birth, who had greatly distinguished himself in the Turkish war, was, at the Cardinal's request, nominated leader of the crusaders. The miserable condition of the peasantry naturally made the crusade most popular, for by joining it they saw a chance of freeing themselves from the yoke of serfdom; the nobles became alarmed, as they feared that all the able-bodied men would join Dózsa, and they would not have people enough to till the ground. An order was therefore sent to him not to enroll any more peasants, and the nobles did their best by threats and the most severe punishments to deter those who lived on their estates from following Dózsa. This brought about an insurrection, the leader of the crusaders assumed the title of prince, and proclaimed a social republic. After having ravaged and destroyed all the houses of the nobility in the neighbourhood of Pesth, killing the proprietors whenever he had a chance, he advanced towards the Theiss, and having taken Szegedin, marched towards Temesvár, his army increasing at every step. His success, coupled with the military skill which he had displayed, spread terror and dismay throughout Hungary. In this extremity, Bathony, whom Dózsa had defeated, applied to Szapolyai, the Woiwode of Transylvania, for assistance. The ambitious chief at once seized this opportunity of increasing his power, and he accordingly marched with his followers on Temesvár for the purpose of raising the siege. The news of his opponents' approach reached Dózsa at a time when he was greatly excited by the large quantity of wine which he had been drinking, and, regardless of his dangerous position, he led his followers against the army of the Hungarian nobles. After a desperate struggle, his army was entirely dispersed, and he himself and his brothers fell into the hands of the victors. Dózsa was seated on an iron throne which had been made red hot; a crown of the same metal, and in the same condition, was placed on his head, and he was forced to grasp a red hot sceptre. Some of his half-starved followers were afterwards compelled to eat his charred remains. The most brutal punishments were inflicted on those who had been taken prisoners, and in the ensuing Landtag the enraged nobles passed the most stringent laws against their unfortunate labourers. It is stated that more than 100,000 nobles, and about 70,000 peasants, lost their lives in this struggle.

Eötvös accepted the post of Minister of Education
under the Hungarian Government, but on the outbreak
of war he resigned his post, as it appears he was not prepared to go to the extreme lengths of the revolutionary
party. During the time that Austria ruled Hungary
as a conquered country, Eötvös led a retired life, but
he did his utmost as a writer to oppose the policy of
Austria. He wrote a very clever and subtle pamphlet
with reference to the rights of nationalities; but he forgot
that the Hungarians are themselves conquerors, and that
those different tribes forming that which he, we suppose,
called Hungary, are far more numerous than his own
race. Eötvös also gave to the world a philosophical work,
which was published in Leipsic in 1858. On the publi-
cation of the Diploma of 1860, and the assembly of the
Landtag, Eötvös was always to be found by the side of
Deák, manfully trying his utmost to bring about the
restoration of the whole Hungarian Constitution; but he
also at the same time wished for a legal change in those
parts of the Constitution which could not well be carried
out to the letter without dismembering Austria, and
urged that a system should be founded in which all the
affairs common to every nationality under the sceptre of
Austria could be treated, without endangering their
mutual rights. There is no doubt that Baron Eötvös
was well adapted for the position he held in the Ministry,
and his post was a most delicate one. The various
nationalities naturally demanded that their religion and
language should not be interfered with; and, as a
reformer, he was bound to do all in his power to develope
and improve the system of education in Hungary. Unfortunately for Hungary, his death deprived her and the
Austrian Empire of the services of a man who fully
understood the political movement of the present day.

COUNT GEORGE FESTETITCS DE FOLNA,
Minister of the Court.

Count George Festetitcs, the brother of the well-known cavalry general, Count Vassilo Festetitcs, who was severely wounded at the battle of Königsgrütz, was born in Vienna on the 23rd of April, 1815.   He was educated by a private tutor.   In the year 1835 he entered the 2nd light cavalry regiment of the Prince of Hohenzollern, with the rank of lieutenant, where he obtained the grade of first lieutenant.   From thence he joined the 14th dragoons of Prince Windischgrätz, with the rank of captain; and at a later period joined as major Baron Piret's 27th regiment of infantry, with which he took part in the Italian campaign of 1848, and was promoted to the rank of lieutenant-colonel.   In the year 1849 he retired from the service.   About this time he was married to the Countess Eugenie Edödy, lady-in-waiting on the Empress of Austria, by whom he had four children.   On his retirement from the army, Count Festetitcs devoted himself to agricultural pursuits, in which his magnificent demesnes offered him a vast field.   We are told that his grandfather had already made himself conspicuous by his efforts to introduce a better system of farming into Hungary ; and, in order to diffuse his ideas, had founded a training-school for agriculturists at Keszthely.   In return for his exertions, Count George Festetitcs was elected president by the Hungarian Royal Agricultural Society.

The Diploma of the 20th of November, 1860, enabled him to place his services at the disposal of the Crown ; and he undertook the superintendence of the jurisdiction of the Comitat of Eisenburg; but the events of the year 1861 compelled him, with many other Hungarians of similar political tendencies, to resign his post.   The favourable turn which affairs took in 1865 gave every

hope for the future consolidation of constitutional institutions in Hungary; and Count Festetitcs again came
forward to assist the Imperial Government. He was
elected lord-lieutenant of the Comitat of Zalada. In
politics he is an adherent of the Deák school, whose
policy he supported in the assemblies of the magnates in
the years 1861 and 1865. At the formation of the Hungarian Ministry he became Minister, and was sent as
Hungarian representative to the Court of Vienna, where
he exercises the most princely hospitality. His charming
manners render him beloved by all who come in contact
with him.

MELCHIOR LÓNYAY,
Minister of Finance.

Melchior Lónyay was born on January 6, 1822, and
was already known in his youth by a clear judgment and
a practical common sense. He left the University in
his twenty-first year, and was shortly afterwards unanimously elected Deputy for the Beregher Comitat, where
his family possessed great interest, not only on account
of their high rank, but also for the interest which they
took in the welfare of the country.

On entering the Landtag, Lónyay joined the liberal
party, and was member of committees on financial and
commercial affairs, acting in the capacity of secretary.
The knowledge which he displayed in this position soon
gained for him a prominent place in the Landtag, where
he distinguished himself, not only as an orator, but also
by his industry and sound judgment. Lónyay had also
acquired great celebrity as a journalist.

He greatly interested himself in the improvement of
agriculture, and there is no doubt that a work which he
wrote about this time on the ' Material Interest of the

Country ' greatly contributed to the development of agriculture in Hungary. In this work he pointed out the necessity of opening out the country by means of roads, railways, and canals.

Lónyay was again elected Deputy in 1847, and in the Landtag was considered one of the first authorities on the above subjects. In 1848 he was elected a member to the first National Hungarian Assembly. He published about this time a work bearing the title ' Letters on Finance,' in which he disapproved of Kossuth's financial plans, and shortly afterwards entered the Ministry with the post of Under-Secretary of Finance.

After the subjugation of Hungary by two Emperors, Lónyay is stated by some to have left his native country; others say that he was concealed in a small secret apartment in the castle of his parents. This latter statement I must myself contradict, for the Minister himself informed me that he fled from Hungary in the disguise of a man servant. In 1850 Lónyay was pardoned. In 1860 we find him occupying his time as a writer on the agriculture of the country, and taking part in all the great undertakings of the day. Through his efforts the first insurance companies were founded. Amongst these was the Hungarian Boden Credit Anstall; and it is not to be wondered at that this able man should, after the death of the energetic and talented Count Emil Desseroff, be elected President of that institution and Vice-president of the Academy of Arts and Sciences. He was over-curator of the Reformed Church of Béké Banal, and special adviser to all the leading societies, not only by name, but by real activity. Lónyay always remained a staunch liberal, and was an intimate friend of Deàk. On the appointment of the Hungarian Ministry, he received the portfolio of Finance, and there is no doubt he was the only one capable of holding that post at that time.

Lónyay is a man of agreeable appearance and polished manners. He is a practical speaker, though his voice is weak; his great *forte* is fluency and conciseness. In dealing with financial affairs he goes at once to the point, and does not weary his hearers with a labyrinth of figures.

In all his acts as a minister, he proves that he fully understands the need of introducing a network of railways in Hungary, together with a regular system of banking, for the purpose of developing its resources and increasing its material wealth. This was shown by the loan which he effected for assisting in opening new means of communication for Hungary. Lónyay, we fear, to satisfy the vanity of the inhabitants of some of the chief county towns, is obliged to expend on small lines large sums of money which ought to be spent on the great national lines. An example of this may be seen on the Transylvanian Line. Temesvár, being one of the most commercial towns of those parts, had its railway; Klausenburg, although much inferior to Temesvár in a commercial point of view, insisted on having also its railway, on account of its being the chief seat of the Magyar population.

COUNT JULIUS ANDRÁSSY.

Count Julius Andrássy is the descendant of a very ancient family, which has given to Hungary many men of note. He was born on March 28, 1823. In his twenty-fourth year we find him in the Diet of Pressburg as Deputy for the Zemplin Comitat, drawing general attention upon himself by his renowned name, his winning appearance, as well as by his polished manners and early matured mind.

In consequence of the February revolution, by which the aristocratic constitution of Hungary was changed into a parliamentary *régime*, we find the young Count occupying the responsible post of Obergespann (lord-lieutenant) of the same comitat; but the reaction which soon took place, through the absolutism of the government in Vienna, prevented Andrássy from proving his abilities as an administrator. When the war with Austria broke out, he headed the volunteers of his comitat, and took an active part in the battle of Schwechak.

The Hungarian army not being sufficiently well organised at the end of 1848 to cope with the Imperial troops, retired to Pesth, and thence to the mountain towns. The Diet and the Provisional Government sought safety at Debreczin, and with them went the patriotic Andrássy.

Soon after he was sent from Debreczin as ambassador of the Hungarian Government to Constantinople, where he still was when the tragic end of the Hungarian war of independence occurred; and when the ever-memorable historical event of the Hungarians surrendering their arms to the Russians took place, Count Andrássy left Constantinople and went to Paris. His high birth, his fortune, his station and personal talents, soon brought the young Count into intimate relations with the leaders of the political circles of Paris. Upon intimate terms with Prince Napoleon, liked by the Emperor, he soon became, next to Count Vladislaus Teleky, the most distinguished diplomatist of the Hungarian Emigration.

The hopes, however, which were founded upon the supposition that the policy of the French Emperor was hostile to Austria were proved to be sterile and vain. After a few years' residence in Paris, Andrássy returned to his native country with an amnesty, and lived there, retired from public life, till 1860, when the October Diploma, the consequence of the Italian war, was published, and it was thus again rendered possible to make

efforts for re-establishing by legal means the Hungarian
Constitution. Andrássy was a second time nominated
Lord-Lieutenant of the Zemplin Comitat, but did not
accept that dignity, the then existing government not
being correctly constitutional, and he appeared in the
Diet opened in 1861, as the representative of the people
in the Lower House. This Diet, as is well known, addressed two petitions to the Monarch, requesting therein
the re-establishment of their laws sanctioned in the year
1848, and the nomination of a parliamentary ministry.
These famous addresses were of Deàk's composition, and
although framed in decisive language, and departing from
a strictly legal point of view, left it however to be understood that the Diet was willing to give to the law of 1848
such a practical execution as the circumstances of the
state-unity of the whole Monarchy and its European
position required. During the sittings of this Diet, Count
Andrássy made a speech in this sense, the statesmanlike
and well-matured views of which increased his reputation,
and added to the consideration in which he was held.

In order to enable our readers to understand why
Count Andrássy, as a constitutional Hungarian, opposed
the policy of Schmerling, we will state what that policy
was, from an Hungarian point of view. Schmerling's
system consisted in governing, by valueless constitutional
forms, the whole Monarchy in an absolute way through
the central Reichsrath, in which an artificial majority
was assured to the German element. This government
was overthrown chiefly through the resistance of Hungary,
which formed the reserve and *arrière garde* for the oppo-
sitional elements of the rest of the monarchy. Towards
the middle of 1865 the Reichsrath ceased to be, having
died of inanition.

With the Minister of State Belcredy, George von
Majláth became again, as Chancellor, the chief of the

Hungarian Government, and with him came into power that aristocratic, strictly honourable, very talented, and in the higher circles greatly esteemed, but in the country not very popular party, which fully desired the re-establishment of the Hungarian Constitution. Standing alone, they had not influence enough to carry into effect by constitutional means that change in the law of 1848, which, having regard to the position of the whole Monarchy, was absolutely required and of prime necessity. As the majority of the country followed in the wake of Deák, the Belcredy-Majláth Government wanted the strength to bring to a successful issue the negotiations which had been re-opened with the Diet that met in December, 1865. On the other hand, those who were in power at Vienna had not yet been able to understand that it was absolutely essential to pacify Hungary, and that the only way to do this was to restore to her the whole of the Constitution of 1848. They comprehended this necessity only when the sorrowful catastrophe of July 3, 1866, had brought the State to the verge of ruin. After Austria had been *de facto* expelled from Germany, her statesmen began to understand that the following up of a preponderant German policy was a mistake, that the centre of gravity of the State was to be looked for in Hungary, and not in Frankfort. It was not the Imperial House alone which began to understand that the Hungarian kingly Crown was a more real benefit to it than the ideal Imperial Crown; the Hungarian politicians themselves began to feel and fear, through the unexpected turn of events in the Austro-Prussian war, the dangers that might result for Hungary in consequence of a dissolution or even a division only of the Austrian Empire; and thus it happened that the Emperor Francis Joseph and the leaders of the nation met each other half-way. Nay, the Deák party, which was very properly considered the *national* party, went even a step farther. They fully understood that the seriousness and difficulties of the position required not only a *partial* reconciliation with the reigning House, but that it was also necessary to come to an agreement and good understanding with the countries of the rest of the Monarchy, which could be done only by giving to these countries an equally liberal Constitution, and to arrange the common affairs of the whole of the Empire—viz., the foreign affairs, war, and finances—in such a manner that the internal independence of the different countries should not suffer thereby. Such a form was decided upon in the Hungarian laws of 1867. It was accepted by the monarch as well as by the Reichsrath of the non-Hungarian provinces, and the institution of the Delegations from both parts of the Empire for the consideration of common affairs was created thereby. This success, by which all the great and many difficulties in the various negotiations were happily surmounted, was, next to Baron Beust, chiefly owing to Count Andrássy. Deàk was the leading idea, Andrássy the diplomatist of the great Hungarian party. As Vice-President of the Diet (1865-1866) he had been repeatedly entrusted with missions from the Diet to the Court. At home in the highest circles, an accomplished cavalier, and a pleasant and most gentlemanly companion, clever and subtle, he had one advantage above all necessary to success, but often denied to the most able and deserving man, namely, luck.

He also succeeded, after having come to an understanding with Baron Beust and the Emperor on the one part, and with Deàk and his more intimate friends on the other, in fixing the basis of an understanding; and having been nominated in the beginning of February, 1867, President of the Ministry in Hungary, he succeeded further in getting that arrangement voted by an immense majority in the Diet, and Francis Joseph and his spouse crowned as King and Queen of Hungary. Thus in the short space of a few weeks he had solved in the Diet, one after the other, in the most satisfactory manner a number of great political State questions, which, during many, many years, almost decennaries, had been considered, so to say, insolvable problems. His triumph, as well as the joy which pervaded the whole of the country was, it is true, somewhat dimmed by the journalistic agitation instigated by Kossuth, who still lurked in Turin. Andrássy resisted the advice and pressure of all those who wanted to induce him to take energetic measures against the revolutionary press. In this he was quite right, considering how small the party is which still follows the *soi-disant* ex-dictator.

Faithful to his belief that these exaggerations would soon evaporate, he allowed things to take their course; and herein he was right, for the noise of the Ultras has gradually lost more and more of its force, and at last has died away in the country without finding an echo.

As a statesman Count Andrássy is persistent even to obstinacy, but at the same time a prudent enemy of extreme measures. Being brought up in a liberal school, he can bear a great deal of opposition. Having constitutional ideas, he rather prefers to give way partly than to oppress, and when that will not do he has the rare faculty of knowing how to wait. By his nervous and restless appearance we might take him to be of a quick and easily excited mind, and his brilliant and spirited *ex improviso* answers to interpellations seem to sanction such an opinion. These, however, are only flashings of the mind, inspirations of the moment, which are due to the excitation occasioned by the attack. He has a superabundance of ideas and thoughts, but he cannot bring them quickly enough into battle array. Whatever he has thoroughly considered becomes in him as clear as conscience. If not a very profound, he is, no doubt. an original and subtle thinker, who can see every object from many points of view. He is, therefore, always an interesting speaker. His general abilities and his education, his comprehensive mind, his entire freedom from prejudice, and his strength of character, make him the most fit person to be placed at the head of a Cabinet, there to give the chief movement and direction, and to sustain unity in the governmental ideas and aims. He is a born diplomatist, remarkable in comprehending the political web, and in winding up and unravelling its threads, skilful in making use of men and their foibles for higher purposes, a faithful patriot, chivalrous, with noble ambition, and equally devoted to his king and his country.

Count Andrássy's conciliatory policy towards the various races which make up the Hungarian kingdom has proved that the Magyars fully understand the true meaning of the expressive obligation of mutual rights, and we trust that the results of his enlightened policy will bring about a similar state of things in the Cis-Leithan kingdom. The greatest proof of the success of his policy was lately afforded by the military manœuvres held in Hungary, in which a force of 40,000 Honvéds took part. This force has been organised and officered by nearly every nationality of the Austro-Hungarian Empire. This splendid body of men which forms only a portion of the large reserve force which Hungary can bring into the field within a few weeks' notice, is, we might say, in its infancy, as it has only been in existence within the last three or four years, and the greatest praise is due to its commander-in-chief, the Archduke Joseph, who was its founder, and the celebrated Marshal Baron von Gablentz.

Andrássy, like most of his countrymen, has English

proclivities, and speaks our language with that fluency which Hungarians only can attain.

Balthasar Horváth,

Minister of Justice.

Balthasar Horváth may be considered to represent the lower classes of Hungary, for he is the only member of the present Ministry who is not connected with the nobility of the land. This fact proves that the possession of great talents alone must have won for him his present position in an aristocratic country like Hungary, which prior to the year 1848 had always been ruled by its nobility.

Horváth was born in the year 1822. He was generally distinguished for his talents during his legal studies; on the completion of which he returned to his native town, Szombathely, to practise as an advocate. Here he was elected to some of the most responsible municipal posts of the town. The year 1848 gave him a favourable opportunity for reaping the fruits of his influence over his fellow-citizens. The results of the French Revolution were then being felt over all Europe, and the town of his birth was also affected with socialist doctrines; but through his influence he induced his fellow-townsmen to listen to the voice of reason; and in return for his patriotic conduct he was elected member of the Reichsrach, where he was selected to act as secretary to several important committees—a post in which he distinguished himself by his industry and ability.

After the capitulation of Világos he returned to his native town to resume his practice as an advocate, which rapidly increased amongst the higher class of nobility, of which the chief was the family Batthyany.

The true reason why the Austrian suspended his prac-
tising as a lawyer for two years was his independent
conduct and his close connexion with those who then unfortunately were termed disloyal; but, in justice to the
Austrian legal authorities, it is stated that they demanded
that Horváth should be reinstated, as his suspension was
a loss to the community at large; and the Austrian
Government acceded to their request.

The October Diploma of 1860 again enabled Horváth
to distinguish himself in the cause of his country. It was
necessary to bring into order the common law of Hungary, which, after the suspension of despotic rule, was a
perfect chaos ; and he was one of those who were selected
for this task

In the year 1861 his townsmen proved that their confidence in him remained unshaken, by electing him as
their representative in the Landtag. Here Horváth
greatly distinguished himself not only as an orator, but
also by his clear and astute powers of discrimination in
the most difficult legal questions of the day, in which he
exhibited a thorough acquaintance with the codes of law
of the different nations of Europe.

Horváth was also elected to assist in the sittings of the
Court of Appeal; but his constitutional ideas prevented
him from accepting this offer. At the dissolution of the
Landtag, he, with the rest of Deák's party, took no active
part in political affairs, as he was a strong opponent of
the Schmerling policy. During this time of his political
inactivity, he was made legal adviser to the Hungarian
Boden Credit Bank. This post compelled Horváth to
take up his residence at Pesth.

In 1865 he was elected as deputy of the Landtag; and
at the formation of the Hungarian Ministry received the
portfolio of Justice. This appointment met with universal approbation, as a great mass of the lower orders

considered it a concession on the part of the nobility, and
as a guarantee that their legal rights would be represented in the councils of their Emperor-King. It is stated
that Horváth was prominent in bringing on the reconciliation between the Hungarians and the King, as in
his judgment the prosperity of Hungary depended on
that of Austria; although we must candidly confess that
his law with reference to the right of purchasing property
in Hungary seems to have been inspired by those liberal
ideas which the early rulers of England possessed, viz.,
by that encouragement to foreign traders to settle in England which has given us our present commercial prosperity. However, Horváth is one of the most independent
speakers in the Hungarian Parliament. He is amiable,
and prepossessing in manners. Although liberal in his
ideas, he is not at all in favour of rapid reform, and
therefore is one of the most energetic opponents of the
extreme party.

We cannot conclude this chapter without offering our
congratulations to Count Wenckheim on his return to
office, for a more thorough specimen of the fine old
English gentleman can scarcely be found.

CHAPTER X.

EMPEROR OF AUSTRO-HUNGARY.

IN the foregoing pages we have given some account of those Hungarians who have aided in bringing about the present compromise. There is no doubt that their labours and those of the Austrian politicians would have been without the slightest effect, had not the Emperor-King of Hungary, impelled by a genuine love of his Hungarian subjects, and longing for the time when he could prove to the world that he had forgotten the past, seized the opportunity, and done his utmost to prove himself a constitutional sovereign. History is rich in examples of rulers who, although actuated themselves by a fatherly feeling towards their subjects, have been forced from their constitutional tendencies to obey the dictates of their Ministers in silence, although they were utterly adverse to them. The facts are undeniable that whatever the present monarch of Austria and Hungary has done was at the advice of his Ministers; that the Hungarian element has always been represented in the councils of the Emperor; and that there have been, and are, many men belonging to the different nationalities of Hungary, some of whom have been Imperial statesmen, who up to the present day have not supported the actual state of things, and must therefore have exercised a certain influence on his opinions. The following Speech, which the Emperor delivered to the Hungarian representatives at the time of the compromise, will give the reader a very fair idea of the feelings which actuated His Majesty in coming to an understanding with his Hungarian subjects:—

Gentlemen, my Lords, and Representatives,—The present Legislature ceases to-day, and we wished to close in person the Diet whose fruitful activity stands unparalleled in the history of Hungary.   We called you together three years ago to accomplish a great task.

Our common aim and endeavour has been to solve all those questions which, not only in these last times, but for centuries, have been the source of distrust and collision.

Although prejudices, inherited from times past, the power of habit, suspicions nourished by events, and the seeming antagonism of interests, contributed to complicate the situation, we have succeeded, nevertheless, in accomplishing our difficult task successfully.

This success is owing to the loyal alliance between the King and the Nation.

To this Diet belongs the glory of having put an end to the political uncertainty which has benumbed the noblest forces of the nation ; mutual friendship and esteem have taken the place of the political struggles between the two States of our Monarchy.

Both States of the Austro-Hungarian Monarchy, by means of their constitutional and parliamentary Government, arrange their own affairs independently ; while in the important questions which concern the common affairs of the Monarchy, as stipulated by mutual consent, each of them exercises in the same measure its constitutional influence.

The Monarchy, having sought and found its centre of gravity within itself, advances with renewed vigour on the new path, the goal of which is peace and prosperity, as well as the maintenance of that position which the Monarchy is called upon to occupy amongst the States of Europe.

Thus the source from which came the evils of the past, is stopped, and over it Hungarian loyalty, patriotism, and moderation, have raised a lasting monument, on which history has already inscribed a long list of great and salutary achievements.

Having been solemnly crowned with the crown of St. Stephen, inherited from my ancestors, the Hungarian Constitution has become a full reality; we have re-established the ancient honour and weight of the title of King of Hungary, and we feel that by this our Empire has not only not been weakened, but, on the contrary, has only regained its old basis and strength. We have, therefore, adopted with regard to foreign countries, a title for our Empire which is in conformity with the laws and with facts. A political compromise, on the basis of equity and of common interests, has been effected with Croatia and Slavonia; thus renewing the link which has existed for centuries, in weal and woe, between the two sister nations. We hope confidently that this alliance will unite again, in devotion to my House, and to the common country, the Hungarian and Croatian nations for centuries to come.

The union of Hungary and Transylvania has become an accomplished fact. Thus the integrity of the Empire of St. Stephen has been restored in a way in which it has not existed for the last three hundred years. One of the guarantees of the integrity, both of the Hungarian Crown and of our Empire, is the new army organisation. Moved by confidence, and judging with deep wisdom, you have recognised the necessity of a common army, and thus the defensive force which is to protect the development of the Monarchy has been created.

The Honvéds (Militia) are called upon to support this force, opening in times of danger a new field of activity to the ancient heroism of which the pages of national history give so brilliant a testimony.

Having thus strengthened the position of Hungary, and of our Monarchy, we find in this likewise the guarantee of peace abroad, the maintenance of which we reckon among our chief tasks.

You have prompted the intellectual welfare of the nation in passing such a law on education, that, if it requires sacrifices from single special interests, it establishes at the same time a system of education which will serve as a support to material and intellectual progress.

You have extended to the use of their language the civil and political rights which the citizens belonging to the different races had already enjoyed, granting all those wishes which are not in opposition to the laws and good government.

We hope that our non-Hungarian subjects will find tranquillity in the conviction that the Constitution insures to every citizen equal freedom, and the development of his mother-tongue.

You have followed the principle of equality of rights in extending political rights to the Israelites, who until now knew only the burdens and not the advantages of the Constitution.

You have regulated the relations of the different confessions on the basis of civil and religious equality.

Not waiting for the constitutional discussion of the law reforms, which demand considerable time, you have by the new regulation of judicial procedure facilitated the prompt administration of justice and the consolidation of private credit.

By regulating the tithe from vineyards, you have insured the free development of an important article of production.

On the financial field you have with great tact struck out the right road; and while on one side you have voted all those expenses which were necessary for the regular functions of the Government, and the maintenance of its credit, you have on the other side subjected to a careful scrutiny the estimates which have been submitted to the Diet.

The progress of Hungary in the field of material prosperity has not been hitherto in proportion to its natural wealth; but the Legislature has understood the importance of material progress in all its bearings. It has ordered the building of new railways, and has concluded several favourable commercial treaties with Foreign Powers.

All these measures could be taken without disturbing the equilibrium of the Budget, and in some respects—as, for instance, the price of salt—it could even lighten the burden of taxation.

The Diet has accomplished great and difficult works, and the result has strengthened the conviction in us that the basis on which, in so short a time, so many salutary institutions could be founded, has all the conditions of solidity; that this basis is good and is conformable to the true interests of the nation.

Gentlemen, my Lords, and Representatives,—After the fatigues of these days you return to your homes.

The symptoms of material and moral improvement which are apparent everywhere may fill your hearts with joy; and if once the success follows with which Providence rewards perseverance and energy, posterity will gratefully remember those who have been the instruments of the welfare of the country.

Receive my best royal thanks, and give them to the whole nation, which, guided by its traditional political tact, has supported you, and thus enabled you to make those salutary and important laws to which we give our sovereign sanction. May the Almighty make this loyal understanding lasting—this understanding which has not only produced great political results, but which has linked together Sovereign and People in the bonds of mutual confidence and love, and which has made us feel that only a happy Nation can have a happy Sovereign.

We declare the Hungarian Diet closed.

Few rulers of the Emperor's age have undergone so many vicissitudes. Time after time has Europe been informed that the dissolution of the Austrian Empire was about to take place, and yet, as if by wonder, it has regained its former position as one of the chief Powers of Europe; and those who have known Austro-Hungary will acknowledge that these constantly-recurring signs of vitality arise from the love and respect which the various races have always entertained for the House of Hapsburg, which they regard as belonging to themselves.

The Emperor possesses the great characteristic of his family, that of making himself at home with his subjects; and if mistakes are made in State affairs, the good people of Austria feel convinced that they do not arise from the Emperor's negligence.

His Majesty is very simple in his habits, and passionately fond of field-sports.

There are many who prophesy that the age of universal anarchy and revolution is near at hand; but the majority of my readers will probably agree with me that, with enlightened and constitutional monarchs like those of

Austria, Brazil, Italy, Spain, Belgium, Holland, and those of Scandinavia and Greece, the different nations over whose destinies they preside have little need to fear this catastrophe, not merely because the institutions which their rulers have introduced guarantee to them those liberties which enable a people to become peaceful, great, and prosperous, but because the continuance of such a state of things is another guarantee, from the fact that the illustrious Ladies who share their thrones have, by their high tone of morality, fully demonstrated that they possess all those attributes of a mother and sovereign which have rendered the name of Maria Theresa so justly famous in the history of the world, and that therefore their children will be taught to follow in the footsteps of their parents.

PART II.

FEMALE MAGYAR CELEBRITIES.

FEMALE MAGYAR CELEBRITIES.

Before giving an account of Female Magyar Celebrities, I think it will interest my readers if I portray some of the attributes of their character. In my belief the features of the females betray to a far greater extent than those of the men the origin of their race, and the same may be said as regards character. One of the greatest virtues in the Magyar mother is that God-like quality, the love of her offspring, whom she cherishes with all the tender devotion of the Hindoo mother. The mother's constant care is the well-being of her children. How often have I heard a mother answer, on my asking whither she was hurrying so early in the morning : 'I am going to offer prayers for the success of my son who is going to pass his examination to-day.' From the peculiar construction of their minds, they require to be fondly and deeply loved by their husbands, for their love is of no common kind. It is life. to them, and without it they are the most miserable and unhappy beings that this world can contain. And it is certain that if they have loving husbands, they will make good domestic wives. It is no uncommon thing to find them not only keeping the accounts of their household, but also that of a business, and in higher life the financial management of extensive estates.

Those who have seen the Magyar wife even of the humblest class doing the honours of the house will, I think, agree with me in saying that in this she is not to

M 2

be surpassed. She has a peculiar unique way of doing it.
Every one is at once at home with her; and even the most
humble and timid person, after having shaken hands with
the hostess, feels as if he were talking to a dear old friend
whom he has not seen for many years. She is always
the same at all times and seasons. The peasantry of her
country look upon her with affectionate regard, and in
every town we find its districts divided among the ladies
of all ranks with the object of affording personal relief
to the humble and indigent. The Magyar lady looks
upon the English wife as the type of this order of beings,
and seeks to follow her good example in all things. She
considers marriage a holy state of existence ; and with
such wives as these we can fully understand how the
husbands must appreciate such sentiments as are thus
expressed by our poet, Campbell :—

> And say without our hopes, without our fears,
> Without the home which plighted love endears,
> Without the smile from partial beauty won,
> Oh, what were man?—a world without a sun !

There is no doubt that they possess great mental capacity ;
and it is extraordinary that they have arrived at so much
knowledge, for they marry very early in life, and the
great difficulties of obtaining first-rate masters, together
with the political agitation which has been for many
years going on in their country, must have been a bar to
their becoming highly educated. Strangers are generally
astonished at their being versed in the politics not only of
the Austro-Hungarian Empire, but of other countries.
They are also well acquainted with the works of the
leading European writers. Their favourite English
authors are Macaulay and Carlyle. They are wonder-
fully quick in picking up information, and possess the
peculiar knack which the French women have of snatch-
ing your thoughts from your mind before you have tim·

to utter them, which is no doubt unpleasant: but the next time you see them you will forgive them, for they will inform you that they have read the work from which you have obtained your opinions.

One of the greatest charms of Hungarian society is to be found in their dear old ladies, who, with any amount of ailments, are always ready to amuse you; and this they can do, for their mind retains the freshness and vigour of youth. I have before said that girls are married when very young, so that there are plenty of grandmothers and great-grandmothers; and one of the most agreeable sights is to see one of these venerable ladies with her third generation. Two generations seem suddenly to be forgotten, for she speaks to her great-granddaughter as if she were speaking to her own child.

And now I suppose I must say something about the young ladies, who, for the information of my readers, I have not the slightest hesitation to own, are the fairest daughters of Eve, and who certainly possess some of those qualities which the wicked world attributes to our good mother. They are fond of admiration, do not object to a little flirtation, nor to your falling desperately in love with them; but they would not hurt your feelings for the world, for they are the most tender-hearted of their sex. And they can be jealous at times, but that is a way they have; they say it is not their fault, it is in their nature, and descended to them from Mrs. Hunyor and Mrs. Magyar. They have two types of beauty and character—Haïdée and Dudu. They are passionately fond of music, singing, and dancing, and if you wish to see them to advantage, gaze on them when they are dancing their national dance, the Csardas—a dangerous experiment; and I should caution my readers not to get in the habit of looking at the dancers, for the Hungarian girl has a way of darting a glance of such an electric

power as will root you to the ground. It is stated that
no one but a Magyar can perform this peculiar measure,
which is no doubt of an Oriental origin. It seems that
the present way of dancing it is far more exciting than
the ancient style.

Most girls speak French, German, and English. The
latter language they are very partial to. As regards
their mental qualities, there is some difficulty at first in
finding out where their strength lies. They never show
their cards before they know yours. They say that they
wish to accommodate their conversation to your ideas,
which is very kind of them; but the ice once broken, you
will be fascinated with the freshness and vigour of their
remarks, for they are not like our English young ladies,
who appear to be totally different in town and country.
The Magyar girl is always the same straightforward,
good-hearted creature.

In conclusion, they are celebrated for four things—the
length and beauty of their hair, the wonderful expression
of their countenance and play of features, their flashing
eyes and finely-formed limbs, and lastly, if not least, for
the smallness of their feet. The world tells us, if we
wish to see a queen-like walker, to go to Toledo, but I
should advise my readers, before so doing, to witness a
Magyar girl moving over rough ground.

CHAPTER I.

ELIZABETH SZILÁGYI.

THE life of Elizabeth Szilágyi constitutes one of the most brilliant episodes in the history of the fifteenth century. Her father, Vladislaus Szilágyi, stood high in the favour of Sigismund, who, as a mark of his special favour, presented him with the estate of Horochszey, which name was afterwards adopted by the Szilágyi family. Her mother was Katharina Bellini. Elizabeth was married early in life to the great John Hunyady, who, as we have before stated, died shortly after one of his most brilliant victories. His death was for his opponents the signal for a round of festivities. At a banquet given to celebrate the fall of his rival, Cilley told his friends that he would never know what rest was until he had utterly destroyed the whole family of Hunyady. The great likeness of character which existed between Vladislaus Hunyady and his father, coupled with his own endearing manners, had rendered him the favourite of the people; and this popularity was increased by the manner in which he and his mother had been treated by their enemies. Ulrich Cilley saw in him an opponent who might stand in his path, as the leader of the people, and prevent him from obtaining the long-cherished object of his ambition—the crown of Hungary. He therefore determined to take his life; and in a letter to his father-in-law, Brankovics, he stated that he would shortly send him the heads of the two Hunyady as a present. This letter fell into the hands of the friends of the Hunyady, and Vladislaus was advised to be prepared for all contingencies. Cilley's great aim was to get himself placed in such a position as would enable him at the first convenient opportunity to arrest the young Hungarian nobleman. He therefore induced the King to call together a Landtag at Futak, to which the patriot's son was summoned; but the wily traitor had beforehand arranged with the King that he should be named Gubernator, and that an accomplice of his should receive command of the forces. This, he thought, would give him sufficient influence amongst the Deputies to obtain their sanction for his iniquitous acts. The Landtag met, Cilley was at once proclaimed Gubernator, and Ujlaky made Commander-in-Chief; but young Hunyady appeared at the head of such a force that Cilley was obliged to give up for the present all thoughts of getting him into his power. It is here, it is said, that the letter of Cilley was put into the hands of Vladislaus; but, such was the respect of the young Hungarian for the laws of the land, that he did not attempt to seek vengeance on his cowardly foe, and followed the King to Belgrade, with the determination of exposing Cilley's conduct at the first convenient opportunity.

One day, during the time that the King was in the chapel, Vladislaus Hunyady met Cilley in one of the royal apartments. The young man upbraided him with honest indignation for his cowardly persecution against his mother and family. One word led to another, and on Vladislaus producing Cilley's letter as a damning proof of his dastardly conduct, the latter broke out in a storm of invectives. Vladislaus called upon him, if he wished to remain unpunished, to resign his post and leave the country; upon which Cilley called the son of the great patriot a traitor! This was too much even for the youth who had been taught from his cradle the principle of restraining passions. In his excitement he grasped his sword, but Cilley who had calculated the effect of his words, had drawn his sabre, and before Vladislaus could unsheath, aimed a deadly blow at the head of his victim. But his weapon having come in contact with a large ring which Vladislaus wore on the finger of his upraised hand, the blow was not fatal: he was, however, wounded. The friends of Vladislaus, who had followed their young lord, fearing that Cilley would take some cowardly advantage over his youthful opponent, hearing the noise of the conflict, entered the room, and on seeing their beloved master covered with blood, rushed madly on Cilley and cut him to pieces, despite the remonstrances and efforts of Vladislaus, who bitterly reproached them for the act which they had committed. Disdaining to seek safety in flight, the young Hungarian noble at once went to the King, and throwing himself on his knees, begged his Majesty's pardon for the tragedy which had taken place, entreating him not to revenge himself on his family and friends. The King, it seems, was moved by the noble sorrow of young Hunyady, and remembering the great deeds and services of his patriotic father, he forgave the son, and solemnly swore that he would take no further step in the matter, however painful the fate of his uncle was to him, and added that he himself would visit his mother at Temeswar. These joyful tidings the loving son at once communicated to his dearly cherished mother, who, on the approach of her sovereign, went to meet him with her son Mathias at the head of a princely retinue. The touching spectacle of this loving woman, on whose face was depicted her sorrow for the great and glorious husband whom she had so lately lost, and the fears which she entertained for the safety of her beloved children, made such an impression on the King, that he did his

utmost to console the bereaved lady; and in order to
remove any doubts which she might have with respect to
his feelings toward her and her sons, he repeated the
solemn oath which he had made to Vladislaus, telling the
widow that from henceforth he should regard her as his
mother, and her two sons as his brothers, and presented
Vladislaus at the same time with a most magnificent
cloak.   The two Hunyady accompanied the King to the
court at Pesth.   The reinstalment of the family of
Hunyady in the Sovereign's good graces was seen with
little pleasure by those who wished to get the King into
their power.   It is true one of the principal, and we
might say most inveterate, enemies of the Hunyady, was
in his last resting-place, but there was still amongst their
enemies a man who of all others should have been a protector to the sons of the great patriot.   This fiend in
human shape was Garay, Palatine of Hungary.   Owing
the post he now occupied to John Hunyady, he not only
calumniated his benefactor, but plotted against his life.
We have seen how this noble man generously forgave
him; and so convinced was he of Garay's future friendship, that he consented to the union of his son with
Maria, the daughter of Garay, and the two lovers had, at
the time of the reconciliation of the King with Hunyady,
exchanged rings.   Garay, who wished to get the King
completely under his authority, caused reports to be
circulated in the country that the Turks intended resuming hostilities; and so well did his agents manage
this, that Vladislaus, believing in the veracity of these
reports, gladly seized an opportunity of proving his
fidelity to his sovereign, and at once set out for the
purpose of collecting all his retainers, and those of his
friends.   No sooner had he left the Court than Garay,
with the rest of the malcontents, insinuated to the King
that Hunyady's party intended to make him their pri-

soner, and raise Vladislaus to the Crown of Hungary.
The King listened to their specious statements, and was
finally convinced of the truth of the pretended treachery.
Vladislaus was therefore recalled to Pesth to have a fare-
well audience with his King before taking command of
his little army; but the moment he entered the royal
castle, he was seized by Garay's satellites, and brought
before a court who pronounced the sentence of death
against him. At the same time his brother Mathias and
all the friends of the Hunyady family who could be
seized were thrown into prison and loaded with chains.

On the third evening of his imprisonment, at the time
when the light of day sinks amongst the western clouds
of the horizon, when labour is rewarded with rest, when
the fond mother, surrounded by her infant children, stands
at the lowly porch with smiling face, waiting for the
return of her husband, when lovers seek the shaded brook
to speak of future joys, Vladislaus passed his prison gates
to meet his doom. His long silken locks fluttered in the
wind as with stately tread and manly countenance he
advanced to the final scene of his life—a life, it is true,
which had been short—but during the time he had been
in this world he had proved himself the worthy representative of his father. The intense love which he entertained towards his widowed mother seems now to have
given him strength. All those who saw him shrank back
with feelings of veneration, for his face beamed with
divine inspiration. Arrived at the scaffold, he turned to
the spectators, and, with burning eloquence, proved the
innocence of his intentions. Then, with dignified composure, he prepared himself for the executioner's fatal
blow. Three times did the deadly instrument sweep
round as it fell in as many successive blows on the neck
of the innocent victim, who now rose to the astonishment
of all, and again protesting his innocence, called upon the

executioner to desist, for, according to the ancient laws
of Hungary, the greatest malefactor is reprieved after
having received three blows of the executioner's axe.
The long cloak which he wore, the gift of the perjured
King, entangled him in his movements, and threw him
to the ground. The executioner again raised his axe,
and this time it proved fatal. Thus fell one of the most
promising youths of Hungary. But what must have
been the feelings of the mother on hearing of the murder
of her darling son, coupled with the knowledge that
Mathias was in the hands of his deadly enemies, and for
all that she might know had already shared his brother's
fate! For some time she was inconsolable, and her
friends thought her reason would forsake her; but suddenly, as if by magic, she became another being; she
whose bosom had known no other thought for years than
domestic love, was now convulsed with the desire for
revenge. When she appeared before her followers they
scarcely knew her, for her magnificent raven-black hair
had now become grey; that voice which had never
uttered an angry word, now quivered with vehement
passion; the beautiful face and eyes, which formerly were
a reflexion of the Madonna-like feelings of her soul, now
gleamed like those of the lioness robbed of her cubs.
The death of her son had raised a storm of indignation
throughout the country. The great nobles had already
forsaken the court of their King, and when the widowed
mother called upon her country for justice and for the
liberation of her child, an army of devoted followers
appeared around her. This force Elizabeth placed under
the command of her brother Szilágyi, who advanced
into Transylvania, destroying all the royal castles without meeting with any resistance. Pongracz von Szent-
miklós, Lord-Lieutenant of Liptau, successfully raised
the standard of revolt in the Upper Provinces, and Ofen

would probably have fallen into the hands of the insurgents, had not the Austrians come to its relief. The Turks also, at this time, began to renew their inroads. The King, finding that his party was not sufficiently strong to support him, fled to Vienna, taking Mathias with him; and then convoked a Landtag at Pressburg, for the purpose of coming to some arrangement with Elizabeth and her brother; but they declined to listen to any argument unless the King, as a guarantee for his good faith, at once delivered Mathias to them. Upon this the King went to Prague with the young Hungarian noble, and placed him in the safe custody of Podiebrad, and, hearing that the Turks had retired, returned to Vienna for the purpose of renewing negotiations with the Hunyady party. Being again unsuccessful, and a regular civil war having now broken out in Hungary with greater fury than ever, the King returned to Prague, where he suddenly died. It is stated that his death was caused by poison administered to him by the agency of Podiebrad.

The tidings of the King's death seem to have divided Hungary into two hostile camps with reference to the monarch's successor. Szilágyi, confiding in the strength of his party and the veneration with which the name of Hunyady was regarded in Hungary, proposed the election of Mathias. This was unanimously adopted by the majority of the nobles. The other party, headed by Garay, who himself wished to be elected King, consisted of several political groups, who represented the interests of the various pretenders to the Crown, and who only acknowledged allegiance to Garay until they should have obtained the downfall of the party of Hunyady. A national assembly for the purpose of electing the future King of Hungary, was convoked for the first day of the ensuing January, by Garay, Ujlaky, Paul Banffy, the

Archbishop Dionysius, and several other ecclesiastical and secular dignitaries. Szilágyi marched to Pesth at the head of 20,000 followers, and accompanied by a large number of magnates. Garay's party, perceiving that the majority were in favour of Mathias, remained at Ofen, and demanded that the envoys of Foreign powers, who represented the interests of the different pretenders to the Crown, should have a voice in the deliberations for the election of a King. Szilágyi, actuated by patriotic feelings, and wishing to save his country from further civil war, guaranteed by oath the safety of Garay and his friends, if they would come over and take part in the deliberations of the Magnates. Garay agreed to this, and for a long time succeeded in preventing the assembly from coming to any unanimous conclusion. But his ambitious aim was defeated in the most singular manner. At the time of the meeting of the Assembly an intense cold prevailed, and the Danube was entirely frozen over, so that thousands of people had collected upon it, while the inhabitants of the town had crowded round the building in which the deliberations were taking place. The severity of the weather and the length of time during which they had been awaiting the result had greatly tried the temper of the multitude, when it appears some sturdy partisan of the family of Hunyady raised the cry of 'Long life to Mathias King of Hungary.' The name which was dearest to their hearts was naturally re-echoed by the thousands who were present, and their exulting cries interrupted the excited debate which was then going on. Garay, like a skilful diplomatist, seeing that all was lost, immediately came to terms with Szilágyi, and the result was that Mathias was solemnly proclaimed King of Hungary. The great difficulty which now arose was to obtain the freedom of Mathias, who, as we have stated, was in the power of Podiebrad. This ambitious

Bohemian, knowing the value of his captive, was in no hurry to deliver him up until he was well recompensed for so doing, and modestly required as the price of his freedom the sum of 40,000 ducats, probably with the understanding that Mathias should not interfere in his election to the Crown of Bohemia, and would marry his (Podiebrad's) daughter.

John Vitéz, an old companion in arms of Hunyady, who had been trusted with the important mission of recovering the King, now hastened to the mother of Mathias, to communicate to her the welcome tidings. Elizabeth, at the head of an immense retinue, proceeded to Strasenitz. Her joy at receiving again into her arms that child whose safety was the theme of her constant prayers through the dreadful scenes of bloodshed which she had witnessed cannot be described.

Their progress to the capital of Hungary presented a spectacle which few Hungarians could ever have hoped to behold during the hundred years of civil discord. When we listen to the descriptions of those who have portrayed this scene, it would seem that the future political horizon of Hungary could never have been again darkened by the smallest cloud of intestine warfare. Unhappily, such was not the case, as we shall see. On the accession of her son to power, Elizabeth Szilágyi seems to have returned to her former self. Neither she nor her son ever once attempted to inflict the slightest injury on those who had so bitterly persecuted their family ; and until her death she might be termed the ministering angel of her son. She died in 1484, six years before her son Mathias, universally mourned ; for even the hearts of her most inveterate enemies must have been softened down when they heard of her death.

CHAPTER II.

ANNA BORNEMISZA.

THE name of Bornemisza belongs to one of the most
ancient and noble families of Transylvania.   One of that
family had two daughters; and the eldest, Anna, possessed so many womanly virtues that her life can
scarcely fail to interest the reader.   It is true she never
interfered in politics, or led her husband's soldiers on to
battle; but her life was spent in giving good advice to
her husband, and acting the part of a mother towards
her subjects.

Anna was born in the year 1626, and in the bloom of
youth married Michael Apafy, Prince of Transylvania.
This young noble seems to have been passionately fond
of his beautiful bride.   He had considerable literary
talents, and possessed many good points of character; but,
unfortunately, he was easily led by others, though, to his
credit be it said, when his wife was near him he always
acted on her advice.

The dreamy days of love of this young pair did not
last long.   Rakóczy II., Prince of Transylvania, had
concluded an alliance with Charles Gustavus, King of
Sweden, for the purpose of dividing Poland between
them.   The whole youth of the Transylvanian nobility
flocked to Rakóczy's standard, and amongst them was
Anna's husband.   In the commencement of the year
1657 they invaded Poland, and effected a junction with
the army of the King of Sweden, at Cracow.   The King

of Denmark, who was then at war with Sweden, compelled Charles Gustavus to return home; and Rakóczy II.
was forced to retreat under the most humiliating circumstances. Kemeny, under whom Michael Apafy served,
was surrounded by the Tartars; and, after a desperate
resistance, he and a large part of his forces were taken
prisoners, amongst whom was Apafy. These tidings
nearly broke the youthful heart of Anna; but, after
some considerable time, through the most unheard-of exertions, in which she expended nearly all her resources,
she was enabled to purchase the freedom of her husband.
Apafy, in the society of his wife, seems to have remained a passive spectator during the turbulent events
which followed each other in rapid succession. Through
the disunion which existed amongst the nobles of Transylvania that unhappy country was nearly turned into
a wilderness. The Turks had played a considerable part
in this devastation, and, in fact, Transylvania might have
been considered as a fief of the Crescent. Kemeny, who
had been elected Prince, was defeated by the Turks, and
the discontented nobles and the Sultan now called upon
the inhabitants to elect another ruler. On their refusal
to do so, he selected Apafy, solemnly acknowledging him
as ruler of Transylvania. Apafy at first declined to occupy this exalted position, and it was only after the most
extreme resistance that he accepted it. The moment
Anna became Princess, the effect of her influence on her
husband was evident by his wise and sensible acts; and
his people, in acknowledgment of his good intentions, sent
envoys to Kemeny to ask him to resign his rank, and allow
them to reap the fruits of peace. This hardy and valiant
prince, however, who had been up to his expulsion the
most devoted patriot, would not listen to their entreaties,
but, entering Transylvania, was defeated, and lost his
life in an engagement with the Turks.

N

When Apafy was acknowledged as ruler, the Turks and the Austrians occupied the greater part of Transylvania, but, acting under the advice of his wife, he adroitly managed to get his country free from these two obnoxious guests; and from this moment his beautiful country began to prosper.

In every act, however, of the Transylvanian Prince the hand of his clever wife was to be seen. In fact, the reins of government may be said to have been wholly in her hands, and her weak but good husband might be considered as the instrument by which she bestowed on the people the blessings of a good administration. Her life must have been a most difficult one, for she could never leave her husband's side for a moment without fear that on her return she would find that he had been induced by the specious flatteries of courtiers to undo some wise plan which he had promised to make the law of the land. By degrees, notwithstanding, Anna induced him to shake off and banish from his court and society those dangerous advisers. The worthy Princess now determined to place near her husband some person on whom she could rely to help her in managing the Prince, and during her absence prevent any of his former associates from approaching him. Her choice fell upon Michael Teleki, a man of considerable talent, but who, under the mask of friendship, concealed the ambitious design of outwitting the wakeful Anna, and getting her weak husband completely into his power. A great hindrance, however, to Teleki's nefarious designs was Dionysius Banfy, the brother-in-law of Anna, who was one of the most powerful supporters of Apafy, and possessed great influence with the Princess and her husband. The wily minister seized a convenient opportunity during the temporary absence of Anna so to work upon the mind of Apafy, that he induced this weak Prince to sign an order for the execution of Banfy. On Anna's return, she, with great difficulty, ascertained the dreadful tidings; and as she knew that, should her brother-in-law be executed, she and her husband would lose their greatest friend, on her knees she implored Apafy to counter-order the execution. When the King was at length induced to sign the order for Banfy's pardon, it was impossible for the messenger to arrive in time to save his life. Great as her distress and misery was, Anna forgave her husband, and did her utmost to counteract the evil designs of the ambitious Teleki, who was now, through the untimely death of his victim, Banfy, the first person in court, and had so got Apafy into his power, that it was with great difficulty that Anna could obtain access to her husband, whose mind now became greatly enfeebled through debauchery and drunkenness, to which he was instigated by his dishonourable minister. Paul Béldi, the leader of the Seklers, was greatly feared by Teleki. This chief was universally respected, not only by his followers but by a large number of the Transylvanian nobles, and was known to be opposed to the ambitious schemes of the minister. The latter, therefore, determined to get rid of him, as he had got rid of Banfy. He caused him to be arrested on a charge of disrespect towards the Prince; and when that unfortunate ruler was in a drunken fit Teleki managed to get his signature to the order for Béldi's execution. Fortunately for the leader of the Seklers, the good Anna obtained access to the King when he was sober, and so well convinced him of the falseness of the accusation brought against Béldi, that, yielding to her prayers, he rescinded his order. This time Anna's messenger of mercy arrived in time to save the name of her husband from being sullied with the murder of one of his most loyal subjects. During the sixteen years that she played the part of the protecting angel to her people,

she seems to have constantly defeated the malevolent
designs of the all-powerful minister; and hers must have
been no easy task when we consider that her very footsteps were watched by the subordinates of her great
enemy.   Up to the last moments of her life, Anna seems
to have retained for her husband the same devoted love
and affection which she had felt for him when he first took
her to the home of his ancestors; and he appears always
to have been ready to follow her advice as long as she
was near him.   The part which he took in the revolutionary wars of Hungary rendered it ten times more difficult for Anna to assist him with her counsels; and we
are certain that, had she been able to do so, the misfortunes which befell the ruler of Transylvania, and which
compelled him eventually to take up his residence at
Fogaros, where he was a mere vassal of the Austrians,
would never have taken place.   Anna was a great patron
of the fine arts, was especially fond of music and singing,
and did her best to develope the blessings of education.
Her son, Michael Apafy II., who had been elected ruler
of Transylvania and Duke of the Holy Roman Empire
during her lifetime, and in whom she trusted that she
had given a good and sagacious ruler to her country, died
a few years after his mother, on the 1st of February,
1712.   With him ended the name of Apafy, and the
independence of Transylvania.

CHAPTER III.

HELEN ZRINYI.

IF the world honours with the name of Great and Good those whose lives, from their early childhood until their spirit was taken away from amongst us, have been passed in the practice of self-denial for the benefit of others, whose sole wish for the prolongation of existence was to alleviate suffering, it must be admitted that Helen Zrinyi deserves to be classed amongst the first of her sex. She not only possessed all those virtues which render a child the darling of her father and mother, and when matured by years, make a wife the pride and consolation of her husband, and a model to her children; but in addition to this, she could, when filial duty demanded it, restrain those feelings which are dearest to a girl; and through her whole life this noble creature seems, in a worldly point of view, to have been the victim of misfortune. Born in the lap of luxury, she was doomed to end her life in penury, subsisting on the charity of the Sultan. At one time Queen of Upper Hungary, and wife of one of the noblest and bravest knights of his time, she was separated from her husband and children, and had to pine for several years immured in the walls of an Austrian cloister. Helen was the eldest daughter of Count Peter Zrinyi, who was married to Anna Katharine Frangipani, and she was born in 1643. The glory which surrounded the deeds of her ancestors seems to have inspired the youthful mind of Helen with an heroic and patriotic

spirit of emulation.   In the year 1665 she was betrothed
to Franz Rakóczy, one of the most powerful and wealthy
Hungarian princes.   In this ceremony, we see this beautiful creature giving the strongest proof of her obedience
to the wishes of her parents, for her youthful heart told
her that she could never return the love which her future
husband felt for her; and thus in the first step of her
eventful life, the feelings natural to her sex were blighted
even before they had begun to bud.   The cause of this
union was a political one, the interests of the houses
of Zrinyi and Rakóczy requiring it in order to enable
them to increase their influence in the country.   A year
later Rakóczy led his lovely bride in great pomp to the
halls of his ancestors, where she was surrounded by a
princely court, and everything seemed to foreshadow
future happiness; but the political horizon of Hungary
soon after darkened, and misfortunes followed each other
in rapid succession.   Many of the nobles, discontented
with the rule of Leopold, who, they considered, had in-
fringed on their constitutional rights, conspired against
him, for the purpose of forcing him to withdraw the
foreign soldiers who were in Hungary, and repeal those
laws which were at variance with their rights and
institutions.   This party had no evil designs against the
person of the King, or the rights of his family to the
Crown, and was supported by a large number of Protestants.   But it seems that Count Zrinyi was actuated by
the idea of placing the crown of Hungary on his own
head; and in order to gain the support of his son-in-law
and Nadasdy, he offered to raise the former to the rank
of Prince of Transylvania, and the latter to that of Palatine.   Fearing, however, that many of the conspirators
would refuse him their support when they became acquainted with his plan, and that his party would not be
strong enough to dethrone Leopold, Zrinyi secretly sent

an envoy to the Porte, offering to pay the Sultan a yearly tribute of 12,000 ducats if he would assist him. This was declined. Zrinyi in this extremity unfurled the banner of revolt, and called upon his son-in-law and relations to assist him. He was defeated and taken prisoner, together with his son and one of his daughters, as well as his brother-in-law. Zrinyi and Frangipani were beheaded. Their death, and the miscarriage of the conspiracy, had such an effect on Helen's mother, who had played one of the principal parts in this rebellion, that she went raving mad and died in a lunatic asylum. Rakóczy had done his best to assist his father-in-law, and it was only through the intervention of his mother that his life was spared, on condition of his paying an immense sum of money. Helen seems to have borne this great loss with the most Christian fortitude; but the blow must have been doubly great by the knowledge that the misfortune which had befallen many of her friends was caused by the unwarrantable ambition of her parents. Scarcely had she recovered from the effects of this great catastrophe than hard fate inflicted upon her another severe blow. Her husband, whom it is true she had never loved, yet whose conduct as a father and husband had animated her to regard him with the noblest and most exalted feelings of friendship, was borne away to the last home of his fathers. Helen now seems to have devoted all her energies to the instruction and bringing up of her children. Her son Franz was afterwards known as the most determined defender of his Protestant countrymen.

The loss of her relations threw the whole management of her fortunes on the head of the widowed mother, who yet found sufficient time to interest herself in the cause of her unfortunate friends and relatives, who were then suffering for having participated in her father's guilt, and it is stated that her efforts were crowned with success.

The miserable state of Hungary, which was devastated
by revolution and by civil and religious discord, re-
awakened in the mind of Helen the dreams of her childhood, but she was not then in a position to assist her
beloved country.   Hungary was now divided into two
parties, loyalists and rebels, who inflicted on each other
the most barbarous cruelties; but still more wretched was
the state of the humble and peaceful cultivator of the
land, for at every opportunity each party plundered his
home and devastated his fields, thus reducing him to
starvation.   Amidst the bloodthirsty revenge of both
parties, Helen was ever to be found ready to encounter
any danger if she could shelter or protect the suffering;
her name was venerated for miles around her.   Count
Emerich Tökölyi, the leader of the Kŭrŭczen, one of the
most determined opponents of Leopold, became acquainted with Helen.   His manly beauty, his great
talents, coupled with the patriotic devotion which he had
always displayed in the defence of his faith and country,
seem to have produced a lasting effect on the sensitive
mind of the lovely and noble Helen, and for the first
time in her life, she found that the presence of man had
given her a new existence.   Tökölyi, on his side, was no
less struck by the grace and beauty of this magnificent
woman, who, in all her actions, displayed the feelings of a
thorough Christian; and the result of their acquaintance
was their betrothal.   Helen's mother-in-law was vio-
lently opposed to the match, and Tökölyi's position and
religion offered little chance of the Court of Vienna ever
allowing Helen to espouse her lover.   She was threatened
that if she married him, the right of being guardian to
her children would be taken away from her.   The
obedience to those whom she considered as her superiors
was here again manifested. Although passionately in love
with Tökölyi, she refused for the space of three years his

proffered hand, until after her mother-in-law's death. The consent of the Emperor depended on the varying success of his arms. Tökölyi was then supported by the deadly enemies of the House of Austria—viz. France and Turkey. At last, the long-wished-for opportunity arrived, and the marriage took place. A few weeks after their espousal, Tökölyi again took the field, and in a short space of time the important towns of Kashau and Tülek fell into his hands. These victories induced the Sultan to acknowledge him King of Upper Hungary. Twelve months afterwards, Helen gave birth to a boy who was named George, and fate, as if determined always to counterbalance her joys by the weight of misfortune, ordained that he should die shortly after his birth. Now followed the bitter days of this Christian woman's life. Tökölyi's allies, the Turks, had been defeated before Vienna; and thus she lost the greater part of her demesnes, and for many years was separated from the man whom she so devotedly loved, for the stern call of duty dragged him reluctantly away. Her husband's partisans, the Protestant clergy, were now the butt of the Austro-Roman-Catholic party, which was headed by Lobkowitz; and we are told that upwards of 450 Protestant priests and teachers were condemned to death.[1]

Once, and once only, during the space of seven years, Tökölyi again sought his bride, and this was for the purpose of inducing her to allow her son Franz to be sent as hostage to the Sultan, in order to regain his confidence, for Tökölyi had been accused of having caused the ill-success of the Turks by betraying them to the Emperor. What a terrible conflict must now have taken

[1] A great number of these had their sentence commuted, and in the year 1675, we find those who were still alive in the galleys of Trieste and Naples liberated through the intercession of the Dutch admiral, Ruyter, and of the Elector of Saxony.

place in the bosom of Helen! She knew that her
husband was innocent, but the love which she bore to her
child told her that it would be unwise to endanger his
life by giving him up into the hands of the Turks. Her
practical mind convinced her that, however faultless might
be the future conduct of her husband, still, if fortune
should again frown on him and his allies, his opponents
at the Turkish Court might again accuse him of treachery,
and perhaps the life of her beloved son would be sacrificed. Tökölyi seems to have agreed with her, for as a
soldier, he boldly went to the Pasha of Grosswardein to
prove his innocence. This officer treated him as a
prisoner, and sent him in irons to Belgrad; but he did
not remain long in disgrace. Shortly after, the Sultan
again placed an army at his disposal, and assisted him in
resuming the war. Scarcely had unfortunate Hungary
begun to breathe the atmosphere of peace, than the
smoke-clouds of the ignited villages wafted across her
plains announced to her children that their greatest
enemy, civil and political discord, was again among
them.

Helen and her children lived in the castle of Munkács,
which was then besieged by the Imperial General Karaffa,
and defended by a skilful soldier named Radics, who was
a most determined and strong adherent to the doctrines
of Luther. For the space of two years the garrison
manfully resisted the efforts of the besiegers; although
they were constantly defeated in all their battles, Helen
induced them to persist, and it was only through pawning
all her valuables that the defenders of the fortress were
able to get provisions. Writers of romances have given
glowing descriptions of the bravery displayed by women
in our wars with the North American Indians, but the
trial of these heroines was of short duration, whereas
Helen Zrinyi for more than two years was to be found,

night and day, in the council chamber, where she displayed the sagacity of a leader; or on the ramparts, in the midst of the greatest dangers, encouraging the soldiers to do their duty; and yet, this noble woman, whose bosom must have been agitated for the safety of her beloved husband, found time to administer to the wants of the sick and wounded, and console the last moments of the dying soldier with prayers for his salvation. Most probably she and her followers would have lost their lives behind the crumbling walls of the fortifications, had not the Governor got possession of a letter of Tökölyi's, who was then in a desperate strait, entreating Helen to write to the Pope, stating that he was ready to become a Catholic, if his Holiness would induce the Emperor to make peace with him. To prevent this, and in order to revenge himself on Tökölyi for this act of apostasy, the hardy Lutheran general began to treat with the Austrian leader for a capitulation, which he forced Helen to accept, and she was compelled to endure the greatest humiliations. The long-cherished right of guardianship over her children was taken from her. Her son Franz Rakóczy, was consigned to the care of the Jesuits, and her daughter Julia was sent to a convent of the Ursulines, to which Helen had shortly after to fly for protection from the many enemies who sought her ruin. On June 24, 1691, Julia was married to the Count of Aspremont. The welfare of her daughter, no doubt, in some degree, compensated Helen for the prolonged separation from her husband; but fickle fate once more smiled upon this faithful and suffering wife. Tökölyi, who had for some time been in ill-favour with the Sultan on account of the defeats of the Turks, was again entrusted with the command of a considerable body of troops by Köprili Mustapha. It is true he did not achieve such brilliant successes as he had formerly done for the Turks, but he

defeated and made prisoners Heissler and Doria, two of
the most celebrated Imperial generals, whom he kept in
his personal custody until his lost wife was delivered into
his arms, on May 13, 1692. So changed in appearance
was the once handsome Tökölyi, that the wife from
whose memory he had never been for a moment absent
scarcely recognised him. The hardships and vicissitudes
of warlike life had left on him their indelible mark.
None but those who have passed in miniature a life like
Tökölyi can picture to themselves the scene of their
meeting. Henceforth we find Helen striving her utmost
to console and enliven the few who were gathered round
her, in order to compensate her husband for the once
magnificent court which he held. The years which
Tökölyi passed in Turkey must have told heavily on the
mind of Helen, for the Turks were now experiencing, at
the hands of the Duke of Lorraine and the celebrated
Prince Eugene of Savoy, a succession of defeats which
had the effect of gradually withdrawing that support
which the Courts of France and Turkey were in the
habit of affording to her husband. About a twelvemonth
after her reunion with Tökölyi, Helen was again blessed
with another child whom she christened Susanna, but
this little creature lived only for a few days. This great
blow seems to have given her renewed courage in life, for
we find her by the side of her husband, manfully facing
every danger which arose in the terrible struggle now
going on between the Turks and the Austrians, where
her motherly feelings made her a ministering angel to
the wounded and the suffering. Her mind was ever
devising fresh plans to insure success to her husband,
but in vain. Step by step they were forced to retreat
before their enemies. The Turks, no longer able to
contend against the masterly skill of the great Austrian
leader, were compelled to ask for peace, and signed

a treaty at Karlovitz in the year 1698. Tökölyi urged the Turks to demand that he should again receive Transylvania; or, at least, if they could not effect this, that his estates should be restored to him; but the Ottomans could not help him and were obliged to submit to a treaty, the conditions of which forbade all Hungarians in the service of the Sultan to reside near the frontiers of their homes. This compelled Tökölyi and his wife to take up their residence at Constantinople, but they were not allowed to remain there long, for the Austrian Government knew too well their talents and character; and, fearing that they might induce the Sultan again to try the chances of war, the Austrian agents persuaded the Sultan to compel them to leave his capital. They were therefore ordered to take up their abode at Nicomedia in Bithynia, where the Sultan put one of his own palaces at their disposal. Helen was for ever by the side of her husband, soothing his broken spirits and enfeebled health; but this joyful occupation did not last long, for she was attacked by some violent bodily complaint which completely prostrated her strength, and consigned her to her couch. Her Christian courage, however, never forsook her, and she underwent the greatest agonies of pain without a murmur. The great enemy had already prepared to carry his victim from the living world; and it is stated that, feeling her end approaching, Helen gathered sufficient strength to rise from her bed and go to the couch of Tökölyi, who was then in great bodily suffering, and in broken accents begged him to forgive her for all the sins that she had committed against him. She died on February 18, 1703, in her sixtieth year, uttering these words: 'In manus tuas, Domine, commendo spiritum meum. Veni, Sancte Spiritus.' She was buried in the chapel of the Jesuits at Galata, and on her coffin were inscribed the words, 'Donec resurgam.' On her tomb of white marble was cut the following inscription :—

Here lie the remains of Helen Zrinyi—a woman whose heroic life and manly spirit were the glory of her sex, and the age in which she lived— the last descendant of the noble families of Zrinyi and Frangipani, the worthy wife of Emerich Tökölyi, and widow of Franz Rakóczy. Celebrated through her rank amongst the Croatians, Transylvanians, Hungarians and Seklers, she was revered by the rest of the world through her great deeds. She boldly bore the vicissitudes of life. In success she was great and good ; in misfortune her virtues appeared in all their splendour. Her military glory was enhanced by her Christian conduct. She departed from this world on the 18th of February, 1703.

Peace be to her ashes. Amen.

Her husband lived two years to mourn the loss of his faithful wife; and thirty-two years later the remains of Helen's son, Franz Rakóczy, were deposited by her side.

CHAPTER IV.

CECILY ROZGONYI.

WOMAN is the consoling, the regulating, the soothing element in the society of the world. Yet history is loud in its praise of Joan of Arc, and we cannot withhold our admiration where we read of a girl leaving the usual sphere of a woman's life for the purpose of serving her king and country. Why should not history render immortal a being who, inspired by a genuine patriotism, leaves her home and hearth, and mingles with hardy and wild soldiers to unfurl the flag of her country? As was Joan of Arc to the French, such was Cecily Rozgonyi to the Magyars. She, too, exchanged the peace of domestic life for the tumult of war and the dangers of death. She, too, girdled the sword around her waist to defend her native country against its enemies. She, too, saved the life of her king at the risk of her own. Her name and career are worthy indeed to be commemorated by the poet and historian in letters of gold, so that after-generations may be inspired to walk in the path that she trod. Yet in all the phases of her military life she never for a moment forgot the duties of a wife and mother.

Cecily was descended from an ancient knightly family who had migrated into Hungary in the reign of King Geiza. Her father's name was Peter Szentgyörgyi, an influential and rich magnate, who lived in the time of the Emperor-King Sigismund. She seems to have been at a very early age betrothed to Stephen Rozgonyi, whom she married, one might say, in her childhood. Her husband, who held the post of Lord-Lieutenant of the county of Ceines, was the beau-ideal of an Hungarian nobleman of that day. A lovelier and more joyous pair perhaps never entered the family home than Rozgonyi and his bride. Although she was young in years, her love for manly sports had invigorated her frame and developed her beauty. She was a fearless horsewoman, a good fencer, and had few equals in handling the crossbow. The history of her country and the times in which she lived led her to take a great interest in the constant wars which were then going on. The Turks, whose continual success had enabled them to overrun and subjugate the greater part of ancient southern Hungary, threatened, if they were not ejected from the many strongholds which they held, shortly to become the masters of the whole of Hungary. The Emperor Sigismund, in his capacity of Emperor of the Romans and King of Hungary, determined to hurl from the battlements of the subjugated fortresses the flag of the Crescent, and replace it with the standard of the Cross. The news of the assembly of the Imperial army had for its consequence the departure of Rozgonyi at the head of his faithful vassals. His wife, who loved him better than herself, would not be parted from him, and it was in vain that he resisted her entreaties and supplications, for she employed those arguments which only a man who disbelieves in the love of woman can withstand; and, with a sorrowful but proud heart, Rozgonyi placed her on the back of her splendid charger amidst the thunders of applause of his brave and determined followers who, like the rest of their countrymen, believed that as long as women were on their side they must be victorious. Yet, how deep must have been the emotion of his heart, when he saw the idol of his affection by his side panting for the moment which would bring into danger that life which he had vowed before the altar of God to watch over and protect! Extraordinary as it may seem, this young and graceful wife actually —through the force of her arguments and the adoration which her presence excited amongst the soldiery—was unanimously proclaimed their leader. Few warriors have ever led their troops against the enemy with a like intrepidity. Onward she ever pressed, regardless of the dreadful carnage which surrounded her.

Her thrilling voice in the hour of emergency aroused the drooping spirits of her followers, determined that they would never outlive her fall. A desperate battle was fought with the Turks. The engagement seems to have begun with the attack of the Turkish fleet by a small Danish squadron. Cecily led the little flotilla, and after a very severe engagement, destroyed the greater part of the vessels of her opponents. Scarcely had the Ottoman fleet been put to flight when Sultan Murad appeared on the scene of action with a large army. A frightful struggle now took place, for Sigismund's soldiers fought under the magic spell of their lovely Amazon, but their bravery was of no avail against the immense numerical superiority of their foes. Step by step they were driven to the banks of the Danube, and crossed it where a short time before they had gained such a splendid victory. The Emperor, regardless of the havoc amongst his troops, did his best to maintain his footing on the opposite bank, when he was suddenly surrounded by a host of the foe. Cecily managed to get her vessel near the King. Not heeding the danger, she rushed up the bank, cut her way through the circle of the King's enemies, dragged him on board her vessel, and triumphantly steered it to the friendly bank. For this daring act of heroic bravery, the King in writing acknowledged not only the services which she had rendered to his royal person, but her share in bringing about the victory by the attack on the Ottoman fleet. Shortly after this event, peace was made, and Rozgonyi with his wife returned home, where Cecily now devoted her whole attention to the education of her children.

CHAPTER V.

CLARA SZÉKELY.

CLARA SZÉKELY was related to the glorious family of Hunyady, which, as we have seen, has rendered Hungary celebrated through the heroic deeds of John Hunyady and his son Mathias, Hungary's greatest king. Jacob Székely, her father, was Statthalter of Syria, and stood in high favour with King Mathias. Her husband, Perenyi, was one of the few who survived the terrible defeat of Mohács. Clara and her husband were afterwards entrusted with the custody of the crown of Hungary. On Szapolyai's retreat from Pesth, they joined Ferdinand, and delivered into his hands the crown of St. Stephen, in order to enable him to be legitimately crowned King of Hungary. After the Emperor had again entrusted them with the custody of the crown, Clara and her husband went to reside at the stronghold of Siklós, where the crown and insignia were placed. Suddenly, one morning, the garrison was alarmed by the intelligence that the Sultan Soliman and Szapolyai, with an immense army, were within a short distance of the castle. Perenyi seems to have lost all presence of mind. Such was not the case with Clara, for she fully understood the responsibility of her position, and in the depth of night the crown and all the jewels were secretly packed in a waggon, and, under the escort of a body of men on whom she could rely, she and her husband started with them for the fortress of Sáros-Patak. Clara managed for some

time to elude successfully the men who were in search of
her and her party, when at last they were surrounded by
a body of Szapolyai's retainers, who had been informed
of the road they had taken by a partisan named Sze-
recsen.   They were now delivered into the hands of the
Sultan.   Clara had here again to play the part of the
man ; and the Sultan and his ally appear to have been
beaten by her diplomatic tact, for she successfully managed to obtain the liberty of herself and her husband,
and nearly that of the crown, which was, however, too
precious an article for the Turks to deliver up.   Perenyi
seems to have been an ambitious man ; and, relying on
the talents of his wife and the desperate contest which
was now going on between Szapolyai and Ferdinand, he
remembered the Latin saying ' Duobus litigantibus ter-
tius gaudet,' and thought he stood a good chance of
obtaining the crown for himself.   With this view he
opened communications with the Sultan, who declined to
have anything to do with him ; and in an interview which
he had with the Vizier Ibrahim, for the purpose of per-
suading that high dignitary to take up his cause, he was
arrested, put in prison, and informed that he would not
be released until he gave his son as hostage for his future
good conduct.   Clara, who was devotedly attached to her
husband, was greatly distressed at his unfortunate fate,
for she feared that unless she sent her son it might go
hard with him.   She therefore obeyed the desire of her
husband, and sent her youthful son to the Turks.   Great
was the joy of Clara when she again saw her husband,
for she trusted that with his assistance they would soon
be able to have their son restored unto them.   In the
year 1541 the war with the Turks recommenced with redoubled violence.   A favourable opportunity now offered
itself to the Perenyi for regaining their lost child, for the
Sultan stood in need of Magyar allies, and had they

joined the enemies of their country Clara would have
recovered her child; but she had sworn the oath of fidelity
to Ferdinand, and come what might she had manfully
resolved to face their destiny without a murmur. Perenyi
now took an active part in the contest, and commanded a
portion of the garrison of Pesth with Joachim the Austrian leader. This important town was then hotly pressed
by numerous bodies of Turks and Szapolyai's followers.
Just at the time when the Austrians believed that they
had gained the battle, by some unfortunate mistake the
approaching victory was turned into a disastrous defeat.
Joachim threw the entire blame of the disaster on the
shoulders of Perenyi, and stated that he had betrayed the
troops into the hands of their opponents. Clara's husband
was without trial thrown into prison, and left to ponder
on the perfidious conduct of his comrade in arms.

Clara now needed all her strength of character to support herself. She knew that her husband was innocent,
and that in attempting to atone for his former dealings
with the Turks he had been rewarded for so doing by
being left to pine in an Austrian dungeon. She was now,
as we may say, alone in the world, and she had no one to
look to for consolation. Kind fate, however, smiled on
her for a short time. Her son, who had been ten years
in the custody of the Turks, managed to escape the vigilance of his guards, and returned to the arms of his half-
broken-hearted mother; but her transports of joy did not
last long. The hardships which he had undergone brought
him to a premature death. What was now her position?
Her future appeared like a bleak and dreary desert; but
Clara's heart was moulded differently from that of many
of her sex. She suffered, but did not repine; and her
great consolation was that through life she had done what
was right. During her husband's imprisonment the
stronghold of her family was surrounded by a large

Turkish force, who had come there for the purpose of razing it to the ground, and taking Clara as captive to the Sultan. Whatever wrongs she had experienced at the hands of the Emperor, she disdained to revenge herself on him by offering to deliver up the fortress to the Turks, unless he liberated her husband. On the contrary, she boldly told her vastly superior adversaries to do their worst, and for the space of three months, at the head of her faithful garrison, defied all their onslaughts; and so great was the loss she inflicted on her Ottoman foes that they raised the siege, and left her to mourn over her absent husband. The news of this heroic deed created so powerful an impression on the followers of the Emperor that they demanded that the case of Perenyi should be inquired into. It was proved that he was entirely innocent, and, to the great joy of Clara, he was released. His imprisonment seems to have driven all ambitious ideas out of his head, and, leaving the scene of their manifold misfortunes, they retired to their family home. Perenyi and Clara now seem to have turned their thoughts in a direction which has for ever made their names great and glorious in the annals of the history of Protestant Hungary. They were the first who seriously undertook to dévelope the doctrines of Luther. Regardless of all opposition, and the loss of many of their greatest and dearest friends, they manfully persisted in sowing those seeds which in the present day have given so abundant a harvest. They built churches and schools, and instructed all those who were willing to listen to the doctrines of a man on whose name every species of calumny has been heaped; and the descendants of Perenyi may well be proud of their forefather, who has been the cause of destroying the bigoted zeal with which Hungarian Catholics regarded all dissenting sects.

CHAPTER VI.

ANNA TARCZAY.

PERHAPS one of the most intrepid acts of daring bravery ever accomplished by an Hungarian girl was the heroic defence of Tarkö by Anna Tarczay. She sprang from one of the most ancient families of Hungary. Her mother was Theodora Bánfy. Her father, Nicolaus Tarczay, lost his life in the unfortunate battle of Mohács, where the flower of the Hungarian nobility fell under the scimitar of the Ottoman. After his death, Anna's mother married a Polish nobleman, and followed him to his country, leaving her young daughter on the family estate in the care of her brother-in-law, who undertook to superintend the child's education. We are told that whenever she was free from lessons, Anna devoted herself to studying the history of her country; and she was never so happy as when able to flourish her little sword on the back of one of her uncle's restive chargers. As she grew up, Anna was always ready to join in any political conversation, and her remarks proved that she possessed great capacity, strengthened by a determination of character seldom to be found in her sex. In fact, she seemed as if destined to play a part in the history of her country. One of Anna's great friends was Isabella, the widow of John Szapolyai. This ambitious woman, knowing the influential position which her young friend occupied, seems to have completely gained her over to assist in raising her son Sigismund to the throne of Hungary.

Anna also became acquainted with a great partisan of Isabella, named Franz Bebeck, who excited her youthful imagination by depicting to her the important part she would play if Sigismund could be elected King of Hungary.   The result was that the enthusiastic maiden supported them heart and soul in their contest with Ferdinand, who had been elected King of Hungary at the instigation of his sister Maria, the widow of Lewis II. Anna's influence and talents seem to have greatly assisted Isabella, for she not only induced many to join the standard of revolt, but also armed and equipped a body of trained soldiers.   The death of her uncle, who fell about this time in the Turkish wars, gave her unlimited command over her estates and vassals.   The pre-eminent part which she played in this intestine struggle attracted the attention of the King, who wrote to her, bidding her to desist from her hostile acts, and at the same time warning her of the evil consequences, should she persist in opposing his authority.   The proud lady, who was then playing the part of the military feudal noble in the stronghold of Tarkö, would not even allow Ferdinand's envoy to appear in her presence, and sent back his letter unopened.   This so excited the King that he ordered a considerable force to advance at once and destroy Anna's burg.   The Austrian general, from the size and position of the stronghold, believed that as soon as Anna perceived the number of his forces, and that they were fully prepared to bombard her fort, she would immediately capitulate; but in this he was deceived.   The young Hungarian girl returned a most scoffing reply to his summons to surrender.   She mounted the battlement, and ordered a black flag to be unfurled from its loftiest point, saying as she pointed to it, that when the Austrian general got it he might use it as a pall for her coffin. Ferdinand's general began the siege of the place, and, after effecting considerable damage on the walls, he attempted to take it by storm, but was driven back with great loss by Anna, who headed her retainers and fought like a common soldier in the breach. This so infuriated the Austrian leader, that, instead of availing himself of his artillery, he persisted in sending forward assaulting parties, who were successively driven back with great havoc by the heroic lady. The severe loss which the Austrian troops were daily experiencing, at last opened the eyes of Ferdinand's general, who not only found himself without officers (for nearly all had fallen in leading the storming parties), but, on account of the thinning which the ranks of his troops had sustained, he believed himself incapable of withstanding a general sortie from the fortress; he therefore retired, and sent for reinforcements. Anna's stronghold was now the scene of a round of festivities, and, yielding to the importunities of her brave and manly lover, George Homonay, she celebrated the joyful event of the retreat of her enemy by her own wedding.

After their nuptials, Anna and her husband retired to their country estates. The news of her departure was very welcome to the Austrian general, who was somewhat at a loss to explain to his sovereign how his army had been defeated and partly annihilated in attempting to capture a small fort defended only by a few retainers under the command of a young Hungarian damsel, and he now experienced little or no difficulty in gaining his object, as Anna was no longer there to inspire its defenders with her beauty, her words, and her deeds. As long as she was in their centre she inspired her soldiers with the belief of their invincibility, but when the magic of her presence was lost they soon fell victims to their enemies. The victorious general now took another stronghold belonging to Anna, and, believing that she was sufficiently humbled by the fall of her fortresses and the occupation of her estates, called upon her to appear before a court of law. This Anna wisely declined to do, but many of her retainers who had been captured by the Austrian leader were compelled to bear testimony as to the part she had taken in resisting Ferdinand's authority. Their evidence was of such a nature that the judges were for some time incredulous with reference to the account they gave of the acts in which this young girl had been engaged for the purpose of assisting and forwarding the interests of her friend. It appears that she not only enlisted and disciplined men, but led them to the standards of her friend Isabella, that she was accustomed to ride alone for miles in the most uninhabited parts of the country, which were frequented only by disbanded soldiers and outlaws, and that she was constantly planning the most daring enterprises, in which she was always ready to take a leading part. In the defence of her fortress she never shrank from any task, and yet with all her manly qualities she made a most loving wife; and few who knew her in after life would have recognised in her the young Amazon who had so boldly confronted the foe.

CHAPTER VII.

MARIA THERESA.

AMONGST the many illustrious and noble daughters which the House of Hapsburg has given to its subjects, Maria Theresa stands pre-eminently the greatest. Her genius, her talents, and the purity of her character, have made for her a name which has seldom if ever been equalled. It is true we can boast of an Elizabeth, Russia of a Catherine, Sweden of an Ulrica—but who has ever attempted to compare these sovereigns with Maria Theresa? She was in every sense of the word the mother of her people; and when we consider the many nationalities over which she ruled, we are astounded to find that they all expressed the same feeling of veneration and respect towards their great Empress. Her sublime motto, 'Justicia et clementia,' is a key to the policy which guided her in all her transactions through her long and glorious reign. In private life, she was equally conspicuous for her virtues, and her married life may serve as a picture of domestic happiness for future generations.

Maria Theresa was born on May 13, 1717, at Vienna. Her mother, the Princess Elizabeth Christine of Brunswick, was famed for her beauty and her womanly virtues. She was christened on the day after her birth, and received the names of Maria Theresa Walburga Amalia Christina. Her titles were—Archduchess of Austria, Princess of Hungary, and Infanta of Spain. Her edu-

cation was superintended by her parents, and under the
care of the Countess Fuchs Fuchsheim. Of the character of this lady we can say but little ; but there
cannot be the slightest doubt that she possessed a considerable amount of learning, and that her talents were
above those of the general class of women.   The respect
which Maria Theresa entertained towards this lady is
fully exemplified by the great honour she did to her in
ordering her coffin to be deposited in the vault intended
to hold her own remains.   In her early childhood, Maria
Theresa displayed great astuteness and wit.   Her merry
nature and loveliness won for her the hearts of all those
with whom she came in contact.   As she grew up, her
budding form foretold that she would become one of the
choicest models of female beauty; and step by step, as
she approached the years of womanhood, nature acknowledged her love of her favourite by additional charms.
Many anecdotes of her girlish frolics still exist among
the venerable domestics of the Court, who with pride
relate the stories which their fathers and mothers handed
down to them.   After the birth of Maria Theresa, the
Emperor redoubled his efforts to bring about the adhesion
of the different European powers to the celebrated
Pragmatic Sanction.

History gives us few instances of crowned heads being
allowed to marry according to the choice of their hearts ;
but with Maria Theresa it was otherwise.   As a girl
she became attached to Franz Stephen, Duke of Lorraine.
It is true there were many applications for the hand of
the Austrian princess, of whom the Infant of Spain was
the chief; and it is stated that Prince Frederic of
Prussia (afterwards Frederic the Great) also wished to
marry her, but his father opposed the idea, as he knew
too well what he would probably have had to expect
should his son become the husband of the presumptive
heir to the dominions of Austria.

Charles VI., who had known the young Duke of Lorraine as a youth, saw in him the promise of a man who could support his daughter with his counsels in the hour of need, for he did not deceive himself with reference to the dangers which would surround his daughter at his death. Through the settlement of the Polish war Franz Stephen received Tuscany as his heritage. On February 12, 1736, Maria Theresa's marriage with the Grand-Duke was celebrated with great festivities. At her nuptials the Archduchess did not forget her beloved governess, for the Countess Fuchs supported her bridal train.

Maria Theresa was about this time doomed to experience a severe bereavement. This was the death of her dear old friend, or, we might say, grandfather, the great Eugene, the most renowned military leader of Austria. As a child, she was a great favourite of the old veteran, and in the hour of danger, when the military talents of Frederic predominated, the advice of her old friend was not forgotten —viz., that treaties were of little avail unless backed by a well-filled purse and a strong army. Prince Eugene was buried with the honours accorded to an archduke, and his death was universally lamented throughout the Austrian dominions. On February 5, 1737, Maria Theresa was safely delivered of a daughter, Maria Elizabeth, who unfortunately died three years afterwards. The misfortunes of the Turkish war, and the unfortunate peace of Belgrade, had no doubt a most distressing effect upon the mind and bodily health of the Emperor, for he seems to have already anticipated his early death, although he was in the prime of life, and externally gave no sign of failing strength. When confined to his couch, he ordered the urn which was to contain his heart after his death to be brought, and, after looking at it for a time, he sighed, ' This is far too small for it.' The unfortunate

fate of Barcelona weighed deeply on his mind in his
dying moments, for one of the last words he uttered was
the name of that town.   He died on October 20, 1740,
without having seen his greatest and most heartfelt
desire accomplished, namely, the birth of a male prince.

Maria Theresa was in her twenty-third year when she
assumed the reins of government.   She had been brought
up in great strictness by her father, and had received
only imperfect instruction; yet she understood how to
make the few blossoms of knowledge ripen into the richest
fruit.   She was considered a delicate young woman, but
with all the energy of a man she seized the helm of state,
and directed it with cleverness and strength.   Even
foreign ministers were surprised to find with what self-
reliance, energy, and diligence she knew how to oppose
the demands which they dared to put to her, favoured
as they thought by circumstances.   Her answers were
striking and decisive; she always knew how to discover
the kernel, and make clear what was entangled.   Maria
Theresa favoured statesmen when she knew that they
wished for the welfare of the country.   She never felt
desponding or discouraged, and possessed much pride,
which often made her hide real dangers.   Yet she was
open to merriment, and by her freshness and genial spirit
influenced all around her.   She was very fortunate in
the choice of her counsellors, and was seldom, if ever,
deceived.   Her kingdom was a living law, and public
interests she considered as her own interests.   The feudal
power had long been abolished in Austria, and the few
traces still remaining of it were soon swept away.   Pro-
vincial forms were torn out by the root where they
hindered the general development.   Her Ministers served
her well, for they saw the result of their labours, and
were rewarded according to their merits.

Nobody could act in a nobler way or be more clear-sighted and judicious about her own duties than Maria Theresa. In her youth, naturally, her beauty had excited enthusiasm. Still, this alone would not have sufficed, for this enthusiasm would have ebbed away with advancing years. Yet we may well say that even in her least prepossessing stage of life, when she was bereaved of her husband, when small-pox had destroyed her beauty, still the love of her nation remained unaltered. Maria Theresa was taller than most women, yet every limb was in proportion. Her stately and graceful bearing remained till her latest age; and perhaps the world has never seen a face which so truly represented the character of its possessor. Her complexion was brilliant, her hair of the most magnificent blond and soft as silk. Her eyes were azure blue, somewhat mild when not in conversation, but the moment the mind was in motion, they were all fire and animation. Her nose was somewhat bent, her mouth finely cut, and the lips not turned up like those of most of the Hapsburgs. The chin, although finely formed and in perfect harmony with the oval shape of the face, displayed great determination. Maria Theresa had a small white hand and beautiful foot; her carriage was light, and a certain freshness seemed to pervade her whole existence and surround her. Her father had led what might be termed a secluded life, but the young and joyous Empress was the most unhappy being unless she was in the midst of her people. On this account, Shönbrunn became her favourite residence, where she was passionately fond of out-door fêtes. She considered that she and her family belonged to the people, and that they therefore had the right, not only of looking at her, but also of sharing her pleasures and sorrows as she did theirs. She was one of the most daring and graceful riders of her day, and very fond of reviewing her troops in the Hungarian uniform, which most admirably suited

her. That she was attached to pomp and splendour, no
one can deny; but this she only displayed on great
Imperial occasions.

Her temperament was naturally sanguine. Every
excitement spread a blush over her countenance, which
greatly heightened its beauty. Maria Theresa possessed
great fluency of speech. Her conversation was animated,
yet her ideas could at once be comprehended by the most
illiterate. She superintended the settlement of all the
great State affairs, and did most of her writing herself; her
style was short and precise. Her discourse was lively,
and she often accompanied her words by merry gestures.
Easily roused and easily pacified, she was scrupulously
just in her dealings. If she believed that she had
wronged anyone, she was always ready to atone for it;
in fact, she often went too far in this respect. The
enemies of the State she considered as her personal
enemies; and hatred was only known to her when she
believed anyone wished to injure her country. She felt
a great aversion for Frederic of Prussia, which was only
too natural, as her inmost being, her religious views, and
her education were in the greatest contrast with those of
that ruler. The accounts of his father's severity towards
him as a youth had excited her pity, and she had strongly
pleaded his cause to her father when he was tried by
court-martial.

She hated his sardonic manners, and called him ' the
evil man.' After the peace of Breslau, she stated that
she did not so much regret the loss of Silesia, as that it
was left to such a man as he.

From her childhood fear was unknown to her. On her
becoming Empress, she was informed that her life was in
danger, but, quoting the words of one of her ancestors,
she boldly replied—' The ball is not cast, nor the dagger
sharpened, that will kill an Empress;' and, regardless of

danger, she availed herself of every opportunity of appearing in public. It is stated that she was once informed that for a certain sum a person was ready to remove Frederic, her most inveterate enemy, out of her path. Maria Theresa at once despatched a messenger to the King of Prussia to warn him that his life was in danger.

It happened sometimes that the Empress broke through all the forms of etiquette, and acted according to impulse and natural sense. For instance, at Pressburg, at the coronation in 1741, as the weight of her crown oppressed her, she took it off and laid it down. Hers was a thorough practical nature; and even in arts and sciences she was eager to see the quick ripening of the fruit. In the most severe trials she was sustained by a faith deeply rooted in her heart. Maria Theresa was a strict Roman Catholic, and anxious to observe outwardly all that religion demanded of her. She rejected all other beliefs as errors which she might tolerate, but in which she could not participate. Her edicts with reference to Church matters fully demonstrated that she was averse to religious persecution, and a strenuous supporter of her sovereign rights against the claims of the papal power; and she did her utmost to insure to all her subjects freedom of worship.

Amongst the multitude of reforms which she instituted with reference to priestly power, was, in 1775, the abolition of the right of asylum, which she saw was incompatible with the ends of justice.

She seemed, however, to entertain an aversion for the Jews. In 1746 she gave orders that they should all be expelled from her dominions; and it was only through the intercession of her husband, Duke Charles, and the Pope himself, that she could be induced to relinquish the idea, and grant them a little more liberty. This aversion seems to have arisen from the belief that they prevented

P

the mass of her subjects participating in the benefits of commerce.

Maria Theresa's feelings concerning all that was becoming and proper were most refined. She watched over the peace and honour of her house, and her love and constancy lasted to her death. No doubt she had her faults; but her mistakes and errors in the Government can be named without throwing a shadow on her fair image. By selecting commissioners for chastity she only wished to do away with the vices of that time and to place spiritual life above the frivolities which then reigned. If she favoured marriage, it was only to improve domestic life; and she would not have been deceived had she not so much trusted. She demanded indefatigable activity from everyone, herself setting the example. She rose in winter at six o'clock, and in summer at five; went to mass, breakfasted, and devoted till nine to the affairs of State, to which the greater part of her day was given. Her subjects easily obtained access to her; for each morning private persons were permitted to give in their written supplications. In her youth Maria Theresa was fond of hunting, games, and the theatre. She was musical, and sang with a sweet voice. With her advancing years she lived more in retirement, and spent her leisure hours almost entirely with her own family. She was a loving mother, and frequently inquired about the progress of her children's studies, and rewarded or punished, as any private person might do. She generally retired early, even at Court festivals seldom remaining later than eleven o'clock.

Maria Theresa did her utmost to increase the prosperity and welfare of the country; and at her death Austria, once so weak, was confirmed in strength, and could raise its voice with effect in Germany, and, indeed, we may say in Europe.

.   .   .   .

On November 22, 1740, Maria Theresa received the oath of allegiance from the great officers of the State. She appeared in a robe of black, her neck and wrists covered with splendid jewels. Her accession to the throne verified the remarks of the great Eugene. Every crowned head in Europe seemed to have some imaginary claim to her dominions. Professor Smyth, of Cambridge, in his lecture on the life of Maria Theresa, says, when speaking of her position on her accession to the Crown: ' Rumours were circulated that the Government was dissolved, that the Elector of Brunswick was hourly expected to take possession of the Austrian territories. Apprehensions were entertained of the distant provinces; that the Hungarians, supported by the Turks, might revive the elective monarchy. Different claimants on the Austrian succession were expected to arise. Besides, the Elector of Bavaria, the Elector of Cologne, and the Elector Palatine, were evidently hostile. The ministers themselves, while the Queen was herself without experience or knowledge of business, were timorous, desponding, irresolute, and worn out with age. " To these ministers," says Mr. Robinson, in his despatches to the English Court, " the Turks seemed already in Hungary, the Hungarians in arms, the Saxons to be in Bohemia, the Bavarians at the gates of Vienna, and France was considered as the soul of the whole." '

By Maria Theresa's firmness towards the Bavarian ambassador, and the peaceful remonstrances of her representatives at the various Courts, a lull took place in the armaments of the ambitious claimants, and each seemed to be afraid of taking upon himself the frightful responsibility of kindling a fire whose limits or duration no human being could foresee.

One of Maria Theresa's first acts on her accession to the throne was the opening of the prison-doors to Neipperg, Seckendorf, and Wallis, who had been imprisoned on account of their ill success in the unfortunate Turkish war.   This act of justice was followed by similar acts to those of her subjects who had any grievances to complain of.   Her readiness to listen to every petition, and the kindness which she exhibited generally in a thousand ways, increased that popularity which she had already secured as a princess.

It may be desirable before going further to give some account of Maria Theresa's husband, of Frederic the Great of Prussia, of Maria Theresa's court, and the great men who surrounded her.

FRANZ STEPHEN.

FRANZ STEPHEN I. was born on December 8, 1708. He spent the greater part of his youth at the Court of Vienna, and became at an early age enamoured of Maria Theresa.   His father-in-law made him generalissimo of the Austrian army; and, from the beginning of her reign, Maria Theresa gave him a share in the Government.   In personal appearance Franz Stephen was handsome, with a noble forehead, fine clear blue eyes, and a good nose; his manners were easy: he was abstemious in his habits, seldom drinking wine.   He was a great horticulturist, and also devoted many of his leisure hours to carving ; and, like his minister Kaunitz, was a good mechanic.   It was a most difficult thing to obtain a promise from him, and his ideas were most strict with reference to keeping his word.   In him reigned that humane feeling which arises from a benevolent heart and lenient judgment. He disliked stiff etiquette, although he had been sur-rounded with it from his infancy, and he tried his utmost to dispense with forms which were disagreeable and repugnant to those who wished to approach royalty. He would not allow the ladies to continue the custom of kissing his hand. In his intercourse with the Court he observed a species of nonchalance. He was not averse to expressing his admiration of any court beauty, yet his friendship never outstepped the ‚boundaries of propriety. The life of the two monarchs flowed on in perfect harmony, and if in course of years there arose little differences, they were soon removed. How could it be otherwise, when each confided so entirely in the other? His political views, however, did not always run in the same groove with those of Maria Theresa. We are told that he never was such a consistent enemy of Frederic II. as was his consort, who looked upon her opponent as a demon in human shape; but Franz Stephen disliked France above all other States, and admired Frederic for his great military talents. He himself was a great financier, but no general. His financial studies had often been a subject of derision to Frederic; yet his talents in this respect were of great benefit to Austria. Although most economical in many matters, he never forgot the poor, and large sums were yearly set aside for their assistance. This amiable and estimable prince died in the year 1765.

FREDERIC II.

FREDERIC WILLIAM, resembling in the worst features of their character those ferocious Scotch sergeants who passed the greater part of their time in the shambles of the thirty years' war, surpassed them in brutality by his unnatural and atrocious thirst for the life of his own flesh and blood. Unlike his son, however, he had his good points. The intercourse between father and son, the conduct of the former towards the latter at the celebrated court-martial, his portentous remarks [1] to those who interceded in that son's behalf, coupled with the tone of the letters which Frederic wrote to his sister in anticipation of his father's death, recall to our minds the fiendish jealousy and distrust which have been so conspicuous amongst Eastern sovereigns. Frederic II., the representative of that peculiar policy the development of which has enabled the descendants of Frederic von Zoller to increase step by step their territory at the expense of the great Teutonic family, ascended the throne in 1740. The absorption of East Friesland, Silesia, and part of Saxony was nothing more nor less than the reaping of the harvest which the schemes of his predecessors had matured. In the same way, the war of 1866 was the accomplishment of the undertakings of Frederic II. and his successors; and in both cases the recasting and riveting the spoils to the Prussian dominions have been the cause of great misery and immense loss of life. But our readers must remember the words of Frederic William: 'Dem ich stabilire die Souveräneté wie einen Rocher von Bronce;' and, when we combine the three words—blood, iron, and divine right—as carried out by a man of Frederic's morality, we have the essence of Prussian policy. His great aim towards England, through his whole life, was to place that country in such a position as to compel her to look upon him as an indispensable ally.

There was a great contrast between the pompous and sometimes tasteless form of court life under Leopold, and the unpretending and simple manners under Joseph. Spanish ceremonies predominated in former times. The merriest time at Court was from 1748 to 1756. The nobility collected around the throne, and Maria Theresa

---

[1] It is stated that, in reply to Seckendorf's intercession, Frederic William answered: 'Sie wissen nicht was Sie erbitten. Sie werden es einmal sehen, was Sie an ihn haben werden.'

was fortunate in all her undertakings. Spanish ceremonies disappeared more and more, and German manners
were adopted. The Court of Vienna displayed great
splendour at the marriage of Joseph II. with Isabella of
Parma, and the royal procession was imposing and magnificent. The splendour of the sovereign power was
fully represented by those who surrounded the throne.
The principal office at Court was that of Lord-Chamber-
lain, and Count Königsegg, who was at the same time
Minister, Field-Marshal, and Commander, occupied that
post in 1747. His predecessor was, till 1743, Count
Stahrennberg. Count Königsegg was followed by Count
Khevenhüller, who was raised to the rank of Prince in
1774, and Count Ulefeld, formerly Chancellor of State,
after whose death came Prince William Trantson, and
the last under Maria Theresa was Prince Schwarzenberg,
who was very much respected at Court. The Austrian
nobility in those days not only played a prominent part
in the pleasures of Court life, but also occupied a high
position in the affairs of state. It was formed of very
mixed ingredients, which consisted of Germanic, Rou-
manian, Sclavonic, and Magyar elements. It was not
only a court nobility on which honours and dignities
were bestowed by right of birth; it occupied a position
which gave great political influence to those of its order
who were possessed of talent. This class, in the eighteenth
century, showed its vitality and intrinsic value in the
most distinguished manner under Maria Theresa, who,
no one can doubt, greatly encouraged it and relied
upon it. By her personal influence on the first families
of the land, this great empress succeeded in bringing
about a more friendly connexion with the Hungarian
nobility. The names of Edödi, Batthyany, Nadasdy,
&c., were to be found among her statesmen. At the
beginning of her reign the chief were the Counts of Zin-

zendorf, Stahremberg, Harrach, Colloredo, Königsegg;
to Count Zinzendorf succeeded Count Ulefeld, and
Stahremberg was followed by Kinsky. In the Ministry
itself there was much discord. The moving powers were
Harrach, Kinsky, and the Secretary of State, Bartenstein. Maria Theresa did not always repose the same
amount of confidence in her Ministers. Charles VI. had
placed little trust in Zinzendorf, who was at the head of
foreign affairs, and the Empress did not find in him the
amount of support which she needed. He was an excellent courtier, but no diplomatist. He had polished
manners, was extremely good-natured, and took more
interest in science than in public affairs. Zinzendorf
was never willing to sacrifice a pleasure. The gratifica-
tion of the table and the gaities of a court life, had
more attraction for him than his official duties. He died
in his seventy-first year. *Ulefeld*, who followed Zinzendorf, was the first to call the attention of Maria Theresa
to Kaunitz, to whom at a later period he willingly re-
linquished his post.

Stahremberg was a man of large means, and a powerful
supporter of the Government. He was born in 1663, and
educated at the universities of Utrecht, Leyden and Leip-
zic, in order to become a clergyman, which profession he
afterwards abandoned. He was President of the Banks,
and as such had to do indirectly with all custom-house
affairs. He rendered great services to Austria.

Kinsky, by birth a Bohemian, was a cavalier of the
old school, of stern manners, outwardly rough and violent, but indefatigable in the discharge of his duties.
Maria Theresa highly esteemed and honoured him. He
was not spoken well of in Prussia on account of his
known loyalty to the Empress of Austria. He died in
the prime of life.

Königsegg was President of the Councils of Ministers

under Maria Theresa. He had formerly been Commander-in-Chief in Italy and in the war with the Turks. His want of success in this war lost him the favour of Charles VI., who recalled him and made him Court-Marshal. Although not an efficient leader in the field, he was generally liked in the army on account of his good-nature, disinterested character, cleverness and wit.

Harrach's talents and high merits were universally acknowledged. This nobleman succeeded to Count Königsegg in the year 1743. His personal appearance was imposing. After the death of Kinsky, Maria Theresa made him Chancellor of Bohemia. He was then fifty years of age, full of experience and energy, and possessed of an acute mind, surpassing the other ministers as regards talent.

Colloredo, his successor, had not, like his predecessor, indefatigable industry, and does not seem to have personally occupied himself much with the affairs of state. He left the greatest amount of work to be done by his secretaries.

Khevenhüller occupied this important post in the year 1748. He was an active little man then about forty, and a perfect courtier. Maria Theresa, as well as Franz Stephen, esteemed him much for his amiable, honest, and modest character.

All these statesmen were selected from the highest nobility, but Maria Theresa was ever ready to reward those who were of humble birth, and who, through their talents, faithfulness and perseverance, had, by their own exertions, raised themselves to her notice, as in the case of Bartenstein and Kaunitz.

Bartenstein was a determined opponent of Prussia, and hated Frederic personally. Through the favour of the Emperor, he had gained a fortune, which was increased by a rich marriage. It was generally believed that he

would never lose his post, but Maria Theresa had in her
service another statesman, whom neither Ulefeld nor
Bartenstein could rival, a statesman who could be placed
side by side with Richelieu and Metternich.   This was
Kaunitz, who directed through nearly forty years the
foreign policy of Austria.   Several individuals of this
name were at different times in the diplomatic service.

Prince *Kaunitz* was born in 1711.   He was the
youngest of nineteen children, and was prepared for the
Church, but, his elder brothers having died, he chose a
diplomatic career, and studied with distinction at Vienna,
Leipzig, and Leyden.   After having finished his studies
he visited France, England, and Italy, where he collected
much valuable information.   We are told he had a great
predilection for England.   As a young man he was
already known for his great love of horses, and in later
years was looked upon as one of the best and hardiest
riders of Austria.   His stables were the admiration of
all who visited them, and he was particularly proud of
his riding-ground.   Kaunitz also possessed a first-rate
collection of pictures of horses as well as of books, written
with reference to this noble animal.   In the first years of
the war of succession, Maria Theresa sent him to Italy
with a confidential mission, and it was his influence which
induced the Italian Court to remain neutral or to vote for
Austria.   In 1742 he was ambassador at Turin, and
accompanied Charles Ferdinand in the campaign against
the French and Spanish forces.   In 1743 he acted in
the capacity of envoy extraordinary in the Netherlands,
which he had to leave on account of the French occupation.   In 1747, Kaunitz represented the Empress at the
Court of St. James', and in 1748 was Austrian representative at the Congress of Aix-la-Chapelle.   It is stated
that the first despatches of Kaunitz were so excellent that
Ulefeld put them before Maria Theresa with these

words :—' Your Majesty sees here her future Prime Minister.' So great were the sagacity and diplomatic tact which he displayed in the conferences of Aix-la-Chapelle, that, as a reward for his services, the Empress made him her Prime Minister. In 1749, Kaunitz was sent as ambassador to France, and by his skilful conduct brought about the Franco-Austrian alliance. With this statesman a new spirit came into the Austrian Government. Through all the reign of Maria Theresa, under Joseph II., up to Leopold II., he directed, in spite of all opposition, the state affairs with unerring judgment and consummate ability. He died in 1794. When he first came to Vienna he was forty-two years of age, tall, slender, and of good deportment, full of physical and moral power. His features were regular, and expressed wit and intelligence. He had a beautiful quick eye ; his look was penetrating. He wore a wig with a mass of curls, and was always dressed tastefully, in the French fashion. He was as particular as regards order and cleanliness in dress as in every other respect. His chief aim was to lengthen his life, and to remain in good health. He was therefore very careful and simple in his manner of living, especially as he grew older, for as a young man he had led rather a wild life. His character was a mixture of great and small qualities. Gradually, his eccentricities became more and more marked and displeasing to the Court of Vienna, the more so perhaps because the world around him had become different. He often astonished the inhabitants of Vienna by driving a team of stags, but it must be admitted that whatever were his pleasures or recreations, they never interfered with his work. Although slow in forming an opinion, the strength and solidity of his judgment always made up for the delay. He spoke fluently French, Italian, and German, and was a good Latin scholar. In his youth he was very fond of the English language. He seems to have preferred French literature to that of the Germans. Voltaire and Molière were his favourite authors. Kaunitz was a great mechanic, and always had in his establishment several workmen, whose labours he superintended himself. He was also a great patron of arts and science, and every celebrity who passed through Vienna was sure to be invited to the Prince's table. As he wore French dress, Kaunitz was also believed to favour French interests, but those who shared that opinion were much mistaken. He only favoured the union of France and Austria so far as it was to the interest of the latter country. He often mocked at the French even at the time when he kept up a secret correspondence with Madame de Pompadour. As to Prussia, he first united all weapons against it in a seven years' war. Then, when Poland became divided, he sided with Frederic, simply because circumstances compelled him to do so. But when that monarch called upon all the European courts to prevent Austria from taking possession of certain Bavarian provinces, Kaunitz again became his adversary. Under his guidance the finances became so well regulated that income and expenditure were equal, and the credit rose. It is said there never was a statesman in whom Maria Theresa had more confidence. He remained at his post after the great Empress's death, highly distinguished by Joseph II., who also reposed great trust in him. Kaunitz is stated to have been opposed to the freedom of the Scheldt, on the ground that Frederic would always be able to defeat Joseph's generous intentions. He was also of the same opinion as regards the exchange of the Netherlands for Bavaria, and strongly opposed the unfortunate Turkish war. His influence was on the decline during the short reign of Leopold, and it is said that the French war broke out without his knowledge and approbation. Amongst the other celebrated men who rose through their own merit, we must not forget to name Van Swieten, Sonnenfelds, Justi, and Horneck.

The greatest military leaders were Prince Charles of Lorraine, Khevenhüller, Traun, Daun, Liechtenstein, Lascy, and Loudon.

Traun is considered by all his contemporaries to have been one of the first military leaders of Austria. He was a man of the most determined character, and of decided opinions.

Daun was the first Austrian military leader in the seven years' war. The crowning points of his life were the days of Kollin, Olmutz, and Hochkirchen. Maria Theresa entertained the highest respect for this general, and, in commemoration of his great victory at Kollin, founded the celebrated order of ' Maria Theresa.'

Liechtenstein held a high post in the army of Prince Eugene in the war with France, and through his talents the Austrian artillery acquired a European celebrity. During his life he was entrusted with several diplomatic missions. He was a straightforward, honest man ; proud, fiery, and full of self-will, yet very benevolent.

Lascy was by birth an Irishman, who had learnt the art of war in the Russian service.

Loudon, next to Daun, exhibited the most eminent talent. By birth he was a Scotchman. In the time of the Silesian war he offered his services to Frederic, who refused him because he did not like his physiognomy. Loudon then came to Vienna. One day, whilst waiting in the ante-chamber for an audience, he was questioned by a stranger as to his wishes and circumstances, and help was offered to him. This stranger, we are told, was Franz Stephen. It is well known that Loudon was the greatest enemy of Frederic the Great. Yet the latter, who was master in every military science, could not help admiring him.   Loudon never looked happier than on the day of battle.   He then became all fire, and was always anxious to act on the offensive.

     .   .   .   .   .   .

    The terrible tempest which seemed about to break over the devoted head of Maria Theresa on her accession to the throne was for a short time postponed, and the weight of anxiety which had so often clouded her brow now disappeared.   She fondly hoped that the birth of her child would mark the beginning of an era of peace and prosperity; but hard fate had decreed that the dreams of the mother should be bitterly dispelled by one who, by the laws of nature, ought to have been the first to sacrifice himself in her defence.   The pause, or as we may say, the retrograde movement, which the adversaries of Maria Theresa had made, did not at all suit the views of Frederic; for he feared that time would introduce moderation into the councils of his future allies, and saw that every day of peace was of untold value in strengthening the government of the Empress.   He therefore determined to take the initiative, and seize a portion of her dominions.   This, he believed, would force the aspirants to the provinces of Austria at once to take the field; but for fear of any mishap, he, with great secrecy and masterly talent—or rather, as Professor Smyth terms it, consummate hypocrisy and cunning—suddenly threw a well-equipped army of 40,000 men into Silesia.   On the accomplishment of this invasion, his ambassador proposed to Maria Theresa an alliance between Frederic, herself, and the Maritime Powers, for the purpose of protecting her dominions.   Frederic also offered to use all his influence to bring about the election of Maria Theresa's husband as Emperor of Germany, and effect a loan of 2,000,000 of thalers.   In return for these favours Frederic demanded that Maria Theresa should give up to him the splendid province of Silesia. He grounded his right on some ancient claim of his family to the districts of Jagerndorf, Liegnitz, and Brieg, which time and treaties had rendered obsolete. The other parts of the province were to be delivered up to him as a set-off against his alliance. If this was not at once acceded to, his money and troops would be placed at the disposal of the Electors of Saxony and Bavaria. We here quote the words of a well-known English writer with reference to Frederic's conduct : ' The common robber has sometimes the excuse of want; banditti, in a disorderly country, may pillage, and when resisted, murder; but the crimes of men, even atrocious as these, are confined at least to a contracted space, and their consequences extend not beyond a limited period. It was not so with Frederic: the outrages of his ambition were to be followed up by an immediate war, then by a revival of it, then by the seven years' war.' All that was wanting to this infamous piece of ingratitude on the part of Frederic towards Maria Theresa was the well-known remark of his father, ' Der mir am meisten giebt, dem adherire ich.' The King of Prussia's proposals would lead one to imagine that he acted with the knowledge and authority of the Maritime Powers, but such was not the case. At first the Viennese Court considered it prudent to treat his offer with silence, and the Prussian ambassador was ordered to leave Vienna in twenty-four hours. But already the news of the invasion of Silesia had caused the adversaries of the Empress to renew their negotiations with each other, and nothing was now left to the Court of Vienna but to prepare themselves for the coming storm. The answer which Maria Theresa gave to Frederic's insolent message was not only worthy of a descendant of the Emperors of Germany, but also of a woman who finds that she has been stung by a viper. We must remember that Frederic, so-called the Great, whether on account of his genius or his crimes, was, before his accession to the Crown of Prussia, a pensioner of the house of Austria; and in fact Maria Theresa had done her utmost to induce her father to prevent his being shot for insubordination. Maria Theresa's notorious answer was probably read with a satanic smile by Frederic of Prussia; as he knew perfectly well before he sent his offers of alliance, that the entrance of his troops into Silesia must bring about a declaration of war, and thus give new strength to the assailants of Maria Theresa.

The duplicity of his character was fully displayed in his communications to the representatives of foreign Powers at his Court, whom he informed that the occupation of Silesia by his troops must not be regarded as an act of hostility towards the Viennese Court, or a wish to disturb the peace of the Empire; but he had done so solely to legalise his claims on that province and prevent its being taken by the other claimants to the dominions of Austria. Silesia, at the time of Frederic's invasion, had only two regiments with whom to oppose his progress, and the fortresses might be considered utterly defenceless in every respect. Maria Theresa's army numbered 30,000 men, and she had about 100,000 florins in her treasury. In consequence of its utter defencelessness, the greater part of Silesia fell into the hands of the Prussians without the striking of a blow. This brought about a coalition of all the claimants to the Austrian provinces, which was organised at Nymphenburg. The parties were France, Spain, Bavaria, and the Electors of Cologne and the Palatinate; Prussia and Saxony also joined. Austria was to be divided among them; Bavaria having for its share Bohemia, Upper Austria, Tyrol, and the district of Breisgau, Saxony, Moravia, and Upper Silesia; Spain was to receive Lombardy, Parma, Piacenza, Mantua;

whilst Prussia kept Silesia, and France should take the Netherlands. The dominions of Maria Theresa were to consist of Hungary, Carinthia, Carniola, and Illyria. With reference to Hungary, Frederic's emissaries were already doing their best in sowing the seeds of disloyalty, and he fondly imagined that the Hungarians, with the assistance of the Turks, would throw off the rule of the House of Hapsburg, and elect a king of their own. The Bavarians stood on the frontiers of Austria; Spanish and Neapolitan troops had entered Lombardy. On March 9 the fortress of Glogau and its whole garrison, commanded by Count Wallis, fell into the hands of the victorious Prussians. On April 10, 1741, the Austrian troops under Count Neipperg encountered those of Frederic at Mollwitz. The Austrians numbered 32.000 men and eighteen guns, the Prussians 60,000 men and sixty guns. In this celebrated battle the Austrian cavalry thoroughly defeated that of Frederic, who himself commanded it. Frederic sought safety in flight. It is stated that he was pursued by an Austrian hussar, who was about to attack him with his sword, when, turning suddenly round, Frederic told him who he was and promised him a high reward if he left him. The hussar, recognising him from the pictures he had seen, left him, saying, ' Very well, after the war ; ' to which the King replied, ' Good-bye, till we meet again.' This hussar was Paul Werner, afterwards colonel of a Prussian regiment of hussars, and knight of the great Prussian order. Frederic's baggage fell into the hands of the Austrians, but the Prussian generals Anhalt-Dessau, and Schwerin rallied the troops ; the precision of the fire of the Prussian infantry told fatally on the ranks of the impetuous Austrian cavalry, and forced them to retreat, leaving on the field of battle two generals and 5,000 rank and file. This success enabled

Q

Frederic to occupy Moravia, and push forward his advanced troops as far as Kornenburg and Stockeran.

Up to this time Maria Theresa had not been crowned Queen of Hungary; but the state of that country rendered it an imperative necessity for her at once to calm the agitation which existed in that part of her dominions. She accordingly invoked a Diet in May, 1741, at Pressburg, and on June 21 was unanimously acknowledged Queen of Hungary, and received the crown of St. Stephen from the hands of the venerable Primate of Hungary, Emerich Esterhazy. The joy of her Hungarian subjects was unbounded, and her grace and dignity were greatly increased by her appearance in a magnificent Hungarian costume. The daring skill with which she managed her impetuous charger during the coronation scene had a most powerful effect on all those who had flocked together to behold her. To the Hungarians the misfortunes of their Queen, it may be said, were welcomed, because they gave them an opportunity of proving the chivalry and loyalty of the nation, and giving the lie to those miscreants who were attempting to sow the seeds of disunion. Maria Theresa shortly after declared her husband co-regent of Hungary, and raised the loyal and devoted Count Palffy to the rank of Palatine. Vienna was the scene of a universal jubilee on her return; all classes vied with each other in doing their utmost to place the country in a state of defence.

The policy of France was at this time guided by the two brothers Bellisle, the one a statesman and the other a marshal; and no one can deny that they could show sufficient reasons for supporting the house of Hohenzollern, who had already helped them to a slice of Germany; and they believed that they could rely on Frederic assisting them to another. Fleury opposed this unjustifiable war; and the strength of his arguments, as well as his opinion of Frederic, were but too truly verified by after events. The only ally on whom Maria Theresa could reckon was England, who had promised her an auxiliary corps of 25,000 men. But the skilful intrigues of France and Prussia, together with the sudden advance of 40,000 French troops into his Hanoverian provinces, prevented the King of England from carrying out his promise.

We shall now notice the efforts of Mr. Robinson and Lord Hyndford to buy off Frederic. Lord Hyndford states that, in answer to his proposals, Frederic replied : ' At the beginning of the war I might have been contented with this proposal, but not now. Shall I again give the Austrians battle, and drive them from Silesia? You will then see I shall have better proposals. At present I will have *four* duchies and not *one*. Do not, my lord, talk of magnanimity. A prince ought first to consult his own interests. · I am not averse to peace, but I expect to have four duchies, and I will have them.' Maria Theresa, in a conversation with Mr. Robinson, told that minister: ' Not only from political reasons, but from conscience and honour, I will not consent to part with much in Silesia. No sooner is one enemy satisfied than another starts up; another, and then another, must be contented, and all at my expense.' ' You must yield to the hard necessity of the times,' said Mr. Robinson. ' What would not I give, except in Silesia ?' replied the impatient Queen. ' Let him take all we have in Guelderland. If he is not gained by that sacrifice, others may be. Let the King, your master, speak to the Elector of Bavaria. Oh! the King, your master!—let him only march!—let him march only !' Her continued losses, however, induced Maria Theresa to consent to make further offers. ' I am afraid,' said Mr. Robinson, ' some of these proposals will be rejected by the King.' ' I wish he may reject them,' said the Queen. ' Save Limburg if possible, were it only for the quiet of my conscience. God knows how I shall answer for the cession, having sworn to the states of Brabant never to alienate any part of this country.'

Mr. Robinson, in his next interview with Frederic, attempted to soften the heart of that monarch. The King, with malignant hypocrisy, replied that ' His ancestors would rise out of their tombs to reproach him if he abandoned the rights that had been transmitted to him; that he could not live with reputation if he lightly abandoned an enterprise which had been the first act of his reign; that he would sooner be crushed with his whole army. If the Queen,' said he at last, ' does not satisfy me in six weeks, I will have four duchies more. They who want peace will give me what I want. I am sick of ultimatums; 1 will hear no more of them. My part is taken; I will have all Lower Silesia. This is my final answer; I will give no other.' And with this he broke off the conference.

The King of England, as we have before said, was unable to give the promised assistance. The French supported the Bavarians with another army of 40,000 men, and granted large subsidies to the Elector, to whom they promised the imperial crown.

Thus Maria Theresa stood alone in the world as regards foreign assistance, but the sequel will prove what the love of a people will do for a sovereign who protects their rights and privileges, and makes it a rule of life to share the sorrows and pleasures of her humblest subjects. About this time Vienna was visited by a frightful waterspout, which broke over the city, creating great loss of property, causing the river to break its banks and inundate the surrounding buildings. Maria Theresa and her husband were to be seen everywhere doing their utmost to appease the sufferings of the inhabitants; and she severely taxed her private means in order to give the people at once pecuniary assistance, which made her ten times more beloved than before.

On August 14, Charles Albert's troops were in possession of Linz and the greater part of Upper Austria; and he had already compelled the inhabitants of Linz to consider him as their ruler. About the end of this month the French and Bavarians occupied St. Polten, and sent a parlementary to Vienna to demand of Count Khevenhüller the surrender of the town. The worthy commander declined to receive him. Lower Austria and the surrounding district offered to Vienna masses of provisions. Everyone flocked to the recruiting-office, where the grey locks of age were to be seen side by side with the silken curls of boyhood. On the fortifications the cavalier, the citizen, and the lower orders vied with each other to prove their devotion for their common mother. Ladies of the first quality were not backward in the hour of danger. Maria Theresa, who was then expecting her confinement, seems to have made up her mind for the worst; for she wrote to her mother-in-law, saying that she did not know whether she would have a town left to her where she could be delivered of her child. In the hour of distress she proceeded to Hungary, for the greater portion of her dominions were already in the occupation of her numerous enemies; and in the celebrated Reichstag of Pressburg she appeared in deep mourning before the assembly of nobles and representatives. Placing the crown upon her head, she strode with majestic dignity to the tribune, from which the kings of Hungary were accustomed to harangue the representatives of the country. We will not attempt to describe the details of this memorable scene, simply because the pen of the illustrious Macaulay has described

it ; we will only quote a part of Maria Theresa's speech :
' Agitur de regno Hungariæ,' said she, ' de personâ nos-
trâ, de prolilus nostris et coronâ; ab omnibus derelicti,
unice ad inclytorum statuum fidelitatem, arma et Hun-
garorum priscam virtutem confugimus.' Professor Smyth,
in his lecture on Maria Theresa's life, describes in the following terms the scene which followed these pathetic
words : ' To the cold and relentless ambition of Frederic—to a prince whose heart had withered at thirty—
an appeal like this had been made in vain; but not so to
the free-born warriors who saw no possessions to be
coveted like the conscious enjoyment of honourable and
noble feelings—no fame, no glory, like the character
of the protectors of the helpless and the avengers of the
innocent.   Youth, beauty, and distress obtained that
triumph which, for the honour of the one sex, it is to be
hoped will never be denied to the merits and afflictions of
the other.   A thousand swords leaped from their scab-
bards, and attested the unbought generosity and courage
of the untutored nation.   " Moriamur pro rege nostro,
Mariâ Theresâ!" was the voice that resounded through
the hall—" Moriamur pro rege nostro, Mariâ Theresâ!" '
The tumultuous shouts which had interrupted her in her
speech, and the flashing of those swords which were soon
to be bathed in the blood of her enemies, overpowered the
feelings of Maria Theresa.   Tears of joy and gratitude
flowed down the cheeks of the glorious Queen, whose
courage no misfortunes or sufferings could conquer.
Again and again the enthusiastic cries of ' Moriamur pro
rege nostro, Mariâ Theresâ, vitam et sanguinem ei damus !'
greeted her ears.   The whole nation rose to a man.
Magyars, Croats, Pandours, Slavonians, Szeklers, Wallachians, Haiducks, &c., rushed to the standards of their
common Queen, and in the ensuing campaign created
dismay and terror in the midst of their disciplined op-

ponents. The celebrated magnats Karoly, Nadasdy, Forgacs, and Andrássy, did their utmost in organising corps for Maria Theresa's service.

We have before mentioned that England recognised the rights of Maria Theresa to her father's dominions. This feeling was not only entertained by his majesty George II., but by the whole people; for large sums of money were subscribed for her assistance, and the ladies of London collected a sum of 150,000*l.* for that purpose; but the Empress graciously and most kindly declined to avail herself of these generous contributions, with the remark that, as a Queen, she could only receive that which the King and Parliament offered to her. In the meantime, the most encouraging success crowned the efforts of the Hungarian magnats. Many of their corps had already joined the imperial standard, and others were operating on the communications of the enemy. One corps, organised by a certain Baron von Trenck, became notorious for the ferocity of its conduct. They were generally considered to be Croats or Wallachians, but were, in fact, the peasants of the neighbourhood of Pandour, in the Sohler comitat, from which they took their name. They were under the command of a sort of chieftain, called Harun Pasha. Their dress consisted of a long cloak, high caps, and long, broad trousers. They were armed with a long gun, and generally carried two pistols and two Turkish poniards in their girdle. Their footsteps were to be marked by the burning homesteads and corpses of their enemies. So great were the atrocities which these wild and desperate men committed, that Baron von Trenck was afterwards tried by court-martial for his conduct, and imprisoned for life. Our readers must not believe, however, that the majority of the Hungarians pursued a similar course.

Although the frightful contributions which had been

levied in the Austrian dominions, especially the troops of Frederic's own corps, had brought about poverty and starvation among thousands of Maria Theresa's subjects, in general the conduct of the Austrian troops in Bavaria deserves the acknowledgment of every unprejudiced mind. The advance of the Hungarians compelled the Elector of Bavaria to fall back upon Linz, whence he proceeded to Budweitz to effect his junction with the French troops.

Maria Theresa, in the course of her long reign, gave many proofs that she had not forgotten the noble conduct of her Hungarian subjects, and by her motherly exertions greatly promoted the welfare of the nation. She never allowed herself to deviate from the path in which she had started, and party spirit was unknown to her. In her eyes all her Hungarian subjects were the same, although gratitude naturally inclined her to favour the Magyar who had so nobly defended the rights of her crown.

In Bohemia, the confederates were successful. Prague was stormed in succession by the French under Bellisle, the Saxons, and the Bavarians, and on December 7 the Elector of Bavaria was crowned in that town King of Bohemia by the Archbishop Manderscheib. A great number of nobles countenanced this proceeding, but the stubborn silence of the people testified their non-adherence and disavowal of what was going on. They knew that this act was the prelude of a series of contributions which would be levied on their scanty means to maintain the court of this prince, and indemnify the allies who had brought him there, and would cause their unfortunate country to be turned into a slaughter-house. A Bohemian Landtag was held, in which the deputies were made acquainted with the French language, for their new ruler paid his ally the high compliment of making known his wishes in French. His first demand was for a sum of 6,000,000 of gulden, to cover the expenses of the first half year.

The tidings of this Bavarian success reached Maria Theresa at a time when she was surrounded by her Hungarian nobility, and she determined at once to proceed to Vienna for the purpose of reconquering Bohemia. Her position was at this time greatly improved by a regular alliance which she had concluded with England and Holland. The British Parliament had voted her liberal subsidies, for it feared that the booty which might fall into the hands of Prussia, France, and Spain would give them undue preponderance in the affairs of Europe. It was therefore the interest of England to break up this formidable coalition; and of all these Powers, Frederic, she knew—in accordance with the traditional policy of his family—would be perfectly willing to sacrifice his allies if he could be made to perceive that it was to his advantage so to do. England therefore gave her ambassador at his Court the necessary instructions. Maria Theresa's return to her capital must indeed have been a touching and interesting spectacle, one that can be enjoyed only by those monarchs who are considered in the light of father or mother of their people. She had left the town when it was threatened by a siege for the purpose of seeking succour in the hour of distress. In this she had been successful, for the enemy had retreated, and her troops were already combating them on their own ground. She entered the town clad in the Hungarian costume, and at the head of the princely retinue of nobles of the different Hungarian nationalities. Her first step was to appoint Count Khevenhüller commander-in-chief of her forces in Bavaria; and the worthy general, on receiving the appointment, fell on his knees before his beloved Queen, and told her that his first report would be dated from Munich.　This promise he fulfilled, after making his triumphal entry into that city on February 12, 1742.　On that same day, Charles Albert of Bavaria was crowned Emperor of Germany at Frankfort by his brother, the Elector of Cologne ; and, by a stranger coincidence still, this day was also the anniversary of Maria Theresa's wedding.　The election of Albert was effected by French money and Prussian influence, through the instrumentality of the clever French diplomatist, Chevalier Bellisle.　The Austrians, reinforced by the Tyrolese, soon became masters of nearly all Bavaria; and the unfortunate and misguided Emperor had to retire to Frankfort and live on the pecuniary assistance afforded him by France, and Prince Thurn and Taxis.　But he did not remain long in his asylum. A French corps under the Duke of Harcourt quickly reconquered Bavaria, and enabled Charles VII. to return to his capital.

We shall now return to Frederic's operations, which had been universally crowned with success.　He had driven Neipperg out of Silesia into Moravia, and defeated the Duke of Lorraine in a pitched battle on May 27.　The fears of a coalition of England, Holland, Russia, and Austria, as well as the discord which prevailed among his allies, induced Frederic to break faith with his partners, to try and secure by diplomacy the booty which his military talents and the bravery of his troops had gained for him.　On June 11, the preliminaries of a peace between the treacherous monarch and Austria were laid ; and a treaty of peace was concluded at Berlin on July 28, the contracting parties being England, Russia, Brunswick, and Saxony.　Prussia received all Lower Silesia, and the greater part of Upper Silesia, with the district of Glatz.　Saxony, to her credit, did not share in the division of the spoils.

In fact, through Frederic's conduct, she sustained severe losses, both in men and money. Thus, freed from her most determined and skilful opponent, Maria Theresa could now turn her whole energies against her remaining enemies. An English fleet compelled the King of the Two Sicilies to become neutral; and an alliance was entered into with the King of Sardinia, who placed his army at the disposal of Austria, and withdrew his troops from Lombardy, where, together with the Spanish forces, they had vainly attempted to effect a footing. The tidings of Frederic's treachery caused a great deal of uneasiness to the French Court, who began to fear for the safety of their army in Bohemia; for already, in June 1742, the Austrians, under the Duke of Lorraine and Prince Lobkowitz, had driven the French from Egar to the walls of Prague. A reinforcement of 60,000 men, which was sent through Hanover, on arriving near the scene of operations, thought it advisable to retire into Bavaria. Marshal de Broglio, at the head of a part of the French army, succeeded in effecting his retreat from Bohemia. No alternative was left to the French commander-in-chief but to treat for terms with his opponents, and the French Court expressed its willingness to conclude a peace, on condition that their army should be allowed to retire without molestation. Maria Theresa demanded their unconditional surrender as prisoners of war. Marshal Bellisle, like a brave and valiant soldier, determined to save the honour of France at any cost, and accordingly, during the night of December 16–17, at the head of 11,000 infantry and 3,000 cavalry, he cut his way through the enemy's lines, and effected his retreat by way of Egar. In his operations of retreat, he lost nearly half of his troops, but he proved himself worthy of the bâton which he carried. The evacuation of Bohemia was celebrated by a *Te Deum* in the Church of St. Stephen on December 30.

On January 2, one of the most magnificent spectacles which Vienna has ever witnessed took place under the superintendence of Maria Theresa. It consisted of eight ladies attired as Amazons, who, on costly war-chariots, drawn by horses whose harnesses were for the greater part of massive silver, performed two sets of quadrilles. After this, these beautiful women, who were chosen from all the different nationalities, went through a series of intricate evolutions, in which they displayed their efficiency with the lance, darts, sword, and pistol. Writers of those days speak of the Oriental splendour of their costumes as unparalleled. As the names of those flowers of Austrian chivalry might interest our readers, we give them in detail as they received their prizes: — The Princesses Auersperg and Esterhazy, Archduchess Maria Anna, Countesses Palffy, Wurmbrand, Althan, Kinsky, Proskay, Kollonitsch, and Baroness Hager. The riding-school was decorated with garlands and damask hangings of a rich blue colour, fringed with silver lace. After the prizes, which were of a most costly nature, had been distributed, Maria Theresa, at the head of her Amazons, passed through the principal streets, and returned to the Burg, where she dined with her companions. The festivities were concluded by a grand ball, which she and her husband opened.

The Duke of Lorraine now advanced into Bavaria, driving back the troops of Charles VII. into Swabia, and occupied Munich, where a regular Austrian Government was organised, the unfortunate Emperor having again to seek safety in Frankfort. The disasters which were experienced by the Spanish forces in Italy produced such indignation, both in Spain and France, that the two Governments determined to despatch a second expedition to Italy. The French Government declared war against the King of Sardinia, and sent an army under the Prince of Condé. The Spanish fleet, which was to help in the operations of Italy, was blockaded in Toulon by an English fleet under Admiral Mathews; but the French fleet having compelled him to raise the blockade, the allies put to sea, whereupon the English admiral attacked and defeated them. The British Government had for some time directed their attention to the formation of a confederate army in the Netherlands, for the purpose of forcing France to conclude peace with Austria. This army was called ' the Pragmatic.' It was composed of English, Hanoverians, Hessians, and Austrians. It first advanced on the Main, for the purpose of protecting the election of the Archbishop of Mainz, and forced the Elector of the Palatinate to become neutral. Frankfort would have fallen into the hands of Lord Stair, but it was not the wish of England and Austria to act with severity against the Emperor. On the contrary, they wished, if possible, to induce him to relinquish his claims on the Austrian dominions, and break with the French. Frankfort was therefore declared neutral, and the Emperor was allowed to remain unmolested in his asylum. Marshal Noailles, the French commander, determined if possible to retrieve the disgrace of the French arms. He accordingly advanced against the Pragmatic army, which was then commanded by the King of England in person and the Duke of Cumberland. The two armies met at Dettingen. The French were defeated, and Marshal Noailles compelled to retreat. The Pragmatic, however, did not follow up their success. The fortifications of Landau were razed, and nothing more was done.

The concentration of the Pragmatic army on the Main, and the success of the Austrians in Bavaria compelled Marshal Seckendorf, the Bavarian general, to demonstrate to Charles VII. the impossibility of continuing the contest; and this ruler, convinced of the helplessness of his cause, ordered him to discontinue hostilities. Peace was concluded between the Emperor and Maria Theresa on the same day on which the battle of Dettingen was fought. By this peace Charles VII. undertook to compel all foreign troops to withdraw from his dominions, and relinquish all claims to the Austrian provinces, on condition that he should be allowed to remain unmolested in Bavaria, and keep the title of Emperor. The French troops, it is true, had again advanced and occupied the greater part of the Netherlands; but they were forced to retire to the frontiers of Lorraine by the rapid advance of the Austrian general, whose troops already threatened Luneville.

Frederic, who had by this time put his army into first-rate condition, and replenished his military treasury, saw that the time had arrived to strike another successful blow, and he accordingly re-opened negotiations with France. That country, forgetful of the past, again renewed her alliance with him, and on May 29, 1744, a coalition was effected between the Emperor, France, Prussia, the Elector of the Palatinate, and the King of Sweden—against Austria, England, Saxony, and Holland. Frederic again displayed in this campaign his usual rapidity of movements, and in the space of three weeks nearly all Bohemia and Moravia were in his power. The victorious advance of the Prussian monarch was checked by the return of the Duke of Lorraine, who compelled Frederic at first to retire to Königsgratz. Prague again fell into the hands of the Austrians. The appearance of an Austrian army in Silesia forced Frederic to give up all idea of retaining his footing in Bohemia and Moravia. He accordingly retreated, and Upper Silesia was now occupied by the victorious Austrians. The retreat of the Austrians from the Rhine left Bavaria without defence, and it was at once re-occupied by the Emperor and his French allies, who advanced across the Austrian frontier.

On January 8, 1745, a quadruple alliance was formed between England, Austria, Holland, and Saxony for the recovery of Silesia. Shortly after this the unfortunate Charles VII. died at Munich, at the age of forty-six, and it may be safely said that the troubles brought upon him by his unwarrantable ambition were the cause of his early death. His son Maximilian Joseph, although only seventeen years of age, had profited enough by this sad experience to see that a continuation of the alliance between Bavaria, France, and Prussia must have eventually caused his downfall, and the ruin of his unfortunate country. He therefore concluded peace with Maria Theresa, relinquishing all claims to the provinces of Austria, and gave his adhesion to the Pragmatic sanction, undertaking, at the same time, to cause the retirement from his dominions of all foreign troops, and promising his support to the Grand Duke of Tuscany in the election to the Imperial crown, on condition that Maria Theresa should acknowledge his right as Elector of Bavaria, and withdraw her troops from his provinces. This was a great advantage for Austria, as all further danger of the molestation of her Bavarian frontiers was thereby removed, and she now could direct all her energies to the recovery of Silesia. The support of the Elector of Bavaria in the election of her husband to the Imperial throne enabled Maria Theresa to bid defiance to the Elector of the Palatinate and Frederic, and although the French had collected an army in the neighbourhood of Frankfort to strengthen the opposition of Prussia and the Palatinate, Franz Stephen was elected Emperor.

Maria Theresa, regardless of danger, proceeded herself to Frankfort for the purpose of being present at the coronation ceremony of her husband. Seated at a balcony, she was the first to raise her voice, in shouting a *vivat* to his accession to power, in which the whole people joined who collected to witness the ceremony. After the coronation, Maria Theresa proceeded to Heidelberg for the purpose of reviewing an army of 60,000 men who were drawn up in order of battle under the command of the Emperor. She visited the encampment, and passed through the ranks of the army, speaking to many of the soldiers. After the review, she dined in a large tent with the chief officers, and on leaving ordered a gulden to be given to each man. Thence, the Empress proceeded with her husband to Vienna, for the purpose of making their triumphal entry into that city, where the new Emperor and Empress were welcomed with unbounded joy.

Frederic, in the ensuing events, deserves great credit for his diplomatic tact and generalship. All the armies which opposed his progress were successively defeated, and he again occupied Bohemia, leaving Maria Theresa no option but to conclude with him a peace which was signed at Dresden on December 25, 1745. Prussia retained possession of Silesia, and received from Saxony the sum of 1,000,000 of thalers, as well as a small portion of territory. But it must not be thought that this was all Frederic's gains out of Saxony. He had extorted the most exorbitant contributions, both in men and money, in every part of the country through which he passed. The Pretender's invasion had forced the English Government to recall their troops from the scene of hostilities, to put down on their own soil a rebellion which, Macaulay says, was due to Frederic's intrigues. It may be noted, in conjunction with this fact, that Prince

Bismarck, in a speech in which he praised the conduct of his own Government towards the House of Hanover, reproached the English with a want of magnanimity towards the Stuarts.

In the middle of the year 1746 the French armies were in possession of all the Austrian Netherlands, Louisburg and Luxemburg being the only fortresses over which the Austrian flag floated.

In Italy the Austrians were triumphant, for Genoa was already in their possession, but at the moment when the Imperialists were about to invade Provence for the purpose of capturing Toulon and Marseilles, the Genoese rose in mass, and, after a severe conflict, Marquis Botta, the commander of the Austrian garrison, was compelled to retire with all his force. This loss, it is true, was in some degree compensated by the victory of the Austrians and Sardinians over the French at Exiles, where the French commander Bellisle lost his life; but the evacuation of Genoa was an irretrievable loss, as it was the key-stone to the southern provinces of France. Towards the end of the year an attempt was made to form a peace congress, but no satisfactory arrangement could be arrived at, and France now declared war against Holland. In a very short time the celebrated French commander-in-chief, Marshal Saxe (Moritz von Sachsen), was master of nearly all the Netherlands, Maestricht alone being still in the possession of the Dutch; but after he had defeated England and her allies at Fontenoy, Marshal Saxe, by a false movement on Luxemburg, lured his adversaries from the neighbourhood of Maestricht, which he immediately surrounded on April 17, 1747. The French commander now devoted all his energies to the taking of that important town, for he knew that if the allies once effected their junction with the Russian troops which had already arrived in

R

Germany, he would be compelled to raise the siege, whereas, if he retained possession of Maestricht, its immense strategical importance would enable him to make his own terms, and thereby compensate the losses which the French navy had experienced at the hands of the Dutch and English fleets.   So rapid was his progress, that the allies, fearing that Maestricht would be compelled to surrender before the Russians had effected a junction, entered into peace negotiations.   On April 30, an armistice was concluded between France, England, and Holland, and the fortifications of Maestricht were, for the time being, handed over to the French.

On October 18, 1748, the ambassadors of France, England, Austria, Holland, Sardinia, Spain, Modena, Sicily, and Genoa, signed a treaty of peace, into the details of which we shall not enter.   All the Powers again renewed their adhesion to the Pragmatic sanction. Hanover was guaranteed to England, Silesia to Frederic; Austria was also called upon to make a partial sacrifice of her influence in Italy.   Dunkirk was dismantled, and the Pretender ordered to leave the French Court.   This peace, however, was not followed by a general disarmament, as no one expected it would be of long duration; but the world was in error.   Europe was tired with the scenes of bloodshed, and by degrees the different Governments felt themselves compelled to yield to the desire of their people.

No ruler, probably, signed the treaty of peace with more unbounded joy than Maria Theresa.   She knew that it would enable her to improve the condition of her people, and develope their social and moral position.   Her ambassadors were ordered to redouble their efforts to remain on the most friendly terms with the different Courts to which they were accredited, and express the wish of their Imperial mistress for the continuance of peace, as well as her wish to observe neutrality in case of war.

In a very short time the fruitful soil had nearly effaced the effects of the scourge of war; but unfortunately, Maria Theresa, through love of peace, and knowing that for the welfare of the country, the greatest possible freedom from military service was urgently needed, never kept up her army on a footing in proportion to the extent of her dominions and the armaments of the neighbouring States. The military quota of the Austrian Government was not 1 per cent., whereas that of Frederic was $4\frac{1}{10}$th, and his army was always on a war footing, ready to take the field at a few days' notice. No doubt financial reasons considerably affected the Empress's policy. During the years of peace which followed the treaty of Aix-la-Chapelle, the State of Austria and its laws underwent a great change for the better. In the year 1751, Maria Theresa issued a severe edict against foreign lotteries, which had formerly been the means of taking large sums of money from the country. In the year 1752, a terrible explosion took place in the saltpetre manufactory belonging to the laboratory for the preparation of explosive materials for warfare, and great damage was done to the surrounding houses. In the year 1755, one of the greatest storms which Vienna had ever experienced took place, accompanied by terrific lightning, and the electric fluid struck many buildings, causing much alarm and damage.

Up to this time, Maria Theresa's Government did not believe in the possibility of a fresh attack on the part of Frederic. The friendly understanding which existed between Austria, France, England, and Russia led the Empress to suppose that he would not again attempt to break the peace of Europe. She had mistaken him. Already that unscrupulous man had prepared for all. To him a continuance of peace was indeed a threatening aspect of things. He believed that it would give the rulers of Europe sufficient time to comprehend the necessity of putting a stop to his aggressive policy, and might ultimately lead to their wrenching from him his illgotten spoils. There were four persons who, he knew, personally disliked him: *Maria Theresa*, whom, together with her subjects, he had constantly insulted; *Kaunitz*, whom he had robbed of his estates in East Friesland; *George II.* of England, who had not forgotten the haughty defiance with which Frederic had treated his claims as Elector of Hanover to the province of East Friesland; and lastly, the *Empress of Russia*, whose pride had been greatly offended by his satirical remarks, and whose indignation he had roused by forcibly enlisting her subjects.

In the year 1754, disputes arose between the English and the French on the frontiers of Canada, and retaliations followed which ended in hostilities. Frederic added fuel to the fire, in the hope that either one or the other of the combatants would require his help. He fully trusted that France, forgetting his previous treachery, would still look upon him as her natural ally. This belief was strengthened by his knowledge of the policy of France, which for more than 200 years had been directed to the humbling of the House of Austria, some of the rulers of France considering the policy of Austria as aggressive, and holding it advisable to foment its internal difficulties, and others from a wish to extend their frontiers at the expense of the German Empire.

Maria Theresa was, however, fully convinced of the fact that an alliance between France and Austria could alone secure the peace of Europe. After the treaty of Aix-la-Chapelle, all the diplomatic talents of Kaunitz had been directed to the realisation of this policy. In this he was most ably seconded by his friend Choiseul. The fruits of his diplomacy, it is true, were not immediately apparent, for all Kaunitz's designs required time, though when accomplished they were perfect. In accordance with this policy, Maria Theresa determined, if possible, to remain neutral in the dispute between France and England, as she considered it her duty to afford indirect assistance to the latter. The French Government knew perfectly well that Frederic was the only monarch who, if handsomely paid, would side with France. The French Minister, in reply to some remarks of a brother diplomatist with reference to the policy of Austria, said, ' You are quite right; Austria may have a diplomatic squabble with England, but a good feeling will always exist between the two.' His remarks to the Prussian ambassador Knyphausen prove how well he understood the character of the denouncer of Machiavelli. ' Write to your king,' said he ; ' tell him that he ought to side with us against Hanover ; there is something to be got by it ; the Elector-King of England has a well-filled exchequer. The King of Prussia will have but to help himself. It will be rare sport.'

George II. knew but too well the character of Frederic. He was fully aware that if he wished to save Hanover from French occupation, he must swallow the bitter pill of becoming the ally of a man for whom he felt the greatest contempt and dislike. More galling still was his knowledge of the fact that, to procure this aid, he must be prepared to outbid France. Two ways were opened to Frederic : he might either attack or defend Hanover. After having sounded the feelings of Russia and Austria, he made up his mind to conclude a defensive alliance with England, which was effected at Westminster on January 16, 1756. If he joined France and attacked Hanover, he would, he thought, most probably have to contend against

England, Austria, Russia, and perhaps Holland, Sweden, and Denmark ; whereas, even if he sided with England, the French troops could not advance into Germany, on account of their alliance with Austria. Moreover, Frederic trusted, with the help of England, to effect a reconciliation with the Empress of Russia, whose nephew, Peter, was a great admirer of his, and who, he believed, had sufficient interest to prevent any hostile movement being undertaken against him.   He would thus be free to undertake the invasion of Saxony and Austria, they not being in a position to cope with him.   But in order more fully to deceive France, with which he had formerly concluded a treaty which had not yet expired at the time of his secret understanding with England, he forbade the passage of Russian troops through his dominions to assist England.   The knowledge of Frederic's transactions caused general indignation in France, but so great was the wish of that country to prevent hostilities breaking out in Germany, that on May 1, 1756, the King of France concluded a defensive treaty with the Empress of Austria, to which was afterwards added a clause by which both States mutually engaged to defend each other with an army of 24,000 men.   The King of France, in the most honourable manner, ordered copies of all the treaties which he had concluded to be forwarded to Frederic, requesting him to join the treaty of May 1.

On July 9, 1756, information was received that Frederic was evidently preparing to strike a decisive blow in some direction.   The French ambassador was ordered to inform Frederic that it was the intention of the French Government to defend the neutrality of Austria.   This alarmed the Prussian King; and by the most extraordinary means he appears to have so completely lulled the suspicions of the French ambassador, that this diplomatist, fourteen days afterwards, led his government to believe that there was nothing to be feared. Frederic, as usual, kept his plans secret, communicating them to only two or three of his most trusty advisers. Even his brothers, William and Henry, were unacquainted with his nefarious designs, and Generals Schwerin, Retzow, and Winterfeld were the only persons whom he consulted as to the carrying out of his purpose. Winterfeld alone did not express his dissent from the proposed iniquitous proceedings; but Frederic was not the man to change his mind, especially when there was a chance of increasing his territory and filling his treasury. Schwerin then informed his royal master that, if he wished to be victorious, he must at once put his plans into execution. Strange as it may seem, it is nevertheless an undoubted fact that Frederic's sagacity had been weakened by the success of his constant treacheries towards France. He felt actually convinced, in his own mind, that if, by a rapid and overwhelming movement, he could absorb a portion of Austria and Saxony, and then express his willingness to join in the treaty of neutrality, France and Russia would not attack him. His strategical plan was to seize the Saxon army, and with it invade Bohemia and Moravia. We hesitate to cast the entire responsibility of the misfortunes which befell Saxony during the seven years' war on the shoulders of the minister Bruhl, because we believe that he wished to preserve an upright neutrality, for he not only declined to join the Russian and Austrian defensive alliance of 1746, but also refused to listen to the earnest solicitations of the Saxon representative at the Court of France, and join in the defensive treaty of Versailles. He also declined to accede to the plan of Marshal Rutowsky, of placing Saxony in a position to resist the advance of Russia, because he stated that he did not wish to give Frederic the opportunity of quarrelling with Saxony on account of its hostile attitude

towards him.　Yet in all his public and private transactions he most explicitly expressed a decided opinion in
favour of the suspicions excited by Frederic's policy.　It
seems that he was either a man in the wrong place, or a
most consummate traitor, for by his policy, he enabled
Frederic to be victorious in his rapid advance.　On
August 29, without a declaration of war, Frederic
occupied Leipzig, and three Prussian columns were
already in Saxony.　He now directed his steps towards
Pirna, in order to compel the whole Saxon army to surrender.　This he succeeded in accomplishing in the
neighbourhood of Konigstein.　We will not here trouble
our readers with the disgusting and revolting means by
which he carried out his plan.　The Austrian General
Browne was defeated at Lobositz.　In a very short time,
all Saxony was in the possession of Frederic; and the
unfortunate Elector-King was compelled to conclude
peace and retire to his kingdom of Poland.

It is unnecessary to say much about Frederic's conduct
towards his unfortunate queen.　His behaviour towards
his wife, and his debased expressions with reference to the
sex, are perhaps sufficiently known to everyone, and therefore we can fully account for his total deadness for that
feeling of pity which every man is supposed to entertain
towards the sufferings of a woman.　The unfortunate
queen died shortly afterwards from a broken heart.

It was only in January 1757, that the Reichstag declared war against Frederic, and even then the Austrian
Government hesitated in their hostile movements against
Prussia, and allowed the golden opportunity of entering
on the offensive against Frederic to slip through their
fingers, simply because they desired to prevent bloodshed,
and prove to Europe that they were not the aggressive
party.　Availing himself of this timidity of the Austrian
Government, Frederic began the campaign as early as

possible, and we find him in April pursuing his career of
rapine and bloodshed, in order to crush Austria before
her allies could take the field. The different corps of the
Austrian army he quickly defeated; and in the space of
twelve days forced the army, which consisted of 40,000
men, under the command of Prince Charles of Lorraine
and Marshal Browne, to retreat to the walls of Prague.
On May 6, Frederic defeated the Austrians, and compelled them to seek refuge behind the fortifications of
that town, which he immediately bombarded, the want
of provisions and the state of its defences giving him
every hope of a speedy surrender. The only disposable
force which the Empress now possessed on the theatre of
war was the right wing of the army, numbering 25,000
men, which was under the command of Daun. The
subjects of Maria Theresa were in dismay; but she, who
knew from the inmost feelings of her heart that her desire
for peace had aided Frederic in his bloodthirsty designs,
now called upon her people, who had never yet deserted
her, and encouraged by that inspiration which the
humblest feels when conscious of the righteousness of his
cause, Maria Theresa, with unshrinking fortitude, set
about placing her empire in a state of defence, and every
subject answered to her call. She at once ordered Daun
at any price to raise the siege of Prague. This the
prudent general accomplished by forcing the Prussians
to attack him, on June 18, in his position at Kollin,
from which the Prussian army in vain attempted to drive
him. With undaunted courage they threw themselves
seven times on Daun's entrenchments, and were each time
driven back with the most frightful loss, and obliged at
last to leave the gallant Austrian leader in peaceful possession of his impregnable position.

This defeat forced Frederic to raise the siege of
Prague and retire into Saxony. On July 26, the defeat

of the English and their allies at Hutenbeck brought about a break-up of this force, namely, by a convention which was signed in September. A part of this army had to take up its quarters in the rear of the Elbe, and the rest to return to their homes, Hanover falling into the hands of the French. This enabled the French general Richelieu to commence active operations against Frederic, and he at once proceeded to effect a junction with the army of the Imperialists, under the command of the Prince of Hildburghausen, who had already been strengthened by the auxiliary French corps under Marshal Soubise, and was advancing to the aid of Saxony. The Russian army, under Apraxine, numbering 100,000 men, had already advanced as far as Jagerndorf. The Swedish forces had effected a footing in the Uckermark, and the French troops had by this time begun to threaten the important town of Magdeburg.

Frederic now felt the full responsibility of his position ; and he knew that in case of defeat, his House and the dominions which had been brought together under its rule, by a series of the gravest offences against the rights of international law, would disappear from the list of European sovereignties. The only Power who he knew did not intend his destruction was Russia. Frederic, it is true, had no troops to oppose to the Russians, Swedes, and French, for already, on October 16, 1757, a body of Austrians had entered Berlin; yet the want of unity and skill which existed amongst the leaders of the armies of his opponents enabled him to defeat them in succession, for suddenly, leaving only a small force in Saxony, he advanced with the rapidity of lightning, and threw himself unexpectedly on the French and Imperialists at Rossbach. The French retreated to Hassen and the Imperialists to Franconia, leaving 2,000 men on the field. It is stated that Frederic directed all his energies to the destruction of the Imperialists, and not only did not pursue the French, but allowed a large number of them who were prisoners to escape, which latter fact was in direct contradiction with his system of enrolling his prisoners under his own flags, a measure generally effected by partial starvation. Frederic was no doubt actuated by the idea that his generosity might bring about a reconciliation with the French. The Austrians, availing themselves of Frederic's absence, advanced into Saxony, took possession of Breslau and Schweidnitz, drove the remnants of the Prussian army from the scene of their former victories, and forced them to take refuge in Glogau. Frederic now appeared on the scene of action, and encountered the Austrians at Leuthen, where he totally defeated them, taking a large number of prisoners and several guns, Silesia again falling into his power. In April 1758, Frederic had not only recovered his lost ground, but threatened the important town of Olmutz. The generalship of Loudon, nevertheless, compelled him to give up all idea of its capture, as a large Prussian convoy had fallen into the hands of this young general. Frederic now hurried to the relief of Kustrin, which was besieged by the Russians, who encountered him at Zorndorf, and a most terrible carnage took place, neither side giving quarter. The Russians were compelled to retreat, but as soon as Frederic's back was turned they again advanced into Prussia, where they remained until they went into winter quarters.

Frederic, on his return to Saxony, took up a strong position at Hochkirchen, where he entrenched himself, and turned it into a kind of fortified camp. It appeared as if it was not the intention of the Austrians to molest him, when suddenly Daun, who had concentrated a considerable force in the early morning of October 14, surprised him. After five hours of hand-to-hand fighting, the Prussians had to leave all their artillery, ammunition, and baggage in the hands of the Austrians, together with 9,000 men, on the ground, amongst these being the Princes of Anhalt-Dessau and Brunswick and Marshal Keith.   Nothing of great importance took place in Westphalia and on the Rhine.   The Russians, after wintering in Poland, again broke into Prussia: and Loudon, who was now known as one of the first generals of Austria, was ordered to effect his junction with the Russians. This he accomplished in July 1759, after totally defeating the Prussians and capturing Frankfort-on-the-Oder. This victory again placed Frederic on the verge of ruin. The presence of Loudon in the vicinity of the Russians, he feared would compel that power to take a more active part in the war; and relying upon the tidings which he had received with reference to the position of the Austrian and Russian forces, he determined to attack the troops of the Czarin, who occupied a fortified camp at Kunnersdorf, and defeat them before they could be reinforced by Loudon.   On August 12, therefore, he attacked the Russians in their position with such desperate valour that he captured seventy pieces of artillery, and after seven hours' resistance had nearly driven the enemy from their entrenchments.   He was thus on the eve of a victory, when suddenly Loudon appeared on the field of battle, and attacked Frederic with his usual impetuosity.   It was in vain that Frederic's veteran troops attempted to withstand the charge of the Austrian cavalry, and the King was compelled to seek safety in flight with the remnants of his army.   Frederic lost all his artillery, and had only 5,000 men with him, the rest of his troops being dispersed.   Peter's friendship here again manifested itself, and the Russian general Rutikow declined to pursue his antagonist.   This enabled Frederic to collect a large portion of his army and effect his junction with his brother Henry. Thus strengthened, he again advanced into Silesia. Daun marched into Saxony; and the Russian general, under the plea of want of provisions, began to fall back in the direction of Poland. The Imperialists, who had now effected their junction with the Austrian troops in Saxony, had been generally successful, and had taken Dresden. On September 4, an army corps, under the Prussian general Fink, was surprised and compelled to surrender, seven generals being taken prisoners. Up to the end of the campaign, fighting was taking place in all parts of Saxony; and Frederic so successfully maintained his footing in that country, that he was enabled to make it his winter quarters. The campaign of 1760 was opened with great vigour on both sides. Loudon totally defeated a Prussian army corps at Landeshut, taking the greater part prisoners. Frederic now retreated from Saxony, and returned with great rapidity, surprising the Austrians on August 14 at Liegnitz; and on the following morning he defeated Loudon before Daun could come to his support. In this engagement Loudon displayed great military talent.

Frederic was now compelled to leave Saxony, as the Austrians and Russians threatened Berlin, which they shortly afterwards captured. Count Esterhazy, the Hungarian general, sent to his Royal mistress Frederic's flute and portrait. During their sojourn in Berlin, the Austrians behaved in the most exemplary way, but the Russians, it appears, carried out Frederic's system of levying contributions. On September 28, the celebrated Hungarian Guard, of whose magnificent uniform and military appointments the world has heard so much, took the oath of allegiance to their Queen at Pressburg, and thereupon became the Hungarian body-guard of the sovereign. A magnificent palace was purchased for them in Vienna. At the coronation of the present King and

Queen of Hungary, this corps was again re-organised, and its present gala uniform is one of the most soldierlike in Europe. On October 1, the Princess Maria Isabella of Parma made her triumphal entry into Vienna, and was married to Prince Joseph. The ceremony was most gorgeous, and the Hungarian Guard attracted great attention. This princess was celebrated for her beauty, and was most passionately loved by her husband. A round of splendid festivities followed this joyful event, and it was considered by many as a lucky omen of a speedy and glorious peace; but such was not to be the case. Daun, who had taken up a position at Torgau, which he had strongly fortified, was attacked by Frederic on November 3. The Austrians offered such desperate and obstinate resistance, that towards evening Frederic began to give up all hopes of defeating his antagonist, when the fortunate arrival of General Leo Thun with reinforcements enabled him to renew the conflict and force the Austrians to withdraw from their position. Daun thereupon retreated to Bohemia. This was one of the most hotly-contested battles of the campaign, and nearly all Frederic's generals and principal officers were wounded. His coat is said to have been riddled with bullets. The French during this campaign kept a firm possession of Hanover and Hesse. The campaign of 1761 opened without any prospect of peace. Two Austrian armies under Daun and Loudon stood opposed to those of the King of Prussia and his brother Henry. Daun's plan was to act on the defensive in Saxony, and wait until Loudon had effected his junction with the Russians, and gained an advantage over Frederic. For four weeks Frederic, with masterly skill, prevented the union of the two armies, but as soon as the Russians had crossed the Oder he retreated and entrenched himself. Here again the Russians, after some time of inaction, retired, under plea of want of provisions;

but the enterprising spirit of Loudon hit upon a plan of forcing Frederic from his stronghold. The Austrian general accordingly advanced and took Schweidneitz, and on September 30, Colberg fell into the hands of the Russians and Swedes.

The French, it is true, received a severe check; but the doubtful battle of Villingshausen left Frederic in about the same position as when he began the campaign. It is accordingly stated that he made several proposals of peace to Maria Theresa; but that noble woman would not forsake her ally Saxony, and allow it to become the price of an alliance with Frederic. In August the celebrated Bourbon contract was executed at Aranjuez, through the talents of the distinguished French Minister, Choiseul. Spain, which up to this time remained neutral, now invaded Portugal, and took part in the hostilities against England. Nothing short of a miracle could save Frederic, when the death of the Empress Elizabeth, on the 5th of January, freed him from all fear of the co-operation of the Russian troops with those of Maria Theresa. She was succeeded by her nephew Peter, who had already done good service to Frederic. Peter at once withdrew his troops from Prussian soil, and concluded a peace, undertaking, at the same time, to induce Sweden to follow his example. On effecting this, he in June formed an alliance with Frederic, and sent an army of 20,000 men to support him. This saved the Prussian king, and he was again able to concentrate his forces against Austria and Saxony.

Peter's accession to the throne of Russia was considered by the opponents of Frederic to be the first step towards their total discomfiture. It was well known that it was entirely through his intrigues that the Russian generals had on several occasions neglected the most favourable opportunities of crushing Prussia; and it would seem evident that Frederic believed he could also rely on Peter's wife, one of the most talented and ambitious rulers which Russia has ever seen on its throne.

There are beings in this world who cannot entertain the idea of the division of power, and Catherine was one of them. At the time of Peter's accession to the throne there existed in Russia a party which believed that Frederic possessed far too great an influence on the mind of Peter, and that eventually the policy of Russia would become subservient to that of Prussia. They fully acknowledged the desirability of being on friendly terms with the unscrupulous sovereign of that country; but at the same time felt the necessity of forcing him to become the instrument of their policy. In Catherine they saw the personification of their wishes and ideas, and Peter was accordingly assassinated.

On her accession to power, in order to obtain a good hold on Frederic, Catherine withdrew the Russian contingent. This led him to imagine that she intended pursuing the policy of Elizabeth; but such was not the case. The Empress gave him to understand that she intended remaining on friendly terms with him. What was the exact nature of the communications which took place between these two rulers no one knows; but Frederic, perceiving signs of a coming understanding between the contending parties, made up his mind to place himself in a favourable position, so that he might conclude an advantageous peace. He accordingly advanced and took Schweidnitz on October 9. On the 29th, his troops were also victorious in Saxony, whilst they maintained their ground in Hesse.

On November 3, England and France began to treat for peace, and on February 10, in the following year, a treaty was signed at Fontainebleau between these two nations, by which France lost some of its finest possessions. On the 15th of the same month, an armistice was concluded at Hubertsburg, in Saxony, between Prussia and Austria. This was also followed by a treaty of peace between these two Powers and Saxony, of which the former treaties of Berlin and Dresden formed the basis, Frederic promising to use his influence in favour of the Archduke Joseph in the election of a king of Rome.

We do not for one moment attempt to deny that Frederic displayed the highest military talent, and also proved that he was one of the most unscrupulous diplomatists ever known. Perhaps some of our readers may object to the title of diplomatist being bestowed on him ; and we own that his intrigues cannot correctly be styled diplomacy. His connexion with the Marquis d'Argent, whose works have been publicly burnt, his intrigues in Hungary and other countries, sufficiently show how debased his mind was, and that there was not one single European statesman who trusted him. He was tolerated solely from the belief entertained by some of the European Powers that he was the best instrument for their purposes. In other words, he was the first mercenary in Europe. At the conclusion of the war he had enriched his treasury by the subsidies which Pitt had granted him, and by the frightful contributions which he had levied on the unfortunate districts through which his armies had passed. His troops cannot be called Prussian, as they consisted of mercenaries, deserters, and, lastly, those miserable men whom he had forced to serve under his colours, and whom the most severe discipline enforced in all its rigour could scarcely keep together.

The principal reason which induced Maria Theresa to come to terms with Frederic was, no doubt, want of money and love of peace. The horrors of war had not, however, this time taken place so near her capital; and the fertility of the Bohemian soil was so prolific that if

s

it had but one good harvest it could make up for the campaigns.

Frederic's remarks with reference to the behaviour of his soldiery proved that he did not trust them ; in fact, the hardiest among his cutthroats began to fear that their own carcasses would enrich the future harvests of the countries they were devastating.[1]

Anyone who has studied attentively the history of this tremendous struggle of Frederic, will perceive that the Austrian generals had displayed in this campaign a far greater amount of talent than they had formerly done, especially where their operations were not made dependant on those of the Russians. The school of adversity had taught Maria Theresa's generals how to counteract the strategy of Frederic. But this was not the only advantage which Maria Theresa had gained. The treaty of peace which England had concluded with France proved that it was highly improbable that Pitt would again subsidise Frederic ; and the Austrian Ministers could also reckon with some degree of certainty that, from the unsettled state of affairs in Russia, Catherine would not give Frederic armed assistance, if Maria Theresa should attempt to carry on single-handed the war with Prussia. Nevertheless, Maria Theresa, with all these advantages on her side, did not hesitate to sign the peace. In a very short time, the three great rulers of Austria, Maria Theresa, her husband, and Kaunitz, through their wise and enlightened policy, not only made up for the losses which the empire had sustained both in men and money, but also had placed the country in a more flourishing condition than it was before the war; and happily the sad experience of Frederic's treachery had a most beneficial effect on her policy with reference to the

---

[1] In fact, even his brother Henry became for him an object of distrust.

organisation of her armies, and the placing her dominions in a proper state of defence.

We shall now give a sketch of Maria Theresa's reign when she acted in the capacity of Regent to her son Joseph. On the accession of that Prince to the rank of Roman King, she gave over to him the direction of the military affairs of the whole empire, and made him Grand Master of the Order of St. Stephen. It is true, St. Stephen of Hungary was the original founder of this order, but no practical use had ever been made of it. Maria Theresa reinstituted it as a civil decoration, with the power of bestowing it on every nationality of the Austrian Empire. The gala costume of these knights is most gorgeous. The one which Maria Theresa wore as Grand Master, she gave on her resignation to Count Franz Esterhazy, Chancellor of the Order.

From the time of August 2, up to its first partition, Poland was the scene of internal feuds, each party relying on foreign influence. We need not go into the unscrupulous intrigues of Frederic for the purpose of bringing about the ruin of Poland. They are too well known to the readers of history, and most undoubtedly he instigated Catherine II. to join with him in compelling Austria to absorb a portion of Poland. His crafty policy was too apparent to Maria Theresa ; she knew that by so doing she was annihilating a Power who, on account of its hostile feelings towards Russia and Prussia, would form a most important ally in case of a coalition of the two before-mentioned Powers against her. It was only to prevent the breaking out of another European war that she most reluctantly submitted to the demands of her two powerful enemies, but no power on earth could force her to take anything besides that part of Poland which formerly belonged to the Crowns of Bohemia,

Hungary, and Austria, namely, Galicia and Lodomeria. In a conversation which she had with the Nuncio, when this question was still in its earliest stage, Maria Theresa remarked : ' I shudder when I think of the amount of blood which has been shed during my reign, and nothing but the most urgent necessity will ever induce me to sanction another drop being shed.'

The news of the Russian advance into Poland appears to have excited great alarm in her mind as to the possibility of maintaining peace, for she told the English ambassador that Austria could not remain a passive spectator to such an unjustifiable proceeding. At a later period she observed : ' For my part, I do not wish to obtain a single village, unless I have a right to it. I will not encroach on the rights of my neighbours, and I will do my best to prevent others doing so. No plan of partition, however advantageous, will have the slightest chance of obtaining my approval; far from it. I shall reject them with the greatest contempt. I do not for a moment make a merit of it, for the principles of sound policy and true wisdom require me to do so, no less than justice and equity.'

Joseph was not so averse as his mother to the plan of partition. In speaking to him on the subject, she said : ' We are pursuing the Prussian policy, and attempt at the same time to preserve the appearance of honesty.' She further assured him that however advantageous any acquisition might be to the monarchy, it was always too dearly paid if purchased at the price of conscience and the honour of the country.[1]

[1] Fearing that her memorable words on the principles which had guided her through life might lose their value by translation, we give them in her own words : ' Vom Beginne meiner unglücklichen Regierung an, haben wir wenigstens uns das zum Ziele gesetzt, nach allen Seiten uns wahr, aufrichtig, zuverlässig maszvoll, treu unsern Verpflichtungen zu beweisen. Das erwarb uns das Vertrauen, ja ich darf sagen, die Bewunderung von Europa,

It appears that great difference of opinion existed in the Council at Vienna as to the policy to be pursued towards Russia and Prussia, for we find Maria Theresa making the following remark : ‘ The whole question is so utterly repugnant to me, so entirely adverse to the principles which have guided my policy, that I cannot bear even to think of it, and I have therefore given the entire management of the affair into the hands of the Emperor, Prince Kaunitz, and Marshal Lascy.’

In a letter which she addressed to Kaunitz, she says : ‘ At the time when all my provinces were being contended for, and I was at a loss to know where to find a place of security, I could place my confidence in my legitimate right and the support of Providence. But here, when not only public right and justice but even common sense is against us, ... I must candidly own that I have never been so troubled in my mind, or felt so ashamed. Consider, Prince, what an example we are giving to the world, if we stake our honour and reputation for the possession of a part of Poland, or of Moldavia and Wallachia. I see plainly that I stand alone and without power. I must, therefore, let things take their course, but I do so with the greatest sorrow.’

It was only in April 1772, that Maria Theresa agreed to the partition treaty ; and, after reading it, she wrote

die Hochachtung und Anerkennung unserer Feinde. Das ist vorbei. In der letzten Zeit ist alles verloren. Ich gestehe, dasz nichts auf der Welt mir so schmerzlich gewesen ist, als dieser Verlust unseres guten Namens. Zu meinem Kummer aber musz ich Dir gegenüber es auch offen aussprechen, dasz wir es verdienen. Und darum wünsche ich, dasz auch jetzt noch geholfen werde, dasz wir jeden Versuch, von diesen Unruhen für uns Nutzen zu ziehen, als schlecht und verderblich von uns weisen, dasz wir vielmehr erwägen, wie wir auf das schnellste aus dieser unglücklichen Lage kommen, nicht dadurch dasz wir sinnen auf Erwerbungen für uns, sondern dadurch, dasz wir streben, den Glauben an uns und unsere Treue und Rechtlichkeit herzustellen, und, in so weit das möglich ist, den Frieden und das Gleichgewicht.’

on the draft the following words: 'Placet, because so many great and learned men deem it necessary. But, when I have long been dead, the world will find out what will be the result of this disregard of all that was formerly considered holy and just.' The division of Poland appears to have haunted her like a spectre, and for years after she was in the habit of constantly reverting to it. In the year 1775, when Marquis Breteuil had his first audience with her, she began the conversation with a passionate outburst of grief at the part she had been compelled to play. 'I know,' she said, 'Your Excellency, I know that the part I have taken in the transactions which have lately occurred in Poland will cast great blemish on my rule; but I assure you that if you only knew how I struggled, and how the various exigencies of the time combined together to put aside all my former precepts and resolutions with reference to the ambition of Russia and Prussia, you would forgive me. I pondered over this subject for a long time, but I found that alone I could not discover means to oppose the plans of these two Powers. I believed that by putting forward the most extravagant demands I should court a refusal, and thus break up the negotiations. But my astonishment and sorrow were inexpressible when I was informed that my demands were accepted. I was never so distressed in my life. I must, in justice to my Minister Kaunitz, own that he did his utmost to prevent this cruel act. I assure you, the manner in which he conducted himself before and after these transactions, have greatly increased my confidence and good-will towards him. What strengthens still more my feelings of respect for him is, that he never gave the slightest sign of the regret which he inwardly felt for the discredit which was attached to his Ministry, and allowed every species of abuse to be heaped upon his head in silence for not having done that which he had striven to his utmost to carry out. And even now he is constantly directing all his strength to put an end to, or at least circumscribe, this unfortunate undertaking. It is but too true, at present I have not the consolation of knowing when this Polish affair will be finally settled. The King of Prussia is constantly deferring, only for the purpose of being able to create new difficulties, and thereby increase his share of territory.'

During these troubles Maria Theresa was unremitting in her endeavours in the development of the fine arts. In 1766, she founded a school for drawing and engraving, and gave its direction to the then well-known Schmuzer, whose father had rendered himself celebrated under Charles VI. She also erected a school for casting and embossing. These two establishments were joined to those already instituted by Leopold I., Joseph I., and Charles VI., for painting and sculpture, and received the name of United Academy for the improvement of the fine arts, and the superintendence of the whole was given over to Kaunitz, who was one of the greatest art patrons at the Court of Vienna. The two Princesses, Maria Anna and Maria Carolina, were elected members of this academy in the year 1766, not on account of their imperial birth, but because they had sent some of their own labours to the collection. Maria Theresa also established the Ritter Academy, the University of Vienna, the Oriental Academy, the High School at Lemberg, the University of Pavia, the Botanical Gardens in Vienna, Milan, and Pavia, &c. &c. Being in the habit of receiving constant reports from her ambassadors on everything that took place in the different countries to which they were accredited, she was enabled to judge the better of the improvements which time rendered necessary, and the different requirements of those who surrounded her, while science and literature were fully represented by men who had raised themselves to eminence by their talents and industry. The great composer Mozart enjoyed her favour.

When Maria Theresa assumed the reins of government, the trade of Austria was in a very low condition; the producing power was represented by a few manufactories of linen, leather, and glass articles; and the state of agriculture was far from flourishing. The Empress instituted a species of Board of Trade and commercial and manufacturing commissioners; she was also the originator of a mercantile marine company at Trieste, and before her death the manufactories were not only able to supply the wants of the people, but also, to some extent, to export. Through her system of canalisation, the internal trade was greatly developed, and the papers which were published by her son Joseph on agricultural statistics led to an improved system of cultivation.

About this time Austria nearly experienced a twofold calamity. The Empress Marie Joseph was suddenly attacked with the small-pox. Maria Theresa, who was then at her favourite summer residence, Schönbrunn, without a moment's consideration, immediately went to nurse her daughter-in-law, and did not for an instant leave her until she herself was attacked with symptoms of the disease. Marie Joseph died on May 28. Maria Theresa's age, and the virulence of the attack, led her physicians for some time to believe that she would not recover. During four days the whole Austrian Empire was the scene of the greatest grief. All places of amusement were closed, and the capital was like a town in mourning. Immense sums of money were lavished in petitions to the Almighty for the restoration of the health of the mother of their country. That merciful and all-seeing Providence was not deaf to the entreaties of her subjects on behalf of a being whose virtues and sufferings were to

be the theme of wonder and admiration for future generations. A great monarch can only feel the love of his
people when his life is in danger, and when that danger
is passed. Such was the case with Maria Theresa. The
empire of grief was converted into a world of tumultuous joy. On July 22, Maria Theresa was present with
the imperial family at a grand *Te Deum*, to return thanks
to Heaven for her restoration to health. After the
service, she and her family passed through the principal
streets of Vienna in the midst of a rapturous ovation.
Nothing was heard but the cries of, ' Long life to the
Empress our Mother !' but her beloved subjects perceived
with mingled feelings of pity that the marks of the small-
pox remained on her magnificent features. Perhaps they
ought not to have thought of such a thing ; but Maria
Theresa was their mother, and, like all children, they
were proud of her personal appearance.

Some time after Maria Theresa's recovery, arrangements were entered into between the Court of Vienna and
that of the Two Sicilies for the marriage of Ferdinand
with the Archduchess Marie Joseph, and their betrothal
took place on August 8, 1767. The Spanish and Sici-
lian ambassadors commemorated this event with the most
gorgeous entertainments, but unfortunately the Archduchess was seized with the small-pox, and expired on
October 15 in the arms of her beloved mother, who had
watched over her night and day during her illness.

These sad bereavements, together with the number of
her subjects who had fallen victims of this virulent dis-
temper, determined Maria Theresa to introduce vacci-
nation into her dominions, and she ordered her Imperial
family to be vaccinated. Sixty-five children who had been
inoculated at the same time with the Imperial family at
the hospital of Meidling were invited, together with
their parents, to visit Her Majesty at Schönbrunn, where

the good Empress intended celebrating the introduction of Jenner's great discovery by a most magnificent festival. Tables were spread on the splendid terrace, at which were seated the sixty-five children; the Empress, with the archdukes and archduchesses, waited upon them. The parents of the children were seated at another table; each of the little ones received at the hands of Maria Theresa a thaler, together with the remnants of the feast. After dinner, the children and their parents accompanied Her Majesty to a theatre which had been erected at Hietzing for the purpose of hearing a new comedy. The immense mass of people who had come from the surrounding districts spent the night in dancing. Maria Theresa was never so happy as when in the midst of her people, and sharing their pleasures, especially among children, and many stories are handed down of her kindness towards them. Maria Theresa's sufferings and motherly conduct always excited the deepest sympathy and admiration amongst all classes of Englishmen, but the following anecdote, which we believe is not generally known in England, cannot fail to increase those sentiments. At the time of which we are writing the whole Austrian nation was in the greatest anxiety with reference to a male heir to the crown. Joseph, who had been twice married, was without male issue, and the only chance which remained was in the marriage of Leopold of Tuscany, whose wife had already borne him a daughter, and at last the inhabitants of Vienna were overjoyed on hearing the news that the Archduchess was again pregnant. As the day approached for the Princess's delivery, the excitement in Vienna increased to such a degree that nothing else was heard in the streets or saloons but the question as to whether any fresh tidings had arrived from Florence. According to all the calculations of the wise mothers and sapient daughters of Vienna, February 14 was supposed to be the day which would bring their fears and anxieties to an end. This was a Sunday, and a very rainy and gloomy one; but the good Viennese are not so easily put out, especially on a Sunday evening, which, in their eyes, is the most agreeable one of the week. All the cafés and places of public resort were crowded with eager inquirers as to the state of the Princess, and lucky were those who were presumed to understand her delicate position. No news having arrived from Florence, the good people of Vienna betook themselves to the usual places of amusement. The Burg Theatre was the greatest point of attraction, first on account of the celebrated comedy, ' Clementia,' by Baron Gebler, one of the most favourite plays of those days, the chief part being taken by Madame Jaquet. It was also believed that the Empress, or some member of the Imperial family, would be present. All eyes were naturally directed to the Imperial box, but in vain; the curtain was drawn up. The play began, and the public now directed their attention to the piece. In the midst of the second act, when the heroine was in the most touching scene, the doors of the Imperial *loge* were thrown open, and Maria Theresa appeared, to the astonishment of her subjects, in her night-toilette, holding a half-open dispatch in her hand, and, with a voice half-choked with tears of joy she exclaimed, ' Der Leopold hat ein Büblein !' Again and again did the public cheer their good mother, and the actors heartily joined. At last the Empress retired. Actors and public by mutual consent considered the best thing they could now do was to go and have their suppers and drink the health of the Empress and her grandson. During the winter of 1768, large quantities of rain had fallen at a time when the Danube was frozen over. This caused a violent thaw, and great blocks of ice were borne with such terrific force against the bridges which connected the two parts of Vienna, that they were entirely carried away, even that on the arm of the Danube which connects the capital with the suburb of Leopoldstadt. The consequence was that the Danube broke its banks, and a large part of the suburbs of Vienna was inundated. Everything that could be done to relieve and assist her unfortunate Viennese, the Empress did. Her son Joseph was to be seen during this time of peril traversing the different districts. Regardless of the danger, he crossed the arm of the Danube in a small boat for the purpose of encouraging the people to repair the damage caused by the inundation. In the midst of his labours, Vienna was visited by an earthquake. It is stated that upwards of a hundred severe shocks took place in the space of thirty seconds. This again caused the Danube to overflow its banks with fresh violence, but the constant presence of Maria Theresa and her son induced the inhabitants to redouble their efforts, and in a very short time the banks of the river were again in good order. With the assistance of pecuniary aid afforded to the sufferers by Imperial generosity, the effects of the two inundations soon disappeared. From the year 1766 to 1770, the great Empress directed her attention to the improvement and embellishment of her capital. To her credit, her labours were specially directed to the founding or enlarging of hospitals and schools. In these patriotic endeavours she was assisted by the celebrated Sonnenfels, the Austrian Montesquieu of his time. This enlightened man had the direction, and in fact seems to have been the originator, of the normal schools in Austria. In every act of Maria Theresa can be clearly distinguished her motherly desire to benefit and improve the condition of every one of her subjects. It is true the great had no opportunity of appreciating these little acts of kindness, but the humble did, and, as they traversed with their joyful families those public walks which her munificence had bestowed on them, they blessed the Almighty who had given them such a benefactress. Maria Theresa was, as we have before said, very fond of hunting, but when she was informed that the game often wandered from the Imperial preserves, and did sad damage to the crops of the poor, she immediately issued an edict granting them permission to shoot them down as wild beasts, and, moreover, made the keepers responsible for the damage if it should be proved to have occurred through their carelessness.

On January 23, 1770, the Emperor Joseph lost his daughter Maria Theresa, a most amiable and promising child, in whom the entire affections of her father were concentrated. So deep was the bereaved father's affliction that for a time he was unable to take any active part in the affairs of the Empire, and sought to regain his peace of mind by travelling in Hungary, nor could anything induce him to marry again. Maria Theresa was not only respected as a great ruler by her subjects, but also for the way in which she brought up her children. In the year 1770, the Princess Marie Antoinette, one of the most beautiful and virtuous princesses of her age, gave her hand to the young Dauphin, afterwards known as Louis XVI. It is stated that the parting between mother and daughter was a most touching scene, and the poor Empress shed showers of tears as if foreboding the unfortunate fate in store for one who, she trusted, would, like herself, become the mother of her people.

The brothers Choiseul, who had been the chief instruments in bringing about the Franco-Austrian alliance, had fallen into disgrace. 'Remember,' said Maria Theresa, at the very last moment, 'remember that those two men were the originators of your marriage, and always be ready to show your gratitude towards them.'

Hearing that Marie Antoinette was trying to imitate the French in their manners, the Empress told her to remain German, and consider it an honour to be one: 'Believe me,' said she, 'the French will respect you far more when they see you behaving like an honest straight-forward German.   Do not be ashamed to be German, even in their awkwardness; if you appear clumsy, make up for it by good-heartedness.   We cannot make our position dependent upon our beauty, our talent, and knowledge, but upon our good-nature.   It is necessary for the internal welfare of our States that we should enjoy the blessings of peace.   If we remain united, nobody will interfere in our good work, and Europe will be at rest.   Not only our own subjects shall enjoy those blessings, but they also whose rulers, on account of their peculiar personal ambition, would wish to disturb this peaceful state of things.   The first twenty years of my reign fully demonstrate the correctness of this assertion. Through our alliance, which is strengthened by so many delicate ties, the foundations of peace and tranquillity have been established, and its continuance will preserve this state of things for years to come.'

A few years later we find the Empress saying, in a letter, 'All that I still desire in this world is the pre-servation of our holy religion, the happiness of my dear children, the prosperity of our States, and the welfare of our subjects.   Because I wish this, I also desire to see those means employed by which these objects, which I have so much at heart, can be attained—namely, that the connexion between the two Houses and our common interests should remain as firmly united as at present, and naturally, that this union should be based upon the mutual inclination and friendship of both sovereigns, in order to prevent ministers or foreign envy causing an estrangement.   The Emperor and the King are both young; both are inspired with great and noble feelings. I am therefore thoroughly satisfied that when they know one another, that mutual understanding which, in their political career, will prove so necessary for them, will at once spring up between them. I know that they will be happy, and will make their people happy. These are the cherished desires of a good old mother for her children. On these grounds I have given my instructions to Mercy, who will inform you how you have to deport yourself.

' The disputes between Turkey and Russia, Spain and Portugal, can easily bring about a general conflagration, in which I shall myself be enveloped against my will. You know our bad neighbour. We must now be all the more wary of him, as the opposition which he has experienced from us in his attempts to carry out his unjustifiable aggressive policy in Poland and other countries will probably redouble his former hatred towards us. He does his utmost to find support in every possible direction, or at least to intrigue against me in every Court. He spreads every possible calumny against us, especially in France. His joy at the slightest misunderstanding between us tells us that we should on no account be disunited. If we hold together, neither he nor anyone else will attempt to break the peace. The idea of our being an aggressive State, is utterly false, and we never have, or ever shall be, unless forced to become one.

' The preponderance of our House no longer exists. If it did, it would be far more advantageous to the welfare of Europe; but our ambitious neighbour has taken good care to prevent it. France cannot enjoy sound tranquillity without us, nor we without France. This alliance is the most natural, the most advantageous, and the most agreeable to me.'

In speaking of the feelings of a people towards its sovereign, Maria Theresa says to her daughter, ' What ecstasy it is to be beloved, especially when you feel inwardly that you deserve it. It is the only reward for our labours.'

It is related that Ferdinand, who had married Maria Beatrix of Este, on being informed by his mother that his appointment to the governorship of Lombardy, prior to his departure for Milan, would be celebrated by a most costly and magnificent illumination, replied : ' Too many festivals have already been given in my honour. How much better I should like to see the large sums of money which this illumination will require distributed among the poor, who are now suffering so much from the high price of bread.' The Empress fondly embraced her son, and with motherly feeling acknowledged the truth of his remarks. The whole sum was privately distributed. Ferdinand returned the next day, and, throwing himself in his mother's arms, said, in a voice choking with emotion : ' O mother, what a happy day this has been for me !' On the arrival of this talented prince in Milan, the inhabitants placed at his disposal 500,000 gulden, to celebrate his installation into office, with which sum the Prince immediately set about improving the roads and canalisation of the country. The total failure of crops in many parts of Europe in the year 1770–71 reduced thousands to the utmost misery. Bohemia was one of the countries which experienced the greatest sufferings. Upwards of 200,000 died from starvation and disease. As soon as the total failure of the crops became known to the Government, Maria Theresa ordered the Treasury to place 500,000 gulden at the disposal of the Bohemian authorities, together with a large quantity of flour and rice. The Emperor Joseph himself traversed in detail the suffering districts, visiting the huts of the poorest

peasants, and with his own hand distributing the neces-
saries of life. As a practical man, he knew that only
immediate assistance would arrest the progress of a deadly
contagion which already made its appearance. He therefore ordered all the military magazines to be placed at
the disposal of the inhabitants. He visited all the
hospitals, regardless of the deadly disease. There his
humane face and kind-hearted words did wonders, and
many a poor wretch died contented, after having pressed
the hand of his beloved Sovereign to his lips. But
Joseph also found time, during his manifold labours, to
ascertain the causes which led to the failure of the
harvest, and on his return to Vienna published many
useful orders with reference to the cultivation of the
ground. Maria Theresa also ordered many exemptions
from the year's taxation, and the patriotic conduct of the
mother and the son was rewarded by beholding Bohemia
reap a most abundant harvest in the following year.

From the year 1772 to 1778 Maria Theresa, with the
assistance of her son and Sonnenfels, did wonders for
Vienna. The Kärntnerthor Theatre was erected, and
the Burg Theatre became the national one. The Imperial picture-gallery was added to that of the Belvedere.
New gardens were built, promenades improved, especially
the Prater. Markets and custom-houses were erected,
and the inner and outer town thoroughly lighted at night;
the principal places paved, and a pavement marked out
for foot-passengers in all the great thoroughfares. Maria
Theresa also introduced several important reforms in the
code of law. Serfdom was done away with in all her
dominions, and Vienna received a regular organised body
of police. The sentence of death was now put into
execution only for the greatest offences.

The Bavarian war of succession would never have
taken place had not Frederic, by his intrigues, brought

T

about disunion amongst the claimants to the dominions
of Bavaria. The hostile position taken up towards him
by the German princes. proved to him that if he wished
to destroy the daily increasing influence of Joseph and
his mother, which might in a short time, by skilful con-
ventions, restore Germany to its ancient federal condition, he must in some way or other pick a quarrel with
Austria, on the plausible pretext that he was defending
the rights of the German princes against the aggressive
policy of the Emperor of Germany.

The death of Maximilian Joseph of Bavaria, the son
of the unfortunate Emperor Charles VII., afforded him a
convenient opportunity for carrying out his plan. This
prince died without issue, and, according to the treaty of
Pavia in 1329, the Golden Bull, and the treaty of
Westphalia, together with the laws of the German
Empire, his successor was Charles Theodore, Elector of
the Palatinate; and, in case of this latter Prince leaving
no male issue, Bavaria was to go to Charles, Duke of
Zweibrücken. It appears that Austria had rightful
claims to a large part of Lower Bavaria, and the
Imperial Crown possessed several fiefs, which had been
held in trust by the rulers of Bavaria. In order that no
disturbance should take place in the empire with reference to the various claimants to small portions of the
Bavarian demesnes, before the death of Maximilian
Joseph, the Emperor attempted to bring about a compromise with that Prince, the Elector of the Palatinate,
and the Duke of Zweibrücken. These princes acknowledged the desirability of a convention being at once
entered into, but the Elector demanded that as a set-off
for his claims he should receive the Netherlands. This
request the Austrian Cabinet, fearing a European compli-
cation, declined to entertain; but on February 14, 1777,
Charles Theodore declared his readiness to forego this

demand, provided Austria would support him in his claim to the Duchy of Julich. This was agreed to on the understanding that he should come to an amicable arrangement with the King of Prussia.

On December 30 Max of Bavaria died. On January 3 following, the Elector of the Palatinate acknowledged the claims of Austria to Mindelheim, and ten days later concluded a treaty with that Power. The Duke of Zweibrücken offered to join this treaty, but the Imperial Cabinet, relying on his fidelity to his former engagements, did not think it necessary, as they considered them sufficiently binding.

Both Russia and France were acquainted with these transactions, but Frederic, with his usual cunning, appeared to take no active part, either for or against the plans of the Austrian Cabinet, although he was doing his utmost, by means of secret agents, to induce both the Elector and the Duke of Zweibrücken to break faith with Joseph. On January 30, Lehrbach, the Austrian envoy, informed his Government that the King of Prussia had offered to guarantee entire Bavaria to the Elector, provided he would oppose the claims of Austria in the Reichstag. At last his intrigues were crowned with success, and the Duke of Zweibrücken was induced to protest against the illegality of the convention which had been concluded. Already, on February 5, Maria Theresa perceived what was Frederic's ultimate object, and entreated her daughter Marie Antoinette to endeavour to induce Louis XVI. to make common cause with Austria. 'Never, perhaps,' said she, 'has there been a time when the stability of our alliance has been more required than at the present moment. The interest, not only of our Houses, but our dominions, yes, of Europe, depends upon it.'

On March 14 she writes: 'If hostilities once break

out, it will become far more difficult to bring about a reconciliation. You know the system of our opponent of always doing his utmost to inflict at the very beginning a decisive blow. Consider my situation. Believe me when I think of it, I lose all self-possession. I feel that I am the mother, not only of my children, but of my subjects. Shall I make them all unhappy? My situation can be figured to one's mind, but it cannot be described.'

' I had always believed,' says this high-minded woman at a later period, ' that there did not really exist a bad feeling against us in France, but only short-sighted and antiquated apprehensions which for the common welfare of both countries ought to have long since disappeared. But I perceive, with the greatest sorrow, how deeply those misapprehensions have taken root, and that the knowledge of this, and moreover the zeal with which the French ministers speak against us, has made our enemy assume so defiant an attitude. They will find out their mistake, but too late for us and our common interest, if we cannot now prevent this war. Not that we have more to fear than on former occasions, for our army was never so strong, so well-equipped, inspired with such courage, and so full of desire to meet the enemy. The prospect has never been so favourable. The Emperor joins the army. But the fortune of war is changeable and uncertain. When I think of the unhappy fate of so many unfortunate beings, I cannot help desiring a peaceful solution, if it can possibly take place, on honourable terms.'

We entreat our readers, to whatever nationality they may belong, to ponder over the following extract: ' Shall such a man become a dictator in Germany? And will not all the Powers unite against such a man, to prevent the great catastrophe which must, sooner or later, overtake them ? For thirty-seven years this man, through his despotism and violence, has been the cause of all the calamities which have overtaken Europe. He has shaken off all restraint imposed by the acknowledged principles of right and morality ; he derides all treaties and alliances. We, from our position, are the most exposed, and yet we are forsaken! This time we may possibly extricate ourselves with or without loss. I do not here speak in the interest of Austria alone, for it concerns far more the interests of all rulers. In my eyes the future seems to be overclouded. I shall not see the storm breaking, but my children, my descendants, our holy religion, and our good subjects will but too soon painfully feel its effects. Do we not already feel this unprincipled and iron despotism which is guided only by one object, its own interests ? If we continue to allow it to gain strength, what a prospect will there be for those who come after us ; for we must not deceive ourselves. This system, it is evident, is gradually developing itself.

‘ Most willingly would I make the sacrifice of my own life, could I only see my children happier than I am, especially as I fondly expect to call a dauphin grandson. Forgive me, daughter, I do not here speak as one princess to another, but as a mother to her child.

‘ It is impossible to be deceived by Frederic's flatteries. He praises only to effect his own object, and when this is attained, he acts quite to the contrary, and never keeps his word. He acts thus towards every country, except the only one he fears, that is, Russia. Just as little can one be deceived in the intentions of the latter. Its principles are the same as those of Prussia, and the heir-apparent advocates them still more strongly than his parents. The Czarina has abated in this policy, but she will never so discard her principles as to act against the King of Prussia. She, also, is generous as regards fine promises, which are either without a meaning, or intended to deceive.

'Is it possible that France could prefer those two Powers to us good honest Germans?

'France and we have the same family and State interests. We shall understand each other still better in future if a change takes place. The unfortunate conquest of Galicia, which was rendered so easy to us, no doubt put us off our guard, but at the same time it has given us a lesson we shall not easily forget.

'The great expense, the cares and disquietudes, the loss of confidence, have pressed so heavily upon us that it will make us remember for a long time that hasty step. The withdrawal of our friend has also contributed a little to this. But we shall forget all this as well as the misapprehensions and bad feelings of the ministers and a great part of the nation, if we can only depend on the loving heart of the King and Queen. We regard their glory and their interest in the same light as our own. They can always be certain that we shall never do anything that could bring them into any kind of embarrassment. On the other hand we are necessary for you. Through our alliance, France can direct her attention to her navy, her colonies, commerce—in fact, to all those things which can never excite our jealousy.

'But for this, we require on our side an equivalent. We also desire to enjoy the benefits arising from this alliance; for I repeat what I formerly maintained, this our alliance alone can, if well consolidated, give peace for ever to Europe.

'It would, on the contrary, be a great misfortune if this peace should be made dependent upon the approbation of the two Powers whose principles are so well known to the world, and have been proved by their despotic conduct towards their own subjects. Our holy religion could only expect its death-blow from such an event. Honour and good faith would then have to be sought for among the savages.

'The picture which I have drawn is not exaggerated. And you can fully comprehend what agony it would be for me to see France become the ally of those two.

'What would be the result? In that case we should have to think only of our own safety. It would not be so difficult to bring about a rupture of the alliance, provided each State could be made to understand its own interest as in the year 1741. Believe me, my dear daughter, I do not express myself too strongly. There is still time to put things in order, but this opportunity may pass away. Profit by the advice of my grey old head, and use it for the benefit of our kingdoms, our families, and our children.'

As the outbreak of hostilities appeared imminent, Maria Theresa again wrote to her daughter as follows : 'Exert yourself to your utmost to assist your House, your brothers. All that I require of the King is an energetic demonstration. France will derive no advantage from our being defeated by our cruel enemy. The question is no longer about the ancient prejudices which should have been long ago buried in oblivion, nor the jealousy between France and Austria. It concerns all that is sacred, even our common interests. We shall be driven back, and forcibly cast down one after the other, if we do not offer a most determined resistance. It is not on account of ourself, or the dangerous position in which we are placed, opposing single-handed this dreadful system; but it is for the common good of Germany, perhaps of all Europe, that I have done all I could to prevent the outbreak of hostilities, hoping that our allies will thereby become convinced of the necessity of coming to our assistance.'

We conclude this remarkable correspondence with an extract from Mr. Harris's Diary, concerning a letter of Maria Theresa to the Empress of Russia. It is dated May 5, 1778:—

' Count Kaunitz's last courier, besides an exact communication of everything which had passed between the Courts of Vienna and Berlin relative to the present altercation till April 1 inclusively, brought a letter from the Empress-Queen, in which, after having fully explained her own conduct and that of his Prussian Majesty, she leaves her Imperial Majesty to decide whether the title of aggressor belongs to this Prince or herself. She then enlarges on the miseries of war, laments the being forced into it at her advanced age, and expresses great horror at the probability of being summoned out of this world at a moment when her mind must necessarily be filled with ideas very improper to carry into the next. The letter concludes with the highest assurances of friendship and attachment, and calls upon the Empress of Russia, both as a Christian and a Sovereign to use her influence with the King of Prussia in endeavouring to dissuade him from persisting in demands so inadmissible as his hitherto have been.'

Frederic, on his side, directed his envoys at the Courts of France and Russia to do their utmost to excite the jealousy of these Courts against the increase of territory on the part of Austria. France was informed that the possession of the upper run of the Danube would be dangerous to her possessions on the Rhine. Frederic wrote also himself to Catherine, and attempted to demonstrate to her that if she wished to be successful in any future war with the Turks, the power of the House of Hapsburg must be curtailed, promising at the same time that should she use her influence in opposing the claims of Austria, he was ready to become her ally in the Turkish war. In vain the Austrian ambassador at the

Court of Frederic offered that monarch every possible concession if he would cease to interfere in the Bavarian question. Joseph, finding all friendly overtures fruitless, occupied Lower Bavaria and the Palatinate with his troops. Thus we again see Prussia intermeddling without any just cause in the affairs of Austria. The King of Prussia, however, did not attempt to do so until he saw that Austria had placed herself in such a position that she must either be ready to pay for an honourable retreat, or stake her fortunes on the fate of war. The transactions between the Austrian and Bavarian Courts were no secret to him, and if he had been an honest man, he ought at once to have expressed his objections. But, like the freebooter that he was, he stealthily waited for a convenient opportunity, as a Jewish money-lender waits to increase his exorbitant demands of interest. At first his ambassador at Vienna expressed his master's opinion in a mild tone; but on a sudden he threw off the mask of moderation, and demanded the instant withdrawal of the Austrian troops, simply because he supposed he was able to throw 200,000 mercenaries into the Austrian provinces without the slightest chance of meeting with resistance. For the first time in his life he found to his dismay that Joseph and Loudon had collected at Königsgrätz a well-disciplined army fully prepared to meet any emergency. The Berlin Court again changed its tone. The man of blood and iron now enlarged upon the dreadful tragedy which awaited Germany should a war occur. He was a stern defender of the Imperial Constitution, and those laws which govern the German Empire. The Austrian Court, taking him at his word, expressed the most perfect readiness to come to some friendly arrangement. To prevent mistakes with reference to any instructions which Frederic might give to his ambassador in Vienna, and avoid their not being properly understood by

Kaunitz, Joseph corresponded himself in person with the King of Prussia. All the Austrian proposals were met on the part of Frederic by counter-propositions, which he was fully convinced the Austrian Government could not accept. The fact was, that he wished to gain time and allies; and this object once attained, his first minister informed the Austrian ambassador that further deliberations must be at once broken off. With his usual strategy, Frederic had attempted to steal a march on his opponent, and was moving rapidly at the head of his army towards the Bohemian frontiers.

It is not our intention to go into the military details of Frederic's campaign. All that is necessary to say is simply that Joseph, by a masterly combination, placed his troops in such a position that they always had a place of refuge to fall back upon, from which they could at any moment act on the offensive; and it was in vain that Frederic, with the most consummate skill, attempted to entice them to take an opposite course. During this campaign Maria Theresa despatched an envoy, Baron Thugus, to endeavour if possible to conclude a peace; but Frederic was deaf to the demands of justice, and trusting that in the ensuing campaign he would by fresh combinations gain over one of the Powers to his cause, he quietly took up his winter-quarters, as usual, in his opponent's dominions, for the purpose of relieving his own from the burden of the war. Both leaders prepared themselves for a tremendous struggle; but, perhaps unfortunately for Austria, Maria Theresa, in her desire to save Germany the horrors of renewed slaughter, in conjunction with France, expressed her readiness to conclude a peace, which was ratified at Teschen. No one can deny that the King of Prussia gained greatly by signing this treaty, for the state of Europe could hardly be regarded in his favour; and had he experienced a crushing defeat, his heavily burdened people were not in a position to give him a second army. The frightful discipline which kept these unfortunate men in the ranks would have been broken, and they would gladly have availed themselves of the opportunity of returning to their homes. The opinion seems warranted that Frederic did not in this campaign prove that former experience had increased his talents; but he was the victor, for he had made the German princes believe that he was ready to act in defence of the weak, although the terms of the treaty proved that he must be paid for pretending to be honourable.

The last public dispute in which Maria Theresa was engaged with Frederic, was on account of his attempting to interfere with the election of her son Maximilian to the coadjutorship of Cologne. The Prussian envoy, seeing that the majority of the chapter were in favour of the Archduke, demanded to know whether they wished to irritate the King, his master, and force him again to take up arms in defence of the peace and liberties of Germany. This insolent speech so exasperated Maria Theresa, that she at once exclaimed: ' Let him do so. He will then see how the lioness can defend her young.'

On July 26, 1779, the good town of Vienna, with its suburbs, was greatly damaged by the explosion of a powder magazine in the Nuszdorf's lines. Extraordinary as it may seem, the sentinels who were standing on duty were not in the slightest degree injured; they were thrown to the ground, and on recovering consciousness found themselves deaf. The neighbouring villages presented the appearance of the effects of a bombardment. Mortars and shells were thrown to immense distances, and the inner part of the town exhibited the effects of an earthquake.

The Emperor Joseph, during his visit to Paris in 1777, had visited the celebrated Deaf and Dumb Asylum of the

Abbé de l'Epée. Sensible of the blessings of so benevolent an institution, he communicated to Maria Theresa the idea of founding a similar one in Vienna, and the celebrated Frederic John Stark was sent to Paris for the purpose of making himself acquainted with the working details of this establishment. A small attempt was made on his return, and it worked so successfully that the present Deaf and Dumb Asylum was instituted.

Maria Theresa, on account of sanitary reasons, ordered that the dead should, for the future, be buried in cemeteries outside the town, thus putting an end to the custom then existing of burying the dead in the churchyards and vaults of the churches. About this time the Empress introduced a tax on drinkables, which does not seem to have met with a very favourable reception from the lower part of the population of Vienna, who, for so long a period had been accustomed to constant reductions in their favour; and they were greatly disgusted with the idea that their good mother should, in her green old age, think of preventing their drinking her health in the usual number of glasses on their Saturday and Sunday festivities. The Empress is stated to have been greatly distressed to think that at the end of her reign she and her beloved Viennese should misunderstand each other.

Up to the year 1780 Maria Theresa enjoyed perfect health. It is true, the outlines of her once graceful figure had altered, and the expression of her finely-cut features had partially disappeared, from the effects of the hand of time; but she still retained that wonderful Madonna-like expression, and her beautiful eyes still shone with their usual intelligence and animation. In her later years she had directed her entire attention to the internal affairs of her people, for whose well-being she had a never-ceasing solicitude. It appears that she was in the habit of being lowered into the vault where her husband's body had been interred by means of a chair, there to pass some time in meditation and prayer. Unfortunately, one day one of the ropes which were attached to her seat broke during the process of her being lowered, and Maria Theresa, who, although possessed of one of the most practical minds was, like most of her sex, rather superstitious, fully believed that this was a warning to prepare for her coming end.

On November 20, she caught a violent cold which ultimately developed itself into an inflammation of the lungs. Maria Theresa daily became worse, and on November 28, all hopes of her recovery were abandoned. She lingered on with Christian fortitude. In the moments during which she was free from pain, she spoke with her son Joseph on State affairs, and even then signed the most important letters. She was constantly expressing her gratitude towards Kaunitz and the whole Hungarian nation. She ordered Count Esterhazy to issue in her name a proclamation to her Hungarian subjects, thanking them for the loyalty and devotion which they had displayed towards her. The last official document she signed was the grant of a pension to an officer's widow. She had to be placed in an arm-chair for fear of suffocation, and declined to take any more medicines.

During the night of the 28th to the 29th, Maria Theresa was seized with the shiverings of death, and at two o'clock the last rites were administered to her. Feeling then somewhat better she began again to speak to Joseph, who begged of her to try and sleep a little. ' In a few moments,' she replied, ' I shall appear before the throne of the Almighty, and you would have me sleep!'

Towards the dawn of day she recovered a little, and regained her whole mental powers—even a calm hilarity. At about five o'clock she asked for coffee, and invited the Emperor to partake of it.

At eight o'clock she saw her children for the last time.
Seeing that they were crying, she told them how deeply
it grieved her to see that they were unable to restrain
their tears, and added : ' I think it would be better for
you to go into the next room and recover your composure.'
She then said with feeble voice : ' Any act of injustice
which took place during my reign happened without my
will, for I always· had the best intentions.'

Joseph, who never left her side but for a few instants,
either to give some directions or speak with some familiar
persons who made inquiries in the adjacent chamber, had
caught a cold in the head. The Empress urged him to
take something for it. As he said he had no care but
about her health and her speedy recovery, she replied :
' That will change ere long. God will have the mercy to
call me soon to peace. How long thinkest thou it will
still last ? Dying appears to me like moving from one
chamber to another.' Then she exclaimed with supreme
cheerfulness : ' I like to see death approaching, in order
not to be taken by it by surprise.' ' I feel chill inter-
nally,' she said later, as she felt gangrene coming on.

A violent thirst began to torment her. As the Emperor
handed her a glass of lemonade, she said : ' Deo gratias.'

It occurred to her that it was the vigil of St. Andrew.
Maria Theresa had always had a special reverence for
that saint, and had put herself under his protection
in all her embarrassments. ' He will come for me, I'm
sure,' she said to the ladies attending her.

Count Sternberg, who saw her, says she was reclining
in her chair, having just had her hair combed. She
appeared wan and worn, but her beautiful features were
not in the least distorted.

The Empress thanked all her female attendants, and
asked their pardon if she had been harsh towards them.

' You're all so downcast,' she said. ' I am not at all

afraid of dying. Fifteen years back I familiarised myself with the thought of it.'

To her dames in waiting, Vasquez, Berchthold, Kallenberg, she uttered, moreover, peculiarly touching words. To Kallenberg, who had been thirty-five years in her service, she added : ' If thou will'st anything, thou may'st tell me, but make haste.'

Her memory being most probably already impaired, she spoke, quite against her usual custom, on the last day nothing but French. At a moment when she was suffering intense agony, she exclaimed : ' Why do you let me suffer so long?'

The bad weather on her dying day seemed to affect her spirits, and, although it was raining, she desired that the windows should remain open in order to enable her again to look upon the world without, for from her child-hood she had been passionately fond of nature. After a short pause she observed : ' What bad weather for such a long journey !'

At about eventide, she said she could see no more. As her features seemed distorted, Joseph asked her if she were suffering. She nodded her head in the affirmative.

At about eight o'clock she rose suddenly from her easy chair and traversed the room without any support.

A quarter of an hour afterwards it was evident that she felt the pangs of approaching death. Her last words were ' God take my soul.' The final act of her life was her endeavouring to behold the last remnant of daylight, and she fell back exhausted in the arms of Joseph. In the eventide, towards nine o'clock, she died, resting on the shoulder of her beloved son.

The heavenly smile of divine triumph which still hovered over those once lovely lips after the last inarticulate prayer for the protection of her beloved children, told that the Almighty, who had protected her through her sufferings in this world, had forbidden that she should feel the agony of death.

Since the spirit of Maria Theresa quitted its human abode, she seems to have been the guardian angel of Austria. The shouts of loyalty which years of oppression had not been able to silence, and which vibrated along the heights of the Blocksberg at the coronation of the Emperor King of Hungary and his Imperial and Royal Consort, told her that woman had for the second time foiled the machinations of Prussia.

Her body having remained exposed, according to custom, in the Imperial chapel during three days, guarded alternately by the German and Hungarian guard, was, on December 3, interred in the Imperial vault of her ancestors, her coffin being placed by the side of her beloved husband.

Maria Theresa had sixteen children, five sons and eleven daughters. Her sons were Joseph II.; Leopold, Grand Duke of Tuscany, and afterwards Emperor; Charles, who died at the age of eighteen; Ferdinand, and the Archduke Maximilian. Of the Archduchesses several died in infancy. Maria Elizabeth, born on February 5, 1737, died in 1740. Maria Carolina Ernestine died a few days after her birth. Another daughter, called Maria Elizabeth, became Abbess of the Community of Innsbruck. Maria Anna was married to the Duke of Parma. Christina, born in 1748, died a few moments after her birth, and Joan Gabrielle when she was only twelve years old. Joseph Gabrielle, betrothed to the King of the Two Sicilies, died a few days after of small-pox. Maria Caroline, born on August 13, 1752, espoused King Ferdinand IV. after the death of her sister. Maria Anna, born on October 26, 1738, displayed in her early childhood great aptitude in acquiring information on all that surrounded her; this gradually increased as she grew up. She was excessively religious, and possessed a most exquisite taste. She was not only a first-rate connoisseur in all the fine arts, but also excelled as a lithographer, and some very fair specimens of her labours are to be found in the Imperial library, which contains also her private collection of prints and books, all tastefully bound in light brown leather, bearing her initials in gold. Her religious feelings and love of secluded life induced her to become Abbess of the Theresian Community for Ladies of noble birth, which the Empress had founded at Prague. Here she passed her remaining days in the pursuit of her favourite studies.

Maria Christine, the favourite of Maria Theresa, was, in her youth, celebrated for her merry and child-like nature, and she was never more contented than when she was able to assist in alleviating the sufferings of the poor, in which her generosity knew no bounds. She was married to Albert Casimir of Poland, to whom she brought as dowry the Dukedom of Teschen, which title he afterwards adopted. This nobleman acted for a long time as Governor of Hungary, and held his Court at Pressburg, which became the bridge on which German and Hungarian State affairs and German and Hungarian aristocracy united and met. Maria Christine accompanied her husband to the Netherlands, where they conjointly exercised the duties of the Governorship. The French Revolution compelled them to leave that country, and they returned to Vienna, where they lived in retirement.

Up to the Princess's death, which took place in June 1798, Vienna and its vicinity were constant recipients of her generosity.

With reference to Marie Antoinette, on whom so much has been written, we think it only necessary to make the following remarks. She was, like her mother, quick,

U

lively, and clever, and very natural in her manners, with an excess of good heart which unfortunately did not suit the taste of the French noblesse, who, fearing that she would become too popular among the lower classes, circulated shameful calumnies against her character, which, for the most part, were ultimately proved to be false.

Whatever may have been her private opinion on the state of France, she unhesitatingly followed the counsels of her husband and those who surrounded him, and heroically shared his fate, although it is well known that a German nobleman could have effected her escape, which she declined to accept on the ground that she should have to leave her children behind her.

THE PRESENT EMPRESS-QUEEN OF AUSTRO-HUNGARY.

After having placed before our readers a sketch of the life of Austria's greatest ruler, it is impossible to conclude these pages without raising our humble voice in the praise of one to whom Hungary is so deeply indebted, and who, by the maternal interest she has always taken in its welfare, has proved herself the worthy representative of the great Empress, and can with justice be styled Hungary's second mother.

The present Empress of Austria, the Empress of Brazil, the Princess of Wales, the Grand Duchess of Russia, the Crown Princess of Prussia, the young Queen of Spain, and the unfortunate Queen of Hanover, are the living proofs of the greatest truism which has ever been spoken : —Train up a child in the way he should go, and when he is old he will not depart from it.

The Empress-Queen of Hungary was born on December 24, 1837; she passed the greatest part of her girlhood in strict privacy, leading a most simple life with her sisters, the Princess Caroline Theresa Helen, afterwards married to the Prince Thurn and Taxis, and Maria Sophia Amalia, afterwards the consort of Francis II. of Naples. The beauty of this noble lady, her daring courage and intense devotion to her husband in all his misfortunes, have gained for her the pity and admiration of all.

From all that is stated of the Empress of Austria's sister, who was at one time to have been betrothed to the King of Bavaria, it would seem that that country would have found in her a true mother, whose well-regulated mind and strength of character would have been of incalculable value in the councils of its King. The Empress of Austria is the mother of two princesses and one prince. She is an excellent linguist, speaking English most fluently, and it is related that she is not only very fond of conversing in that language, but is also very partial to our country. One of the chief attendants of the little Archduchess is an English lady.

Her subjects say that Her Majesty is not very fond of grand Court ceremonies, and prefers the wild flowers of her country seat to those of the Imperial gardens at Vienna. Her beauty, her winning manners, and generosity of heart proclaim to the world that nature has given to Austria one of her choicest gifts. Happy, indeed, has the present Emperor of Austria been in finding such a consort; for no ruler has needed more than he that counsel and consolation which only loving wives can give. It is our most fervent and heartfelt wish that they may long live to be the expounders of Maria Theresa's sublime motto —

JUSTICIA ET CLEMENTIA.

APPENDIX.

CYGANIS.

ANYONE who has been in Hungary must have been astonished with the effect which music has upon the Hungarian, especially when the performer is a Cyganis, or gypsy; and on this account I have given a sketch of the origin and character of this remarkable tribe. We have no certainty as to the origin of the gypsies, but, amongst the various conjectures which have been advanced, the remarks of Grelman carry with them the greatest amount of probability.

This author, drawing his hypothesis from the similarity of words, construction of sentences, and many habits and customs, as well as from the time of their first appearance in Europe, believes that the gypsies were originally Hindus of a low caste, who were expelled from their country by the cruel war of devastation carried on in 1408–9 by Timur-Beg. They migrated to Egypt, and from thence entered Europe. The antiquity of their race is proved by the many precious vases which they have in their possession, guarding them with the most zealous care, and of which no amount of money and persuasion can ever induce them to dispossess themselves.

The earliest mention of them is in the year 1414, when they were first observed in Germany, whence they soon spread all over Europe.

The common origin of the Cyganis with the hordes of gypsies, which are to be found not only in all parts of Europe, but also in the East, is proved by their peculiar kind of countenance as much as by the similarity of their language, customs, and manners. It is everywhere the same round form of the face, the same dark and swarthy complexion, small, curved nose, and black eyes, the same gay and cheerful turn of mind and bodily agility.

On their first arrival in Europe they represented themselves as

Egyptians, and for the space of half a century, under that character, were received with favour and protection by different potentates. Gradually, however, they were (we will not say whether rightly or wrongly) considered troublesome; and, as they had no regular means of subsistence, they were accused of supporting themselves chiefly by pilfering, the females having the credit of using their fingers with greater dexterity than the men.

Though spread through the whole of Hungary and distributed in every village, the Cyganis always remain a distinct race, for they very seldom marry out of their own body. They seem to entertain a great aversion for field labour, and are, in fact, considered inferior even to the peasants; they are generally employed either as smiths, carpenters, or to carry messages. Many attempts have been made to civilise them, but with little success, as the following account of their present condition sufficiently shows.

The Cyganis may be divided into two distinct classes—the nomadic tribes, which have at present almost entirely disappeared, and the more civilised ' Neubauern,' or New Peasants. The former live, in summer, under a tattered tent of coarse woollen material, moving from place to place to exercise their calling, which is generally that of a smith. An old horse, which carries their tent, a pair of hand-bellows, a stone anvil, a pair of pincers, and a couple of hammers, a spoon, an earthen pot, an iron pan, a water jug sometimes, together with a dish, form all their inventory. In winter they live in caves.

The Neubauern, who received this title (probably as an encouragement) from Maria Theresa, are in a somewhat better condition, though in their person they are quite as filthy as their nomadic brethren. Their habitations, which, though small and poor in appearance, contain a few more articles of comfort than the tents already described, generally stand on the outskirts of the villages in the neighbourhood of some thicket or rough land. Their occupations are generally the same as those of the wandering tribes, and in Transylvania they are also sometimes employed in gold-washing; but even amongst the New Peasants there are but very few cases of Cyganis having become regular agriculturists. With reference to their morality, on which so much has been said, we quote the following from Dr. Bright:

'For my own part, I have not been able to discover all those marks of natural and inherent depravity in the gypsy character which have been so obvious to others; and I am inclined to think that by far the most depraved members of their little community are such as, having married gypsy women, become its adopted and not its natural associates, of which many instances have come within my knowledge; and I am confident that we are apt to appreciate much too lightly the actual happiness enjoyed by this class of people, who, beneath their ragged tent, in the pure air of the heath, may well excite the envy of the majority of the poor, though better provided with domestic accommodation, in the unwholesome haunts of the town.

* * * * * * *

'I leave it to those who have been accustomed to visit the habitations of the poor in the metropolis, in great cities, in country towns, or in any but those Arcadian cottages which exist only in the fancy of the poet, to draw a comparison between the activity, the free condition, and the pure air enjoyed by the gypsy, and the idleness, the debauchery, and the filth in which a large part of the poorer classes are employed . . . . In all attempts to change their habits, and to reduce their enjoyments to our own standard of happiness, we should carefully bear in mind that the gypsies are a distinct and separate people, and that it is rather their misfortune than their fault to have wandered into a country where property is so strictly appropriated as in Europe.

'The troops of wandering musicians and dancers seem also to belong to this race, from which they have separated themselves, for Spain and Russia are the only countries in which gypsy dancing can now be found. With reference to those in Russia, it would be useless for us to dilate upon the excellence of the Russian gypsy dancing-girl, as the elaborate descriptions given by most of our English journals of the magnificent entertainment given by the Governor of Moscow to H.R.H. the Prince of Wales, in which the most celebrated gypsy dancers were called upon to display their talents, will, in our mind, fully suffice. We will therefore proceed to those of Spain.

'Those who have beheld the fandango and bolero danced by

Spanish girls sigh when they behold the miserable attempts of some of the greatest danseuses to represent those sensuous scenes; but those who wish really to know to what a pitch excitement can go should frequent those places where the gitanas, through the marvellous suppleness of their limbs, as well as their graceful and lascivious movements, seem to be in reality those beings whom the devout Mussulman supposes will surround the true believers in Paradise. With reference to female gypsy life in England, those who heard Miss Herbert describe it in her lively song, " The Merry Zingara," will agree with us that the gitana's life is not without its charms.

'We now come to the Hungarian gypsy musicians, who generally perform on stringed instruments, chiefly the fiddle and violoncello. It is a miracle to find one who can read a single note of music; their instruments are generally handed down from father to son as a family heirloom. Their power of endurance is something wonderful; they never seem to tire, and, as long as there are dancers, they are ready to play with the same force and execution as when they commenced; indeed, the later in the evening (I mean the morning) the better their performance seems to be. Those who have witnessed the Csardas properly danced by Hungarians, especially after supper, and have looked at the faces of both dancers and musicians, will, I believe, agree with me that music is the connecting link between them, and there can be but little doubt that they have the same common Eastern origin. . . . Dr. Vambery has himself told me that the Hungarian national music is to be met with in Central Asia, and there is great similarity of the national airs in vogue among the Don Cossacks and those of the Hungarians. The national music of Hungary is perhaps the most inspiring in the world. We remember hearing one of Wellington's veterans tell us, after having heard some Hungarian ladies singing and playing, that he now fully understood why a man could blow out his brains on account of a woman.'

www.ingramcontent.com/pod-product-compliance
Lightning Source LLC
Chambersburg PA
CBHW031409270326
41929CB00010BA/1383